HEALTHY HAPPY VEGAN KITCHEN

HEALTHY HAPPY VEGAN KITCHEN

KATHY PATALSKY

Houghton Mifflin Harcourt
Boston New York 2015

For information about permission to reproduce selections from this book,
write to Permissions, Houghton Mifflin Harcourt Publishing Company,
215 Park Avenue South, New York, New York 10003.

www.hmhco.com

Library of Congress Cataloging-in-Publication Data is available upon request.
ISBN 978-0-544-37980-0 (pbk.); 978-0-544-37696-0 (ebk.)

Design by Amy Sly
Printed in China
C&C 10 9 8 7 6 5 4 3 2 1

TO
NELLY

CONTENTS

ACKNOWLEDGMENTS

Thank you to my supportive family, including my amazing husband. You know there is no one else on earth I would rather share a "table for two" with.

Thank you to everyone at Houghton Mifflin Harcourt for turning my cookbook dreams into reality. A special thank-you to Justin Schwartz. And thank you to my agent, Holly Schmidt, and Hollan Publishing.

And most importantly, thank you to all my HealthyHappyLife.com readers and FindingVegan.com fans. You are the reason I am able to do what I love for a living, creating recipes and sharing them with the world. The kindness and compassion I have received from my loyal blog readers is beyond priceless to me. Thank you. I cannot wait to continue to share my crazy, amazing, food-infused journey with you guys!

Thank you to YOU for buying this book. I want to wish you all the success in the world when it comes to your wellness goals. Believe in yourself, be kind to yourself, and you can do anything.

Love, light, and happy wishes to you all. Xo

—Kathy

INTRODUCTION
WELCOME TO THE PLANT-BASED PARTY

a pause before entering the kitchen

This book, this journey, is about more than learning new recipes. It is about finding a healthy, happy lifestyle that works for you. With each new recipe or kitchen discovery, step back and gaze at the big picture view of the newfound lifestyle habits you are embracing, the transformation that is occurring. Every meal is another small step down your healthy, happy life path. Let this moment be your starting place. Let my recipes and kitchen chatter inspire your journey.

This path has endless possibilities. Dreams, goals, aspirations. I believe all corners of life are expanded when you take care of yourself. And feeding yourself well is a large part of that. Happiness, energy, community, and love can all be born from a healthy diet, enriching your life on a grand scale.

Why vegan? I believe that there is no diet on earth more uplifting to one's body, mind, and soul than a vegan one. Plant-based foods are the ultimate path toward total body and spirit enlightenment. A vegan diet consists of foods that are rich in life, rather than death. Vegan foods are energizing, healing, kindness-infused, sunshine-filled, and overflowing with vitality-enhancing nutrients, enzymes, and phytochemicals. Talk about superfoods!

Long story short, embracing a vegan diet is a worthy starting point for positive changes in your life!

Let your starting point begin today. Look in the mirror—your partner for this journey is you. (And me!)

This food-filled, wellness-seeking, happiness-embracing adventure starts in your kitchen and ends wherever you wish. Let your kitchen serve as a place where creation, discovery, beauty, love, and light are unending.

Feeding your body well is also a way to feed your soul.

on deliciousness

These recipes. I adore them. But the real genius comes from how *you* serve them. How you pair my dishes, creatively marry flavors, and immerse yourself in the meals you craft—that is where culinary magic will be born. What do I mean? Well for example, last night, hurried between recipe testing and photo shoots, my dinner plans included a leftover steamy bowl of my Rainy Day Tomato Soup (page 258). I casually paired the soup with leftover vegan cheese sauce from my Favorite Vegan Mac and Cheese recipe (page 224), as well as a slice of my Walnut Lentil Mushroom Retro Loaf (page 246). The trio of flavors from these dishes was a symphony of yum. These favorite dishes tasted even better together than on their own!

The number of flavor and meal combinations from recipes in this book is practically endless. Old recipes can be given new life by creative pairing. I could easily write an entire book on flavor pairings of vegan foods, but the truth is that the real fun comes from discovering them by yourself. Happy accidents.

My advice is to never be afraid of pairing foods together that may seem strange or odd. Could you imagine if someone long ago had said, *Hm, I should not pair peanut butter and chocolate together, those two things are so different! Or Why would I put tomato sauce and cheese on baked dough? Or Wait, jam and nut butter? Madness!* Take chances—you never know what you will create and discover. Eat with abandon and inspiration and challenge your taste buds as often as you'd like.

let's begin!

Welcome to my healthy, happy, vegan kitchen! I am so excited to share more than 220 of my favorite vegan recipes with you. (That is a lot of vegan deliciousness!) Now, if you are a bit uncertain about stepping into a vegan kitchen, maybe even for the first time, let me first and foremost assure you that I wrote this book for everyone. And I mean *everyone*! I'm inviting everyone on the block to this vegan recipe party. So put on something sparkly or snazzy and come knocking on my door. Let yourself in. You will find me in the kitchen, dancing around amid a slew of steamy dishes wafting yummy aromas through the air.

this book is for you

Just like on my popular vegan recipe blog HealthyHappyLife.com, these recipes were created to be accessible and appealing to everyone. New vegans, savvy longtime vegans, non-vegans, part-time vegans, wannabe vegans, and even "I will never be" vegans. I am excited to take all of you on this delicious journey through my vegan kitchen.

"But I don't like vegan food." Ah, the skeptics. I love them. The only reason anyone could ever have a negative view of vegan food is if they have only ever had *bad* vegan food. (And yes, it does exist.) So the immediate solution to fixing those wayward souls is to sit them down at my table, link them over to my blog, or get their noses in this cookbook. A few taste tests of real deal amazing vegan food, and skeptics usually see the light, the sparkly green vegan-loving light. Taste buds do not lie. And while I understand that the lifestyle practice of veganism may not be for everyone, vegan food is for everyone to reach out and embrace! So if I can at least get everyone skimming these pages to realize how delicious and accessible vegan meals can be, and in turn eating more vegan meals, my job here is done.

How do I know my vegan recipes will impress even the pickiest of taste buds? Because of my taste buds! I don't settle when it comes to food. I hate eating anything that doesn't taste delicious. Life is just too short. And food is so important to life! Food can easily influence my mood, my energy levels, and my entire day, so every recipe in this book has been personally approved by my mouth. These are recipes I eat and enjoy every day, and I want you to be able to squeeze them into your cooking routine as well.

it takes work

Our lives have always been influenced by the food choices we make. Since day one we were shifting our eyes around the room, searching for something delicious to satisfy our tiny rumbling tummies. And that never changes! But figuring out what to eat for optimal wellness (and deliciousness) isn't always easy. No one is born knowing exactly what to eat. And most vegans, myself included, did not even grow up eating all plant-based meals. But I discovered that eating is one of the greatest adventures in life—for me, it's a lifelong journey toward discovering my perfect diet! I learn new lessons from food every single day.

You see, your relationship with food is just like any successful relationship in life: You have to work at it and pay attention. Awareness. Reading, discovering, and eventually cooking my own meals at home helped me deeply connect to what I was putting into my body. I learned that our daily meals should not be taken for granted. Food is of great importance to how our lives unfold. Food *is* life.

food is life

Our lives are intertwined with our diets, our schedules are tangled with the meals we eat, and our values are mingled with the foods on our plate. Food is the fuel that propels us through our day. It brings shine and shimmer to social situations. Food can transform your day and showcase your personality. Food is essential to life, and our relationship with it is a lifelong one. You will always eat, so make it a priority to figure out how to allow food to nurture you, rather than frustrate you; enlighten you, rather than weigh you down; be something you anticipate, rather than dread.

my solution

For me, veganism brought me that solace. It was a peacemaker in my relationship with food. It even changed the way I viewed myself. My soul glows with pride knowing I eat a compassion-filled diet. I found that veganism starts healing your body from the inside out. It starts in your heart, dances in your mind, and seeps into your spirit in a way that makes you feel different. And that glow is eventually something that is projected to the world.

on my menu

In these pages you will find sprouts, tofu, kale, raw desserts, smoothies, and other standard, obviously healthy, vegan things that scream "good-for-you" and "plant-based." But you will also find things like melty vegan cheese sandwiches, classic pasta dishes, stacked veggie burgers, creamy soups, decadent desserts, fluffy muffins and pancakes, colorful hearty bowls, and more—all recipes that totally make you forget you are eating "vegan food." Because yes, I love eating giant vegan salads and sipping on green smoothies, but let's be clear: Sometimes a girl just wants to devour a plate of fried risotto balls. Are you with me?

on cooking

"But I am a busy, busy person." Busy bees, pull on an apron! (Or not—I don't actually own one of those. But if *you* do, go for it.) Let's talk about scheduling. Yes, some of my recipes are fancy and time intensive. But others are super-fast and easy. I completely understand that sometimes dinner needs to be on the table in fifteen minutes, or *else*. I know my competition! I know the takeout deliveryman is just a phone call or iPhone app order away.

So whether you adore cooking your meals at home every day, slowly and relaxed like classical music humming through the kitchen, you fear recipes that take longer than a commercial break on your favorite television show, or you have a serious eating-out addiction (been there!), I hope together we can start a loyal, healthy, and balanced mealtime relationship. You and me.

I want cooking at home to be something you do not force yourself to do, but something you truly love to do. You dream about it. You wake up thinking about flipping on your kitchen lights like an artist setting up a fresh canvas. What do you think? You and me, in the kitchen, six nights a week? Five? Four dinners, four breakfasts? I will even throw in a few desserts. Deal? I think this could be the start of a beautiful plant-based relationship, don't you?

veggie girl: my story

From an early age, I was conflicted about the food on my plate. When I was a kid, something inside of me just gravitated toward vegetarianism. I pushed aside animal products from a very early age, picking the pepperonis off my pizza, scowling at steaks, pouting at chicken wings. I ended up requesting veggie-based entrées as my favorite meals: spinach enchiladas, veggie lasagna, big bowls of kale drowning in olive oil and garlic.

My lack of love for animal products as a child is not something I can fully explain. But when I analyze it enough, for me, being a veggie girl has always stemmed from my intense love of animals. As a child, I felt much more like myself when I was petting a bunny rabbit's soft fur or smiling at the cows grazing in a hillside pasture, rather than when I was eating a beef burger or picking at my pork chops. I adored my childhood pets, my cats and my bird, my bunny and my goldfish, and all the animal wildlife around me. The seagulls soaring over the crashing Pacific Ocean waves a block from my house. The friendly neighborhood animals, the timid raccoons, fluffy skunks, and sly opossums, that would sneak up to our back porch at night and nibble scraps of leftovers off paper plates that my mom would leave out for them. And also the magical exotic creatures like lions and whales that I saw on TV. My heart ached from the conflict between my plate and my heart. Why would I ever want to eat some of my favorite creatures?

Vegetarianism came quite naturally to me.

Then when I learned that animal products like eggs and dairy can be just as cruel on animals in factory-farming environments, I knew I had to extend my veg status to become vegan. But it was not an overnight change. Before my switch, I was a bit lost. I had wrestled with defining my perfect diet for most of my teenage and college years. I tried every "diet" under the sun until I realized that so many of my instincts about food in my life were right. My gravitation toward plant-based foods was something that ended up being 100% right for me and for furthering my state of wellness while setting my heart at ease. It took me about three years, while I was in college, to fully switch over from a vegetarian diet to a vegan diet.

I have been vegan since around 2002. I can firmly say that I am a veggie girl for life.

But I can also say this: Perfection is overrated. For anyone considering a vegan diet, please do not let the finality of the dietary restrictions deter you from the big picture view of what every vegan meal you have means for you and for the planet. Everyone is different and you should always let your heart and body lead the way. Your body speaks to you often, so perk up and listen to it! That goes for your heart, too.

to all the wannabe vegans

I love wannabe vegans. You inspire me. I want to hug you all and say thank you for seeing the glimmer of genius in vegan cuisine. Even if you are very far from actually being vegan, just that thought of *Gosh, it would be good to eat more vegan meals* can be a life-changing spark in your brain! Do not ignore your instincts when it comes to your body, soul, and food. Always explore them. And right or wrong, learn from every exploration you make.

the basics

Vegan cooking involves using ingredients that are free of all animal-derived products. Vegan ingredients do not contain dairy, eggs, meat, or products that are processed using animal products. For example, sugar might appear "vegan" at first glance but many white sugars are processed using animal bone char. (But here is a quick tip for you about sugar: Since bone char is not a certified-organic ingredient, any sugar labeled "organic" is most likely vegan.)

That example aside, you really can choose for yourself how strict you want to be. Through my years of interacting with a wide variety of vegans and veg-curious people, I have found that the successful long-term vegans are those who start very casually with a vegan diet and those who remember first and foremost that a vegan diet is not a cure-all. The reality is that no diet can guarantee lifelong wellness because throughout life, all of us will experience wellness highs and lows.

vegan newbies

If you are just starting out, be very easy on yourself. Do not worry about scrutinizing every label, or being vegan at every single meal. Seriously, you will drive yourself crazy. Pay attention to ingredients and labels as much as possible, but the moment you start to feel overwhelmed, obsessive, or anxious about it, step back and give yourself some space to breathe. Being vegan should be something that comes to your life with a smile. The "diet mentality" will not work for a long-term plant-based diet. What will work is if you suddenly wake up one day and realize you love every single second of being vegan and you wouldn't dream of filling your plate with anything other than delicious, kind, clean vegan foods.

To propel yourself forward, fill your journey with loads of self-reflection, experimentation, and education.

Why vegan? Fruits, vegetables, legumes, seeds, nuts, and other plant-based foods have been shown to be health-enhancing foods that inspire positive wellness changes in our bodies. The simple phrase "Eat more plants" is a good place to start on any path to improving your wellness. I have personally seen friends, family members, and readers of my blog make huge wellness strides simply by going vegan. My favorite example is that of my mom, who finally lost a significant amount of weight—weight she had been carrying around for close to twenty-five years—after going mostly vegan. With the vegan changes in her life, she also watched her energy levels soar and her heart health increase, among other positive effects.

get in the kitchen

Okay, the best part is here! The cooking fun. This big journey all starts in one place with this quiet scene: you, in your kitchen, doing a scan of your refrigerator and pantry with one simple question on your mind—what do I eat now?

Your next amazing meal is at your fingertips!

Nutrition Included! A helpful feature of each recipe is that nutritional information is included. Please use as a guideline estimate, since specific brands and ingredients will vary. The recommended daily allowance (RDA) percentages are based on a 2,000-calorie diet. Modifying the recipes will change these estimates.

TEN TIPS FOR NEW OR TEST-RUN VEGANS

1 **Play.** Experiment with a wide variety of new and known vegan foods. Make it a habit to buy at least one "new" food at the grocery store or farmers' market each week.

2 **Cook.** Get in the kitchen and cook. Try different methods of preparation for foods new and familiar.

3 **Read.** Feed your craving for knowledge by reading cookbooks and other vegan lifestyle books. The bookstore shelves (real and virtual) are filled with talented vegan authors!

4 **Explore.** Taste test, shop around, dine out. Start out by trying a wide variety of plant-based whole foods, brands, and products, recipes, and restaurants. Every city usually has at least one "veg-friendly" restaurant. Try it! But even go to mainstream restaurants and challenge the chef to create something plant-based for you. Food is a social thing, so you will need to get used to discussing your vegan status when dining out with friends. Work on shedding your shyness. Be proud of the positive lifestyle changes you are embracing.

5 **Talk.** Share your new diet with anyone who will listen. Hopefully you will find at least one supportive friend or family member who will act as a cheerleader (or even join you) as you experiment with vegan living.

6 **Reach.** Embrace community. Read blogs to hear others' experiences and pitfalls. Check out my website FindingVegan.com to browse recipes by talented vegan bloggers. Or stop by my blog, HealthyHappyLife.com. Tweet @lunchboxbunch or say hi to me online!

I am eager to help in any way I can, as are many vegan bloggers online. Seek out fellow vegans in person or online so that you do not feel so alone during this transition.

7 **Tune in.** Pay attention to your body and see what foods work for you. Because above all, remember that everyone is different. Each of us will respond to foods differently, so paying attention is your key to success. Realize that each new meal is an experiment.

8 **Write.** Write it down. Start a food diary. Or download a smartphone app that helps you track what you eat and allows you to make notes about how you respond to certain meals.

9 **Seek expert advice.** Consult a doctor or dietitian. Each person has varying nutritional needs, so checking in with your physician or starting a relationship with a vegan-friendly dietician is key to your journey. A doctor will be able to test your levels of important nutrients like vitamin D and vitamin B_{12} and more. One of my favorite vegan dieticians and authors is Ginny Messina, RD.

10 **Find your yum.** Huh you say? What this means is that everyone has different favorite recipes. Start off your mealtime exploration by veganizing your favorite non-vegan meals. Or look for vegan recipes that are similar to your favorites. Next, keep an eye out for brand-new meals that make you swoon. Once you discover your favorite vegan foods, you can create a cornerstone set of go-to meals that will keep your vegan diet humming along quite easily.

KITCHEN TOOLS
TOOLS FOR BUILDING A VEGAN KITCHEN

Stocking your kitchen is fun! Filling your cooking space with tools you love will help you look forward to your cooking sessions and sometimes even make cooking a little easier too! But do not get overwhelmed by this list of suggested kitchen tools. You do not need to zoom over to Crate & Barrel, Target, or Williams-Sonoma and max out your credit card (which could be quite easy to do at kitchen stores!). The trick to stocking your kitchen with tools and gadgets is to start small, go slowly, and build.

You want to start out with a few basics like a sturdy chef's knife, a reliable wooden cutting board, quality measuring cups and spoons (for both liquids and dry ingredients), and a few go-to pans and pots. Then, as you become more familiar with your recipe favorites and recipes you want to try, you can add to your list of goodies.

As you browse cooking supply stores you may notice that some pots, gadgets, and electronics can be incredibly expensive, so how do you know where you want to splurge and where to stay thrifty? One tip is to start out with cheaper versions of a few cooking tools, wait and see how much use they receive, and then if you use them a lot, buy a more expensive, higher quality version. I did this with my blender. My "cheap" blenders kept breaking and losing their edge from so much use, so I eventually gave in and invested in a Vitamix. I was thrilled with my kitchen upgrade and truly appreciated the quality of this investment-purchase kitchen gadget!

Another tip is to choose tools that are reliable in quality and made from natural materials, like wood, porcelain, and glass as opposed to plastic and aluminum. (And when you do buy plastic, look for BPA-free.)

Sturdy, eco-friendly nonstick skillet— Useful for sautéing tofu scrambles and omelets, for pancakes, and French toast. For those quick sautés with little cleanup choose an eco-friendly (PTFE- and Teflon-free) nonstick skillet.

Cast-iron skillet—A healthy choice for any sauté, a cast-iron skillet requires a bit more muscle power to handle, but it can actually infuse small amounts of iron into your meal, which may be helpful to some vegans. Also, cast iron can provide a rustic, seasoned flavor to food.

Large soup pot—A must-have item for boiling pasta and veggies, making large batches of soup, and much more.

Strainer—For straining veggies, pasta, seeds, juices, and more.

Chef's knife—A sharp, high-quality knife makes kitchen prep so much easier.

Wooden cutting board—Be sure you have a clean, sturdy wooden cutting board for recipe prep.

Baking sheet—A standard flat or rimmed baking sheet is a must-have for cookies, biscuits, and roasting veggies. Parchment paper is my favorite way to line baking sheets for recipes like cookies. Silicone baking mats can also be helpful.

Loaf pan—For baking bread loaves and veggie loaves.

Nut milk bag—For making homemade nut milks. There are several varieties available. Hemp canvas bags are nice but my preference is nylon bags because they dry quickly for easy cleanup.

High-quality blender, like a Vitamix, or food processor—A high-speed blender can take the place of a fancy food processor. It does in my kitchen. My Vitamix is my favorite kitchen appliance. I simply could not cook without it! It blends up thick smoothies, purees hot creamy soups, and helps me make homemade flour by processing oats and nuts. You can buy a separate dry container for perfectly processed grains and nuts, or use your standard Vitamix container—both will work with varying degrees of success.

Yes, a Vitamix has a high price tag at first glance, but in my opinion, it is an investment worth making. In my recipes ahead, any time I mention using a high-speed blender, I am referring to my Vitamix.

BPA-free plastic or glass food storage containers—Useful for storing leftovers or large batches of juices or nut milks.

Reusable grocery bags—Useful for grocery shopping and loading up with fresh farmers' market produce.

Can opener—A basic tool for opening cans of coconut milk, beans, tomatoes, and more.

Fruit and veggie juicer—A juicer is a wonderful wellness addition to any kitchen. None of my recipes call for fresh-pressed juice, but drinking fresh juice is a healthy wellness habit.

Grill press or panini press—For perfect grilled cheese sandwiches and paninis every time, a panini press can't be beat!

Crock-Pot or slow cooker—For slow-cooking soups and stews, grains, and a wide array of other recipes.

Glass drinking straws—Invest in a few glass straws for your smoothies and other beverages. They last forever and make your drinks taste cool through the glass straw.

Spatulas—I use small spatulas every day for scraping out the contents of my Vitamix. Large spatulas are useful during sauté sessions or when making pancakes, fritters, tofu steaks, and more.

Waffle maker—If you love waffles as much as me, invest in a good waffle maker. I prefer the Belgium waffle makers because they have a "flip" feature that makes vegan waffles extra crisp and fluffy.

Large stainless-steel or glass bowl—A large bowl, or two, is a must-have item for just about everything from whipping up cookie dough and batter to tossing salads with dressing.

Muffin pan—A standard 12-cup muffin tin is a must-have for making delicious vegan muffins.

Round cake pans—For flat cakes and layer cakes. I recommend having two pans around.

Glass casserole dish—For making lasagnas, casseroles, roasting veggies, and more. Oven-to-table dishes are very helpful when cooking for a family. They allow you to keep dishes warm in the oven until ready to serve.

Pie dish—For making pies, savory and sweet.

VEGAN PANTRY
FAVORITE VEGAN INGREDIENTS

on buying organic

Over the years I have acquired the desire to stick to this phrase: Always buy organic when possible. That being said, organic products are usually more expensive than their non-organic counterparts, so the decision is ultimately up to you.

A good plan is to at least try to buy organic when it comes to produce and ingredients that have thin skin and would be more directly exposed to pesticides. This includes foods like: berries, grapes, tomatoes, potatoes, carrots, apples, peaches, plums, mushrooms, leafy greens, among other fruits and vegetables without thick skins. And don't forget that this applies to dried fruit too, foods like raisins are simply dried grapes and are preferably always organic.

Foods that have thick skins and are more protected from pesticides are bananas, thick-skinned citrus, and more. However, some argue that the non-organic exposure can seep into even these protected foods.

Other foods like rice, beans, and processed foods that contain more than one ingredient (like crackers, snack bars, sauces, and more) can also be organic.

But organic food production is about more than simply pesticides on your plate. It is about pesticides in the environment and the long-term environmental effects of various non-organic farming practices on nearby ecosystems. And the long-term effects on our crops and farms. Buying organic is a choice you can make for your family's budget and your own personal environmental values and goals.

Organic or not, always make sure to wash your produce very well. I suggest buying a good fruit and vegetable cleaning spray. This can help remove bacteria, dirt, and debris and even pesticide residue! I am a big fan of fruit and veggie sprays. You can buy them at most grocery stores.

a few of my favorite vegan ingredients

Get to know the foods in my recipes a bit more. If you see an unfamiliar ingredient in one of my recipes, come back here to get a bit more info.

Açai—Açai berries are tiny purple berries with a chocolaty berry flavor and loaded with antioxidants. My favorite way to enjoy açai is via an açai bowl. You can buy açai products via frozen smoothie packs (choose unsweetened varieties!) and via açai powder and açai juice. Açai is delicious for breakfast, and bowls can be dressed up with added fruit, nuts, and seeds.

Almond butter—Almond butter is a nut butter made from ground almonds. It is rich in healthy fats and minerals and contains some protein and fiber. You may use almond butter in place of peanut butter whenever desired. Almond butter is easy to find in both raw and unsalted varieties. It is usually a bit more expensive than peanut butter and drier in texture. Almond butter is a healthy ingredient to have on hand since it can be used in a variety of snacks, sandwiches, and dessert recipes. It should be stored in the fridge and has a long shelf life.

Almond milk—Almond milk is a popular nondairy alternative to dairy milks. It can be bought in the shelf-stable nondairy milk section or in the refrigerated nondairy milk section. When store-bought, almond milk is usually slightly less creamy than soy milk, but has a very easy to drink, nutty flavor that most people love. Homemade almond milk is very silky and creamy with a fresh, amazing nutty flavor. When lightly sweetened and flavored with vanilla and cinnamon it tastes reminiscent of vanilla ice cream. Homemade is the best way to enjoy almond milk—there is really no comparison on a grocery store shelf. Try it (my recipe) and you will be amazed at its creamy, fresh flavor. Almond milk contains protein, iron, vitamin E, calcium, magnesium, manganese, and phosphorus. You can find fortified store-bought versions with even more calcium.

Apple cider vinegar—Apple cider vinegar is vinegar made from apple cider. You will want to buy raw, unpasteurized apple cider vinegar (like the kind produced by Bragg). I use this vinegar in baked goods, as well as in dressings, sauces, and more. I even enjoy drinking it straight from the fridge by the spoonful, for it wellness benefits, which may include digestive health and more.

Avocado—Avocados are rich in healthy fats and have that signature green buttery texture and nutty, luscious flavor. Avocados are one of my favorite wellness foods. They're delicious sliced over salads, added to sandwiches, or used to make super-easy avocado toast.

Bananas—Bananas are always in my kitchen. Frozen bananas are my favorite ingredient for creamy, frosty, shakelike smoothies. And when fresh bananas turn too ripe on my countertop, I can easily peel them, slice them, and place them in plastic baggies in my freezer. Ripe bananas are also wonderful in baked goods like banana bread and other muffins and loaves. They act as an excellent egg replacer, too. They are sweet, creamy, and loaded with potassium. They also contain fiber, vitamins C and B_6, and magnesium.

Bay leaves—I add bay leaves to brothy soups and stews to add a complex, rustic flavor. Just one bay leaf added to a veggie stew can add a lot of unique flavor. A must-have item for soup lovers.

Blueberries—Blueberries are a superfood. Their signature blue color is from the unique antioxidants that these berries contain. Blueberries can be used in smoothies, baked goods, or salads, or eaten raw. Blueberries contain fiber, vitamin C, vitamin K, manganese, and antioxidant power! They may be helpful in preventing a wide variety of health ailments, from cancer to hypertension.

Brazil nuts—One Brazil nut contains more than 100 percent of the recommended daily allowance of selenium. I eat 2 or 3 Brazil nuts each morning alongside my lemon tea. Brazil nuts are large and long compared to other nuts. They have a buttery, crisp texture and mild creamy flavor. Choose raw Brazil nuts instead of roasted and salted.

Brown rice—Brown rice is nuttier, chewier, and contains more fiber than plain white rice. Brown rice contains the whole grain and is less processed than white rice. Short-grain brown rice is my go-to pick.

Carrots—Carrots are sweet, crunchy, and versatile. They contain fiber and loads of vitamin A. You can shred raw carrots for adding to sandwiches and salads or baked goods like carrot cake. Slice carrots for soups and stews or roast carrots until they are soft and sweet. Carrots can also be sliced into sticks, perfect with dips for a snack.

Cayenne—Cayenne is made from ground dried chile peppers. A pinch adds a mild spiciness to recipes. I add cayenne to my morning lemon tea each day and I use it often in soups, stews, veggie dishes, and more. It is one of my favorite spices. Cayenne may even have a wide variety of health benefits including aiding digestion, detoxification, and more.

Chia seeds—Chia seeds are tiny poppy seed–like seeds that are purplish or white in color. Chia seeds are a good source of omega-3 fatty acids and can absorb up to thirty times their weight in water. Chia seeds are useful as a thickening agent or egg replacer in a variety of recipes. And they are delicious when made into chia pudding.

Cocoa powder—Cocoa powder is made from cocoa beans. It is a good source of antioxidants and of course has that amazing chocolate flavor. I love using cocoa powder for chocolate baking recipes, in chocolate puddings, pies, and smoothies, and of course for homemade hot cocoa. Be sure to buy cocoa powder that is dairy-free and unsweetened. Cacao powder can also be used. Cacao powder is simply a less processed form of cocoa powder and is therefore preferred in my kitchen.

Coconut water—Coconut water is the liquid from young green coconuts. It is rich in potassium and is an excellent beverage for hydration. It has a mild, sweet flavor. I love it in smoothies or straight from the fridge. I also use it to make coconut water ice cubes. Always buy coconut water that is 100% pure and unsweetened. I prefer coconut water that is not from concentrate. Raw, unpasteurized, straight-from-the-coconut coconut water is my preference when possible.

Extra-virgin olive oil—A go-to oil in my kitchen. Extra-virgin olive oil can have a grassy, lemony, fruity, or buttery flavor. High-quality extra-virgin olive oil has a smoke point high enough for roasting or sautéing veggies, which is just another reason to love it. I also love it for salads. This oil is so easy to find and quite versatile.

Farro—Farro is a whole grain that is super nutty and minimally processed. It looks similar to barley, but with a thicker outer layer, and is longer, like rice. It takes longer to cook than less hearty grains, but it is incredibly flavorful and wonderfully chewy in texture. I love it tossed with roasted veggies or simmered to make farro porridge breakfast cereal.

Flaxseeds—Flaxseeds contain healthy fats and omega-3 fatty acids. They also work wonderfully as an egg replacer, often referred to as a "flax egg," in baked goods. To make one flax egg, simply combine 1 teaspoon ground flaxseeds with ¼ cup water. I also often add ground flaxseeds to baked goods recipes where I want additional nuttiness and binding. Flaxseeds get very sticky when wet. They also go rancid very quickly when ground, so freshly grinding seeds is always best. I grind my seeds using my high-speed blender, but a nut-and-seed or coffee grinder also works. Store whole flaxseeds in the fridge to prevent rancidity.

Garlic—Having a head of garlic in your kitchen is always helpful. Garlic adds instant flavor to soups, stews, and veggies. Garlic is a heart-healthy ingredient and may help boost the immune system as well. Garlic can be added raw to dressings and sauces, sautéed, or roasted to sweet, sticky perfection.

Ginger—Ginger is a rhizome that is twisted and hard. It has a very thin skin and the beige flesh is thick and stringy. I use raw ginger a lot in my recipes. I love adding it to hot teas, juices, and smoothies and grating it into recipes for baked goods. Ginger can also be finely chopped and added to soups and stir-fries. Ginger is good for healthy digestion and may aid upset tummies. It is warming, soothing, and stimulating.

Grade B maple syrup—I simply adore this stuff. Grade B maple syrup is darker in color and has a more caramel flavor than grade A. Plus, the darker color means that there are more nutrients and minerals in the syrup. I use maple syrup in just about everything. Salad dressings, baked goods, sauces, teas, desserts, and more. It is not a cheap sweetener, but if you splurge on a few new ingredients, let this be one!

Kale—Kale has had its fair share of time in the spotlight these past few years, and for good reason! It's a superfood, containing fiber, vitamins C, A, and K, copper, calcium, potassium, and manganese. This leafy green is delicious in raw kale salads, soups, and stews, dried into kale chips, sautéed, wilted, and more. Kale is a hearty green so it will keep for a few days longer than some delicate greens that wilt very easily. When preparing kale, it is best to remove the thick, chewy stalk and just use the leaves. There are a few varieties of kale you can easily find, including dinosaur kale, also called Lacinato kale, which has long, narrow leaves. There is also red kale and purple kale, which have tones ranging from green to red and purple. And then there's the typical dark green kale with ruffled edges and that classic sturdy kale texture.

Kombucha—Kombucha is a fermented beverage rich in probiotics, vitamins, and enzymes. It can be bought in a wide variety of flavors or made at home. It has a fizzy flavor that is perfect for drinking in place of sugary sodas.

Lemons—Lemons are another ingredient that I always have in my kitchen. Fresh lemon juice and zest are found in many of my recipes. Lemon juice is a healthy way to add loads of perky flavor without adding fat or salt. They're also rich in vitamin C. Lemon juice is a perfect acid in baked goods, and I also use it every day in my morning lemon tea. Try to use organic lemons when a recipe calls for lemon zest.

Lentils—Lentils are a tender, flat legume rich in protein and iron. They are an ideal superfood for vegans because of their hearty nutrient profile and mild nutty flavor. I love lentils mashed into veggie burger patties or sizzled in a skillet and served alongside veggies.

Matcha green tea—I like to always have a tin of matcha on hand. I adore this stuff. Matcha green tea is made from ground green tea leaves. So you are actually ingesting the whole green tea leaf, as opposed to soaking the tea leaves in a liquid and then straining them out. I love adding matcha to smoothies and lattes. You can even add it to baked goods, waffles, and pancakes. The flavor is refreshingly grassy and bittersweet with a slightly nutty texture. Do your research before buying matcha, as the brands and quality levels vary greatly. I did a review on my website of over twenty different brands of matcha and found great variations in the price, color, and flavor. On average, you get what you pay for. The higher priced matcha brands do tend to have better quality. Look for brands whose matcha is a super-bright green color. Brands whose matcha is faded green or brownish green in color will likely not taste very pleasant.

Mushrooms—Mushrooms are a wellness vegetable. They are actually one of the few vegan foods that may contain natural amounts of vitamin D. I choose shiitake, maitake, oyster, and portobello mushrooms for most of my recipes.

Mustard—Mustard, a versatile condiment for your kitchen, adds zingy flavor to a dish or dressing. I prefer to keep spicy Dijon or whole-grain mustard on hand. Steer clear of any mustard that is neon yellow.

Nutritional yeast—Nutritional yeast is a flaky, powdered yellow food that contains a wide variety of nutrients including protein and B vitamins. But the best part about nutritional yeast is its cheesy flavor. It is delicious sprinkled on a wide variety of dishes in place of dairy cheese. I add it to soups, stews, pasta, pizza, and more.

Organic virgin coconut oil—Coconut oil has really only emerged on the mainstream cooking scene in the past few years. It is a very flavorful and versatile oil. You can use it in most baking recipes and for sautéing, and it is a secret "firming" ingredient for raw pies and desserts. Coconut oil becomes very hard when chilled and is usually soft like butter at room temperature. When heated, it melts and becomes silky and thin. When using coconut oil in baking recipes, just be sure that all the ingredients are at room

temperature so that the oil does not bead up when it comes in contact with cooler ingredients. Always look for virgin or extra-virgin coconut oil, which indicates that it is unrefined. Never use refined or bleached coconut oil.

Pumpkin seeds—Pumpkin seeds are rich in minerals like magnesium and are delicious sprinkled over salads or blended into pesto and dressing recipes. I always keep a bag of salted sprouted pumpkin seeds in my fridge for snacking. Superfood seed! Pumpkin seed oil is another delicious ingredient to try.

Quinoa—Quinoa is a gluten-free grain (well, actually a seed!) that is perfect for using in place of rice. It cooks up light, nutty, and fluffy and can be eaten as a side or stirred into soups and stews. It is higher in protein than other grains like brown rice.

Raw cashews—Raw cashews are a must-have item in any vegan kitchen. Raw cashews can be soaked and blended into cashew cream, which mimics creamy dairy products like sour cream and yogurt quite nicely. Cashews can also be made into cashew cheese and cashew milk. Raw cashews are also delicious added whole to sautés. Cashews, like most nuts and seeds, are a good source of healthy fats and contain various minerals and a bit of protein, too.

Rolled oats—Rolled oats are an essential ingredient to any vegan kitchen. Rolled oats can be used in basic hot oatmeal recipes, processed into gluten-free oat flour, or used in various baked goods recipes. Rolled oats are also a key ingredient in most vegan granola bars and homemade granola. Rolled oats are a good source of fiber and other nutrients. Oats also come in steel-cut varieties, which are delicious for hot cereal, but are too hard to process into flour with a blender. They also take a bit longer to cook.

Sauerkraut—Sauerkraut is rich in healthy probiotics since it is a pickled food. For the most healthy digestion benefits, choose raw sauerkraut. I love eating sauerkraut raw or warming it a bit and serving it on sandwiches like a Tempeh Reuben (page 92). Kimchi is another probiotic-rich pickled veggie product.

Soy milk—Soy milk is still my favorite milk for hot beverages like lattes and hot cocoa. I think it has the creamiest texture and foams up quite nicely when latte foam is desired. I always choose organic soy milk that is fortified to include nutrients like calcium and vitamin B_{12}. If you have trouble digesting carrageenan, a thickening agent derived from seaweed, look for carrageenan-free brands. Soy milk is a good source of plant-based protein: 1 cup usually contains 6 to 8 grams of protein.

Sprouted grain bread—This variety of bread is made using sprouted wheat berries. It is less processed than flour-based breads and thus contains more fiber and nutrients. It may also be easier for some people to digest than highly processed flours. It is one of my favorite breads for toasting and serving alongside breakfast dishes, and for using as a base for sandwiches. I store mine in the freezer and toast it to warm.

Sweet potatoes—Sweet potatoes are my favorite food ever. And that is quite a statement coming from me! They are packed with vitamin A, and they contain fiber, potassium,

vitamin B_6, and more. They are known for their creamy, sweet, irresistible flavor. The best way to prepare sweet potatoes is by baking them in the oven until the edges of the skin become crisp and sticky-sweet. The skin should easily fold off a sweet potato when it has been baked long enough. The inside flesh will be sweet and steamy. Be sure to poke holes in the potato before baking so that plenty of steam can escape. Sweet potatoes are incredibly versatile. I love them mashed, stuffed, blended into sauces, pureed into soups, and diced for stews. They are also the main ingredient in my favorite veggie burger recipe. Sweet potatoes come in a variety of colors. You can find white Japanese yams with purple skin and creamy white flesh, golden sweet potatoes, and garnet sweet potatoes. All delicious and satisfying. And always in my kitchen.

Tahini—Tahini is a paste made from ground sesame seeds. It is reminiscent of peanut butter, but it has a much stronger and more bitter flavor. A little tahini goes a long way! Tahini is wonderful for adding a bit of creaminess to salad dressings and sauces, and it is also important for hummus recipes. It adds flavor to and helps bind veggie burger patties and more. I usually work with roasted tahini, but raw tahini is available. Raw tahini has a bright and bitter flavor and is super thick and creamy.

Tempeh—Tempeh is made from whole fermented soybeans. It comes in thin planks and is less processed than tofu. Tempeh has a nutty, slightly bitter flavor and meaty, beany texture. It can be thickly or very thinly sliced, cubed, or crumbled. Tempeh is a great source of vegan protein and is my favorite soy product at dinnertime. It can be seasoned in a wide variety of ways and is super easy to prepare. Some people like to remove the bitterness by steaming the tempeh as a first prep step, but I personally do not mind the slight hint of bitterness. Tempeh is the main ingredient in tempeh bacon!

Vegan mayonnaise—I never liked traditional mayonnaise when I was a kid. But vegan mayo, I am addicted to! Vegenaise is a creamy white, slightly sweet vegan spread that can be used on sandwiches, slathered on toast alongside soup, or added to creamy salad dressing and slaw recipes. It comes in a variety of flavors including grapeseed, soy-free, organic, and reduced fat.

Tumeric—Tumeric is a root that is ground into a spice. It provides a bright orange-yellow color to foods with a mild savory flavor. I love adding it to smoothies, entrées, and lattes. It has anti-inflammatory benefits.

Watermelon—I eat watermelon year-round. Every day, really. It's true! Frozen watermelon cubes are my secret ingredient for achieving a perfectly frosty, ice cream–like texture in my smoothies and shakes. Watermelon is low in calories, contains potassium, lycopene, and has a subtle sweet flavor. Watermelon is incredibly hydrating as well. For the frostiest smoothies ever, slice up a watermelon, store the cubes in the freezer, and use a few cubes or more in your smoothies. You can easily use watermelon in place of ice in most smoothie recipes.

White miso paste—White miso paste is a fermented soybean product that has a salty, unique flavor. Miso is used for flavoring soups and stews as well as pasta sauces and marinades, among other things. Miso is a wellness food and contains probiotics, protein, and a wide variety of vitamins and minerals. You can also buy other varieties of miso, like red miso, but I use white miso in all my recipes. The flavor is appealing and versatile. It is also vitamin-A rich when orange fleshed.

Winter and summer squash—Come fall, I fall in love with anything squash infused. Winter squash like butternut and pumpkin are so delicious pureed for soups, roasted, and used in a wide variety of savory and sweet dishes. Summer squash is a bit lighter, and foods like zucchini and yellow squash are delicious roasted, shredded for raw pasta, or added to veggie sautés. Squash is usually very low in calories, while being high in fiber and water content, smart choices if you are watching your weight.

10 WELLNESS TIPS

KATHY'S FAVORITE HEALTHY HABITS

"what is wellness, really?"

Wellness Kitchen Girl. While most kids were cracking open cans of soda pop and crunching on neon orange tortilla chips, I was in my Santa Cruz, California, backyard picking plums, apples, figs, and cherries while pondering the merits of "an apple a day." Each week, I anxiously awaited the Saturday morning farmers' market trips with my mom. I was a student of wellness and healthy living from the start! I loved thumbing through nutrition books, wellness cookbooks, and magazines, hopping in the kitchen to try out a few recipes and pitching in with family meal prep every chance I found.

But before I share my tips, here are some basics.

Wellness Defined. There is so much more to wellness than simply diet and exercise. The term *wellness* actually defines much more than most of us know.

In 1976, Bill Hettler, MD, the cofounder of the National Wellness Institute (NWI), created the Six Dimensions of Wellness. They are: physical, emotional, occupational, spiritual, intellectual, and social. Feeling your best isn't just about shopping at Whole Foods and going to the gym. Having a healthy social circle, being happy in your workplace, being able to manage stress, having outlets to express your creativity and expand and enrich your mental capacity, getting enough quality sleep, feeling spiritually connected to something greater than yourself and feeling the meaning and importance of your life, and being able to analyze and express your emotions in a healthy way—all these factors contribute to wellness.

So as you sit down to enjoy one of these healthy, happy, vegan recipes, give your mind a few moments to ponder how you can improve the wellness in your life today. If you make wellness a priority right now, just think how much better you will feel ten years from now.

In today's fast-paced society, wellness goals often have many barriers and conflicts to overcome. But keep up the fight and find that inner passion, the desire that is built into each one of us to improve our state of wellness. Improving wellness can change every aspect of your life.

An easy way to improve your wellness is to upgrade your diet to include healthy, plant-based, nutrient-dense, clean, cruelty-free foods. But there are many other facets of wellness and tips to try for yourself. Here are a few of my favorites that have stuck in my routine and become part of my personal wellness mantra.

TEN WELLNESS TIPS AND LESSONS

1 Healthy Weight: Weight loss—I get it. Many of you want to lose five, ten, fifteen, or many more pounds. Obesity is a huge problem here in the United States, and it is easy to get off track with wellness in a society obsessed with convenience and processed foods, refined sugars, alcohol, and caffeine. For me, my epiphany came when I decided to do two things:

Food. I stopped counting calories and started saying YES to everything. If I wanted a bite of something or if I wanted to eat the entire giant slice of carrot cake, I would. Eventually, over time, I found that I felt so much better when I restrained my portions and ate feel-good foods. I never felt great after overindulging, so the habit of restraint actually came by choice rather than by fear.

Self-esteem and exercise. I decided to throw away my scale and stop caring about maintaining a healthy weight for anyone other than myself. The most important step in that was to start exercising in ways that I loved (dancing, biking, tennis, and more). I made the choice to stop chasing "skinny" and just worry about sticking to being vegan, loving myself, and being as kind to myself as I am to animals, my friends, and my family.

Long story short, it worked. And the success is not about what I weigh or how I look— nope! The success is that I have accepted my body no matter what it decides to do. Bodies change and shift every second of every day. So looking in the mirror and saying, "I love myself like *this* but not like *that*" is pretty silly. The bottom line is that if I feel good, I have won the healthy weight battle. Looking good usually comes whenever you *feel* good, healthy, happy, and confident first.

And yes, veganism has really helped me in my healthy body challenges throughout the years. Without my commitment to my vegan lifestyle, I am certain that I would still be diet-hopping, chasing skinny, counting calories, and just basically totally confused about my diet. Veganism grounds me. Rather than obsessing about a "diet," I am free to focus on eating foods that make me feel healthy and happy.

2 Hot- and Cold-Water Therapy: This is an easy daily practice I love. You can do it in the shower or tub, or if you have a bathroom with both a shower and a tub, even better. First, take a warm to hot shower or bath, as hot as you can. Then, switch over to cold water for as long as you can stand. Then go back to the warm. And back to cold again. Repeat this process. The idea is that the hot and cold variations are constricting and opening your blood vessels, increasing your blood flow. This energizing therapy always perks me up. Whenever I am at hotels that have a giant Jacuzzi tub and a separate shower I fill the tub with warm to hot water, soak, and then go hop in an ice-cold shower for a few minutes, then back in the warm tub. So energizing! You will see the results as your skin perks up to a rosy pink from the stimulated blood flow.

*Disclaimer: Please consult your physician on all matters concerning your health and wellness, and consult a physician regarding the activities and actions described below.

3 The Only Question: What Is healthy for You? If you compare yourself to others during your plight for wellness, you will always come out feeling like you are "less than." But the reality is that health looks so different on each and every person reading this. Our body types and energy levels are all so different. "Healthy" looks different on me than it may on you. Learn from others' experiences and stories, but keep in mind that you are a one-of-a-kind body and soul and only you will be able to evaluate your progress on your road to total body and soul wellness.

Your wellness journey, crafting your perfect plant-based diet and wellness lifestyle, will be unique for you. Notice the changes you feel and see. And notice how your energy shifts and changes and how your heart swells with pride and confidence from the strides you make toward your wellness goals.

4 Skin Brushing: I love this simple technique of removing dead skin cells and stimulating skin cell renewal. Buy a simple "skin brush" made of natural bristles and wood. Then brush your skin in long upward strokes right before a bath or shower. Easy!

5 Probiotics: I am a big fan of probiotics. Probiotics help boost our immune systems and aid digestion. Find a quality vegan brand you love and make a habit of taking your probiotic pill every day. And beyond just supplements, you can find probiotics naturally in a wide variety of vegan foods: kombucha beverages, raw fermented foods like kimchi and sauerkraut, pickled veggies, and nondairy yogurt.

6 Juicing and Smoothies: I am a big fan of smoothies and juicing, which is not surprising considering my first book is called *365 Vegan Smoothies*. Sometimes our digestive systems need a pause while being infused with plenty of nutrients. Juicing is the easiest on your digestive system since there is no fiber being consumed. Your digestive system gets a true "break" while being infused with nutrient-dense liquid. Juice fasts for a few days may even be your thing. I have done fasts for two to three days and I enjoy them, but only once or twice a year. I usually just add juices into my normal routine. Raw juices like ginger-carrot, beet, green blends, and more are hydrating wellness boosts.

But for my daily routine, I am more a smoothie girl. Smoothies are awesome because they contain fiber, but the fiber has been preblended so your digestive system doesn't have to work as hard to break down heavy fiber-ful foods. I have either a smoothie or a juice at least once a day. And take note: Sweet green smoothies are wellness game changers for anyone who isn't a "salad lover."

7 Morning Tea: I love my morning habit of lemon tea. In its simplest form, you can add some lemon to warm water and drink that upon rising. I like to make my tea a bit more intricate and add grade B maple syrup, cayenne, and tea bags. See my recipe on page 334.

8 Spices: I am a huge fan of adding spices to your menu for wellness. Spices like turmeric, cayenne, cinnamon, pepper, and more have been delicious wellness enhancers for my diet. I add turmeric to soups and drinks, and stimulating cayenne and black pepper to just about anything. And warming cinnamon is an easy spice to love. Embrace spices, try new ones, and infuse even more wellness into each meal.

9 Awareness: Wellness requires awareness. You have to pay attention. Just by reading this book I know that you have already tuned in to your health, happiness, and wellness. Well, take your self-reflection even further and start making a mental note of how specific foods, activities, people, and places make you feel. Really notice when you feel your best and when you feel your worst. Stop and take inventory of what leads you to those positive and negative states of being. And when you find something—a place, food, person, activity, or thought—that makes you feel better and "works," keep doing that! Eventually you will have a long list of feel-good go-to resources for wellness. A fun exercise to take inventory of what you already know is to make a list of "Things That Make Me Happy." Start from there and keep building!

10 Long-term Wellness Goals: Long-term wellness is not a sprint. And a high-maintenance "diet mentality" will only drain you of energy and happiness. Your biggest challenge and your greatest rewards in this journey will come from being like a snail in this race toward wellness. By working day by day to add healthy habits to your routine, like the ones I just mentioned, you are slowly building a lifelong foundation of health and happiness.

Eventually you will notice that you begin to shed your feel-bad, unhealthy habits without really even trying. With so many healthy habits to fill your day, you will simply have less time and desire to devote to the "bad" habits—things like smoking, excess drinking, overloading on caffeine, drinking soda, avoiding exercise, bingeing on junk food, skipping meals, negative thinking, and more. The goal is that all your energy goes into positive things so that negativity is diminished and slowly fades away from your everyday life, leaving you feeling clean, whole, happy, healthy, strong, loved, and capable of just about *anything*.

BREAKFAST

Breakfast is a time to wake up, fuel up, and start your day feeling cleansed, energized, and ready to take on the world. Breakfast will often change greatly based on your schedule and cravings, but making it a habit to hydrate upon rising and put something, anything, into your stomach is a great wellness habit to start.

I always start my day with some warm Every Morning Lemon Tea (page 334) and then proceed to enjoy whatever I crave. Breakfast can easily set the tone for your day of eating, so fill your plate, bowl, or glass with something delicious and energizing and your day will be better for it.

Light starts may include chia pudding, smoothies, juices, toasts, muffins, big bowls of fresh fruit, and more. Heartier breakfasts can include protein from tofu, tempeh and beans, filling potato hashes, veggies, and grains. And sweeter treats may include pancakes and waffles. I also love cozy grain bowls to start my day, with loads of fresh fruit on top. Start your day with a plant-based breakfast and feel the glow all day long.

EASY TOFU SCRAMBLE

This is my go-to tofu scramble recipe. It can be whipped up in just a few minutes and provides a protein-rich hot breakfast. You can even make this on a busy weekday morning! And the best part about this simple recipe is that you can change it up as you'd like based on the veggies and spices you have on hand. Toss in a handful of spinach. Add some vegan cheese shreds. Sprinkle in some Cajun spices or add diced bell pepper, mushrooms, or kale. So many variation possibilities! Keep some tofu in your fridge so you'll always be ready to make this recipe.

SERVES 2

12 ounces firm or extra-firm tofu

Nonstick cooking spray or oil

1 teaspoon vegan buttery spread

½ cup diced onion

Other veggies (mushrooms, bell pepper, carrots, scallions, etc.; optional)

1 cup chopped greens, such as fresh baby spinach, kale, or chard

1 tablespoon tamari

1 teaspoon grade B maple syrup

⅓ cup nutritional yeast, plus more as desired

¼ teaspoon freshly ground black pepper, plus more as desired

½ to 1 teaspoon ground turmeric

A few pinches of freshly grated orange zest (optional)

Sea salt

Optional add-ins: vegan cheese shreds, Tempeh Bacon Bits (page 62), additional spices

1 Drain the tofu of excess liquid and press it dry with paper towels.

2 Coat a nonstick or cast-iron skillet with nonstick spray. Heat the pan over high heat. Add the vegan buttery spread. When the butter has melted and coats the pan, add the onion and any additional chopped veggies (if using). If the greens you're using are hearty, like kale or chard, add them now. Cook the veggies, flipping them with a spatula, until the edges brown and caramelize, about 2 minutes.

3 Using your hands, crumble the tofu into the pan. Break apart any big pieces using a spatula. Drizzle the tamari and maple syrup over the top. Sprinkle the nutritional yeast, pepper, turmeric, and orange zest (if using), over the top as well. Flip and toss the tofu with the seasonings and veggies. Continue cooking until the tofu appears to have firmed up a bit as it absorbs the flavors and lets off steam, 2 to 3 minutes more. Fold in the more delicate greens like spinach (if using). Allow the hot pan and tofu to gently wilt the greens into the mixture.

4 Taste a bit of the tofu and add nutritional yeast, pepper, and salt to taste. Remove the pan from the heat and transfer to serving plates. Serve warm.

Tip: Black salt and truffle salt both add a wonderful savory flavor to tofu scrambles. Pink salt is another favorite.

Tip: Some flavor boosters to make your tofu scramble more "eggy" are truffle oil or salt, black salt, or ume vinegar.

| **NUTRITION FACTS** (per serving–252g) | Calories: 248; Fat: 10g; Carbs: 17g; Protein: 25g; Fiber: 7g | Vitamin C: 15%; Iron: 34%; Calcium: 37%; Vitamin A: 22% |

GARDEN VEGGIE FRITTATA

This colorful garden veggie–filled frittata cooks up light and fluffy. Full of vitamin A–rich carrots, superfood kale, and plenty of cheesy, savory spices, this soy-based frittata is a healthy entrée for a veggie-filled breakfast. Make it in advance and simply warm to reheat and serve. Have a brunch garden party and let this be the star of your table.

MAKES ONE 9- TO 10-INCH FRITTATA; SERVES 6

TOFU BASE

18 ounces silken tofu

½ cup nutritional yeast

2½ tablespoons arrowroot powder or cornstarch

1 tablespoon tahini or almond butter

1½ teaspoons ground turmeric

1 teaspoon sea salt

½ teaspoon garlic powder

½ teaspoon freshly ground black pepper

VEGGIES

1 teaspoon extra-virgin olive oil

½ cup diced zucchini

½ cup diced carrot

¼ cup diced portobello or shiitake mushrooms

3 cups chopped kale

TOPPINGS

½ cup canned diced fire-roasted tomatoes or diced fresh tomatoes

Handful of vegan cheddar cheese (optional)

3 tablespoons sliced black olives

Sprinkle of freshly ground black pepper

1   Preheat the oven to 375°F. Grease a 9- to 10-inch round baking pan. You could also use a cast-iron skillet.

2   **For the Tofu Base:** In a blender or food processor, combine the tofu base ingredients and blend until smooth. Pour the mixture into a large bowl.

3   **For the Veggies:** In a skillet, heat the oil over high heat. Add the zucchini, carrot, and mushrooms and cook, stirring, until the edges are browned. Fold in the kale and cook until it has wilted. Remove the pan from the heat.

4   Fold the warm veggie mixture into the tofu base. Pour the mixture into the prepared baking pan. Top with the tomatoes, vegan cheese (if using), olives, and pepper.

5   Bake until the top and edges of the frittata are nice and browned, about 1 hour. Let the frittata cool in the pan on a wire rack for at least 30 minutes before serving. You can make this dish a day ahead of time, store it in the refrigerator, covered, and reheat in the oven to serve.

NUTRITION FACTS (per serving–193g) Calories: 169; Fat: 6g; Carbs: 18g; Protein: 14g; Fiber: 6g   Vitamin C: 76%; Iron: 28%; Calcium: 10%; Vitamin A: 138%

PANCAKES BASIC PANCAKE DIRECTIONS

1 Slowly warm a nonstick skillet over low heat. Pancakes cook best on a skillet that is evenly and fully warmed up to prevent burning or uneven cooking (gooey insides). Raise the heat to medium when ready to cook. Slow cooking on a properly warmed skillet will yield golden and fluffy pancakes. A good 3 to 5 minutes is needed to warm the skillet.

2 While the skillet is warming up, place the dry ingredients in a bowl. Blend them together, using a sifter to remove any clumps in the flour. Stir in the wet ingredients until the batter is smooth and silky. Fold in any accent ingredients like fruit, nuts, or seeds. You could also add these directly to the pancakes while they are cooking on the first side. For example, you can press fresh blueberries into the just-poured pancakes.

3 Once the skillet is warmed evenly, coat the pan with a drizzle of oil so the pancakes do not stick. I like to use safflower or virgin coconut oil for my pancakes. The oil also adds toasty, buttery edges to the pancakes. Wait another minute and then start adding the batter about 2 tablespoons per pancake for small pancakes or 3 to 4 tablespoons for large pancakes. Allow the pancake to slowly cook, as tiny bubbles form through the surface of the batter, until the edges are firmed, cooked, fluffy, and not wet, 2 to 3 minutes. Lift the bottom edges of the pancake with a spatula and flip the pancake. Cook for 2 to 3 minutes on the second side.

4 Transfer the cooked pancakes to a paper towel–lined plate and repeat until all the batter has been used. Add oil to the pan before each new batch of pancakes.

5 Serve warm with vegan buttery spread, jam, fruit toppings, and/or maple syrup, if desired.

Note: Most of the cooking should be done before that first flip, so just another minute or two on the other side should do it.

Tip: If you are worried about the pancakes sticking when flipped, add a spray of oil to the top side of the uncooked pancake just before flipping.

Tip: To speed up the cooking process, cover the skillet with a lid for the first minute of cooking to trap in the heat and cook the top side of the pancake a bit faster, still using low heat.

GLUTEN-FREE OAT FLOUR PANCAKES

These gluten-free pancakes are fluffy, cozy, and craveable. This easily modifiable recipe can include a wide array of healthy fold-in ingredients like fresh blueberries, sliced bananas, chopped nuts, toasted coconut, sliced apples, and more! For everyone seeking gluten-free pancake bliss, this recipe is for you.

MAKES 4 LARGE PANCAKES OR 8 SMALL; SERVES 4

1 cup plus 1 tablespoon homemade oat flour (from rolled oats; see Sidebar)

1 tablespoon baking powder

1 teaspoon ground flaxseeds

1/8 to 1/4 teaspoon sea salt

Few pinches of ground cinnamon

1 cup vanilla soy or almond milk

1 ripe banana, mashed

2 teaspoons fresh lemon juice

2 teaspoons vegan sugar or agave syrup

2 teaspoons safflower, sunflower, or melted virgin coconut oil

1/4 teaspoon pure vanilla extract

Optional fruit, nuts, and more

Oil, for the pan

Follow the directions on page 37 to prepare the pancakes.

HOMEMADE FLOURS: OAT, ALMOND, AND MORE

Homemade flour will change the way you bake and cook! Flours made from processed whole oats, nuts, and seeds can bring new life to your recipes. Plus, these flours are gluten-free! My favorite homemade flours are almond and rolled oat. Simply place the ingredient in a high-speed blender or food processor and blend from low to high power until powdery and soft. Just be careful with nuts. Blend too long and you will have nut butter. Blenders like Vitamix give you the option of purchasing a dry container made specifically for processing dry ingredients like flour. But the standard container will usually work, too. A food processor can also be used. Store leftover flour in an airtight container in the fridge and use it within a few weeks for oats and within a few days for nuts for the freshest flavors and textures. For longer storage, keep the flour in your freezer. Nut flour, which is high in fat, freezes very well. However, using it the same day is best.

NUTRITION FACTS (per serving–151g) Calories: 225; Fat: 11g; Carbs: 27g; Protein: 6g; Fiber: 4g | Vitamin C: 3%; Iron: 10%; Calcium: 25%; Vitamin A: 3%

STRAWBERRY BUCKWHEAT PANCAKES

Healthy buckwheat flour, all nutty and rustic, provides the perfect accent to sweet, juicy, antioxidant-rich strawberries. You could also try blueberries, raspberries, or sliced cherries!

SERVES 4

---

1 | Follow the directions on page 37 to prepare the pancakes.

¾ cup all-purpose white flour

½ cup buckwheat flour

1 tablespoon baking powder

1 teaspoon ground flaxseed

⅛ to ¼ teaspoon sea salt

Few pinches of ground cinnamon

1 cup vanilla soy or almond milk

⅓ cup applesauce or mashed banana

2 teaspoons fresh lemon juice

2 teaspoons vegan sugar or agave syrup

2 teaspoons safflower, sunflower, or melted virgin coconut oil

¼ teaspoon pure vanilla extract

1 cup thinly sliced fresh strawberries

Oil, for the pan

NUTRITION FACTS
(per serving–211g)

Calories: 261; Fat: 10g; Carbs: 38g; Protein: 6g; Fiber: 4g

Vitamin C: 8%; Iron: 11%; Calcium: 25%; Vitamin A: 3%

MOM'S APPLE PANCAKES WITH CINNAMON-MAPLE "BUTTER" SYRUP

These are the pancakes I grew up eating! Made using organic green and golden apples from the tree in our backyard in Santa Cruz, California, these pancakes were always my favorite. I never cared that they were not perfectly round because I actually liked seeing odd-shaped pancakes, different sizes and tones of doneness. Speckled with thinly sliced cubes of freshly chopped apples, these fluffy pancakes taste like home. Serve with a drizzle of maple syrup or cinnamon-maple "butter" spread on top!

SERVES 4

1 Follow the directions on page 37 to prepare the pancakes.

2 **For the Cinnamon-Maple "Butter":** Combine all the ingredients together in a bowl and microwave for 10 to 15 seconds. Stir to combine. Serve warm, over the pancakes.

1 cup plus 1 tablespoon all-purpose white flour

1 tablespoon baking powder

1 teaspoon ground flaxseeds (optional)

⅛ to ¼ teaspoon sea salt

Few pinches of ground cinnamon

1 cup vanilla soy or almond milk

1 ripe banana, mashed

2 teaspoons fresh lemon juice

Pinch of freshly grated lemon zest

2 teaspoons vegan sugar or agave syrup

2 teaspoons safflower, sunflower, or melted virgin coconut oil

¼ teaspoon pure vanilla extract

1 cup finely diced green apples

Oil, for the pan

CINNAMON-MAPLE "BUTTER"

2 tablespoons grade B maple syrup

1 teaspoon vegan buttery spread

A few pinches ground cinnamon

NUTRITION FACTS
(per serving–174g)

Calories: 263; Fat: 6g; Carbs: 48g; Protein: 6g; Fiber: 6g

Vitamin C: 8%; Iron: 14%; Calcium: 19%; Vitamin A: 2%

DOUBLE CHOCOLATE WAFFLES WITH FRESHLY SLICED STRAWBERRIES AND COCONUT WHIP

These craveable waffles combine the delicious flavor combo of healthy sweet strawberries and rich dark chocolate. Top it off with some silky soy or coconut milk whip for the perfect chocolate-covered strawberry–inspired waffle breakfast. If you'll be serving the waffles with Coconut Whip, be sure to keep it chilled in the refrigerator until ready to serve.

1 In a medium bowl, combine the flour, cacao powder, baking powder, instant coffee, cinnamon, and salt. Stir in the soy milk, 1 tablespoon of the agave, the vinegar, and the vanilla. Fold in the chocolate chips.

2 In a small bowl or cup, combine the sliced strawberries with the lemon juice and remaining 1 teaspoon agave.

3 Heat the waffle maker. Spray the plates with coconut oil spray. Pour half of the batter into the waffle maker. Cook until the waffles are dark brown in color, 2 to 3 minutes depending on the waffle iron. Carefully remove the waffle and let cool for 1 to 2 minutes. Repeat with the remaining batter.

4 Serve each waffle topped with half of the berries and 2 tablespoons of the coconut whip, if desired.

½ cup all-purpose white flour or spelt flour

2 tablespoons cacao powder

1 teaspoon baking powder

¼ teaspoon instant coffee

¼ teaspoon ground cinnamon

⅛ teaspoon sea salt

¾ cup plain soy milk

1 tablespoon plus 1 teaspoon agave syrup

½ teaspoon apple cider vinegar

⅛ teaspoon pure vanilla extract

¼ cup dark chocolate chips

1 cup sliced strawberries

1 teaspoon fresh lemon juice

Coconut oil spray

4 tablespoons Coconut Whip (page 304; optional), for serving

NUTRITION FACTS (per serving–160g)	Calories: 217; Fat: 5g; Carbs: 42g; Protein: 7g; Fiber: 7g	Vitamin C: 80%; Iron: 16%; Calcium: 31%; Vitamin A: 4%

GLUTEN-FREE BLUEBERRY ORANGE PEEL WAFFLES

These gluten-free blueberry waffles are accented with sweet candied orange peel, cinnamon, and ginger.

— SERVES 2 —

¾ cup homemade oat flour (from rolled oats; see Sidebar, page 38)

1 teaspoon ground flaxseeds (for extra binding; optional)

1 teaspoon baking powder

¼ teaspoon ground cinnamon

¼ teaspoon sea salt

¾ cup crumbled silken tofu

1 tablespoon agave syrup

1 tablespoon melted virgin coconut oil

¼ teaspoon apple cider vinegar or fresh orange juice

¼ teaspoon pure vanilla extract

¾ cup fresh or frozen blueberries, warmed

1½ tablespoons chopped Candied Orange Peel (page 45)

Pinch of grated peeled fresh ginger

Coconut oil spray

1. In a small bowl, combine the oat flour, flaxseeds (if using), baking powder, cinnamon, and salt. Set aside.

2. In a blender, combine the tofu, agave, coconut oil, vinegar, vanilla, and 2 tablespoons water and blend until smooth. The total liquid volume should be just over ¾ cup.

3. Stir the tofu mixture into the flour mixture and let sit for a minute to allow the oat flour to moisten. Fold in the blueberries, orange peel, and ginger.

4. Heat the waffle iron. Spray the plates with coconut oil spray. Pour 4 heaping tablespoons into the waffle maker. Cook until the waffles are formed and fluffy, 2 to 3 minutes. The waffle will have a slightly spongy texture. Carefully remove the waffle—it will be delicate upon removal from the griddle—and let cool slightly before transferring to a serving plate. Repeat with the remaining batter. Serve warm.

NUTRITION FACTS
(per serving–185g)

Calories: 279; Fat: 11g; Carbs: 42g; Protein: 9g; Fiber: 6g

Vitamin C: 25%; Iron: 17%; Calcium: 16%; Vitamin A: 0%

CANDIED ORANGES

This is a fun little recipe that I adore. I add candied oranges as a garnish to salads and entrée platters. They are so pretty and really give a plate a gourmet tone. The roasted oranges are a bit more meaty and savory-sweet, while the candied orange peels are pure sweet!

- Roasted Oranges: Slice several oranges or tangerines into thin wedges and remove any visible seeds. In a bowl, toss the citrus with a drizzle of oil—try safflower, virgin coconut, or sunflower—and a generous amount of sweetener (liquid sweetener or dry vegan). Place the oranges on a parchment paper–lined baking sheet and roast at 400°F until the edges caramelize, about 15 minutes. Serve as a garnish or a sweet treat. The edges should candy enough so that you can nibble the peel, too! Extra-sweet: Toss the finished orange wedges in fine vegan sugar just as they come out of the oven.

- Candied Orange Peel: Slice the rind of 1 orange into long, thin strips. Bring ½ cup water and ¾ cup sugar to a boil and add the orange rind. Simmer for about 15 minutes. Drain the liquid syrup from the pan (or re-serve it and use as a seasoned simple syrup). Toss the orange peels in sugar and spices, such as cinnamon, if desired, and lay flat to dry on parchment paper for at least 1 hour.

EASY CITRUS AND SPICE FRENCH TOAST

This delicious vegan French toast is easy to make and includes some very lovely breakfast flavors, including cinnamon, orange zest, maple syrup, and vanilla. The result is a tender and moist egg-free French toast with just enough toasty browned edges to keep you very happy. Top with some fresh berries, chopped walnuts, maple syrup, and/or Coconut Whip (page 304) for a very welcoming start to your day! You can use a wide variety of breads for this recipe. Day-old or crusty bread works best to keep your French toast from becoming soggy, but if you are using fresh bread, lightly toast it before soaking to remove some moisture.

MAKES 4 SLICES; SERVES 2

SPICED SOAKING LIQUID

½ cup vanilla nondairy milk

¼ cup fresh orange juice

½ teaspoon ground cinnamon

¼ teaspoon freshly grated orange zest

¼ teaspoon freshly grated nutmeg or ground ginger

⅛ teaspoon pure vanilla extract

Pinch of sea salt

FRENCH TOAST

Vegan buttery spread or virgin coconut oil (about ½ teaspoon per slice of French toast)

4 slices bread (any variety)

Freshly grated orange zest

Few pinches of ground cinnamon

Drizzle of grade B maple syrup

Tip: Baking the French toast in a warm oven after the pan sauté can help to gently "dry out" toast that is a bit too soggy!

1 **For the Spiced Soaking Liquid:** In a small bowl, combine the soaking liquid mixture.

2 **For the French Toast:** If using fresh bread, toast it lightly before proceeding. Day-old, crusty, or slightly dried-out bread works best to prevent "soggy" toast.

3 In a nonstick skillet, melt the buttery spread over medium-high heat. Soak 1 slice of bread in the soaking liquid, then transfer to the pan. Sprinkle some orange zest and cinnamon over the bread and drizzle with a bit of maple syrup. Cook for about 2 minutes, then flip the toast and continue to cook until the edges are browned and all the liquid has been absorbed, 1 to 2 minutes more.

4 Transfer the cooked French toast to a serving plate and let cool for a few minutes before serving. Repeat with the remaining bread slices.

5 To serve, sprinkle additional orange zest and cinnamon over the French toast and drizzle with maple syrup. Serve warm.

NUTRITION FACTS
(per serving-161g)

Calories: 233; Fat: 4g; Carbs: 42g; Protein: 8g; Fiber: 3g

Vitamin C: 43%; Iron: 16%; Calcium: 14%; Vitamin A: 3%

CHOP 'N' TOSS
RAINBOW FRUIT SALAD

This fruit salad is filled with fiber, antioxidants, and energizing flavors and colors. The bright aroma of fresh citrus fills the kitchen when you whip up this bowl. This familiar fruit salad has been boosted with superfood goji berries and selenium-rich Brazil nuts. Serve right away or allow it to marinate and chill in the fridge for a few hours. Choose organic fruit when possible, especially fruit (and veggies) with thin skins like berries, grapes, peaches, and apples.

MAKES 5 TO 6 CUPS; SERVES 4

1 Roughly dice the apple. Place in a large bowl.

2 Squeeze 1 orange into the bowl. From the second orange, use a Microplane to grate about 1 teaspoon of zest into the bowl. Cut away the remaining rind. Roughly slice the orange, remove any seeds, and place in the bowl.

3 Peel the kiwi, dice it, and add it to the bowl. Peel and slice the banana into large rounds and add them to the bowl. Halve the grapes and add to the bowl. Remove the rind from the cantaloupe, dice the flesh into large cubes, and add to the bowl. Rinse the blueberries under cold water, drain well, and toss into the bowl.

4 Add the Brazil nuts, goji berries (if using), maple syrup, cinnamon, and cayenne and fold very well so all the flavors combine. Serve right away or cover and chill for up to half a day before serving. This salad is best the same day it is made.

1 apple

2 oranges

1 kiwi

1 ripe banana

½ cup red grapes

½ cantaloupe

1 cup blueberries

7 Brazil nuts, chopped

2 tablespoons goji berries (optional)

1 tablespoon grade B maple syrup

Few pinches of ground cinnamon

Few pinches of cayenne

NUTRITION FACTS
(per serving–275g)

Calories: 216; Fat: 5g; Carbs: 43g; Protein: 3g; Fiber: 7g

Vitamin C: 137%; Iron: 5%; Calcium: 7%; Vitamin A: 34%

MAPLE-LIME PAPAYA

This is one of my favorite morning fruit recipes. The combination of dark, rich, grade B maple syrup with bright, zesty lime juice accents the sweet, juicy papaya perfectly. Papaya is naturally rich in the enzyme papain, which is beneficial for healthy digestion. There are two main varieties of papaya at the grocery store: large red-fleshed papaya and golden Hawaiian papaya. Red papaya is my preference for this recipe because of its large boat-like shape, and I find it has a more dependable sweeter flavor and creamier texture. However, if you can find very fresh and sweet Hawaiian papaya, go for those!

SERVES 1

½ large red papaya, or 1 Hawaiian papaya

1 tablespoon grade B maple syrup

Juice of 1 lime

Pinch of freshly grated lime zest

Pinch of pink salt

1 Remove the seeds from the papaya.

2 Drizzle the maple syrup and lime juice over the papaya and into the center where the seeds were scraped out. Sprinkle with the zest and salt. Serve.

NUTRITION FACTS
(per serving-227g)

Calories: 122; Fat: 0g; Carbs: 35g; Protein: 2g; Fiber: 5g

Vitamin C: 173%; Iron: 4%; Calcium: 8%; Vitamin A: 9%

MINTED AVOCADO–GRAPEFRUIT SALAD WITH TOASTED PISTACHIOS

Green and pink, with an accent of fresh mint and rich earthy molasses make this grapefruit salad one to crave! Creamy, healthy-fat avocado is the perfect accent to sassy citrus. And did you know that molasses is rich in vegan iron, and iron is more easily absorbed when eaten with vitamin C? Grapefruit is a great source of citrus C, so call this a super-wellness fruit salad, and dive in!

SERVES 2

1. Slice or peel away the grapefruit rind. Carefully cut out the grapefruit sections using a paring knife. Or, if you do not mind thickly cut grapefruit slices, rough chop the peeled grapefruit with the membrane still intact. Remove the seeds. Place the grapefruit in a large bowl.

2. Heat a dry skillet over high heat. Add the pistachios and toast for just a minute or two. (This brings out the warm, nutty flavor without overcooking the healthy nuts.) Add the pistachios and pumpkin seeds to the bowl with the grapefruit.

3. Dice the avocado and add it to the bowl along with the mint, molasses, and salt. Add the cayenne, if desired. Gently toss the salad and serve.

1 large pink grapefruit

¼ cup roughly chopped pistachios

2 tablespoons raw pumpkin seeds (I like sprouted and salted varieties)

½ avocado

1 tablespoon chopped fresh mint leaves

2 teaspoons molasses or grade B maple syrup

Pinch of pink salt

Pinch of cayenne (optional)

Tip: If using molasses as the sweetener, you could also serve it drizzled over the salad instead of folding it in.

NUTRITION FACTS (per serving–209g) Calories: 311; Fat: 20g; Carbs: 26g; Protein: 7g; Fiber: 6g Vitamin C: 11%; Iron: 16%; Calcium: 5%; Vitamin A: 6%

PRETTY IN PINK LEMONADE PARFAIT

Pretty in pink! This fun, refreshing pudding parfait uses protein-rich silken tofu as the base ingredient. Antioxidant-rich berries and lemon add zesty-sweet flavor and pink color. Add fresh fruit and vegan granola to complete your parfait breakfast. This also makes a lovely afternoon snack or healthy dessert.

SERVES 3

PINK LEMONADE–TOFU PUDDING

12 ounces silken tofu

1 cup strawberries, washed and stems removed

¼ cup agave syrup

¼ cup fresh lemon juice

½ teaspoon freshly grated lemon zest

⅛ teaspoon sea salt

1 tablespoon arrowroot powder or chia seeds (for additional thickening power; optional)

PARFAITS

½ cup Easy Vegan Granola (page 66) or chopped nuts (optional)

1 banana, sliced

1 cup sliced strawberries

1 **For the Pink Lemonade–Tofu Pudding:** In a blender, combine the tofu, strawberries, agave, lemon juice, lemon zest, and salt. For a thicker texture, add the arrowroot powder to the blender as well. Blend until smooth. Pour the mixture into a medium bowl, cover, and chill in the refrigerator for at least 2 hours. You can make the pudding up to 1 day in advance; refrigerate until ready to use.

2 **For the Parfaits:** Divide the pudding among 3 parfait glasses, layering it with the granola (if using), banana, and strawberries. Serve right away or place in the fridge to chill until ready to serve.

Tip: For added protein, blend in 1 scoop of your favorite plain or vanilla-flavored vegan protein powder.

NUTRITION FACTS (per serving—296g) Calories: 227; Fat: 4g; Carbs: 41g; Protein: 9g; Fiber: 3g Vitamin C: 126%; Iron: 10%; Calcium: 1%; Vitamin A: 1%

CHIA SEED PUDDING

Chia seeds are rich in healthy fats and fiber. They are magical in the way that they plump up and absorb liquid to create a thickened texture. Plain nondairy milk briskly stirred with chia seeds becomes a thick, silky pudding in just a few hours. Prepare your chia pudding ingredients at bedtime and wake up to a chia pudding breakfast the next day. This is a basic recipe that can be easily modified to suit your sweetness and flavoring tastes. Add nuts or fruit to your pudding to complete the dish. Chia pudding is delicious served at breakfast, as a snack, or even sweetened a bit to be served as dessert!

SERVES 2

1. **For the Chia Seed Pudding:** Prepare the pudding at least 4 to 6 hours before serving.

2. In a bowl, briskly stir together all the ingredients. Alternatively, in a blender, combine the milk, sweetener, cinnamon, vanilla, and salt. Blend on the lowest speed while you slowly pour in the chia seeds so they do not stick to the sides of the blender. Blend on low for 2 to 3 minutes to jumpstart the chia seed plumping process.

3. Divide the chia mixture between two serving glasses or pour it into a large jar. Cover and place in the fridge for at least 6 hours. After 30 minutes to 1 hour, give the pudding a few stirs to swirl the chia seeds a bit. This prevents them from clumping up at the bottom or top of the container. (This step is optional. You can always do a brisk stir right before serving, too.)

4. To serve, top with any add-in ingredients you'd like or fold them into the pudding. Serve the chia seed pudding nice and chilled. Any leftover pudding will keep in the refrigerator for up to 2 days.

Tip: Reduce the sweetener by 1 tablespoon if the nondairy milk is on the sweet side.

CHIA SEED PUDDING

2 cups plain almond milk or soy milk

2 tablespoons liquid sweetener, such as grade B maple syrup, coconut syrup, or agave syrup

¼ teaspoon ground cinnamon

⅛ teaspoon pure vanilla extract

Pinch of sea salt

6 tablespoons chia seeds

OPTIONAL ADD-INS

Fresh fruit

Chopped nuts

Additional spices

1 tbsp cacao powder

NUTRITION FACTS
(per serving–283g)

Calories: 212; Fat: 10g; Carbs: 35g; Protein: 6g; Fiber: 9g

Vitamin C: 2%; Iron: 13%; Calcium: 64%; Vitamin A: 10%

SOUTH BEACH AÇAI BOWL

If you have ever been to Miami, Florida, you may have spotted a specialty item on the menu at smoothie shops and beach cafes. Fresh açai bowls are purple bliss! Açai has a creamy and frosty texture, a sweet chocolate-berry sort of flavor. Açai bowls are basically thick açai smoothies. You enjoy them in a bowl, with a spoon instead of a glass and a straw. You can add whatever healthy toppings you'd like to your bowl, including fresh fruit, nuts, seeds, superfoods like cacao nibs, spices, and more. You can even blend some cacao powder right into the açai blend to boost the natural chocolaty flavor of the açai. Açai is rich in antioxidants, and this recipe is a super-healthy way to start your day! Perfect on a warm, sunny day—crashing waves, beach, and blue ocean view optional.

SERVES 1

1 tablespoon shredded unsweetened coconut

2 frozen açai smoothie packs (unsweetened or sweetened; see Note)

½ to ¾ cup vanilla nondairy milk (I like almond milk for this bowl)

1 banana, frozen

¼ cup sliced raw banana

¼ cup sliced fresh strawberries

1 teaspoon raw pumpkin seeds

1 teaspoon raw cacao nibs (optional)

Note: If using unsweetened açai you may want to add a drizzle of agave syrup to the blend.

Boost It! Blend in a scoop of your favorite vegan protein powder.

1　Heat a small skillet over high heat. Add the coconut and toast until the edges brown, usually under a minute. Remove from the pan and set aside.

2　In a high-speed blender or food processor, combine the açai smoothie packs, ½ cup of the nondairy milk, and the frozen banana. Blend on low until the smoothie packs break down. Add a few more splashes of nondairy milk, if needed—just try to add as little liquid as possible so that the açai blends up very thick. (If you accidentally add too much liquid, thicken things up by adding frozen fruit or ice. Frozen blueberries pair very well with açai!)

3　Pour the blended açai mixture into a bowl and top with the raw banana, strawberries, pumpkin seeds, and cacao nibs (if using). Sprinkle the toasted coconut over the top. Serve with a spoon. Enjoy right away.

NUTRITION FACTS (per serving–379g)	Calories: 320; Fat: 13g; Carbs: 50g; Protein: 4g; Fiber: 6g	Vitamin C: 14%; Iron: 9%; Calcium: 19%; Vitamin A: 36%

MOM'S BROWN SUGAR RAISIN PORRIDGE WITH CINNAMON ALMOND MILK

This is a veganized version of the family-style pot of porridge my mom used to make for our family on many mornings. I requested this porridge almost as much as I begged for her apple pancakes. The super-creamy rice or wheat-style porridge is accented with tender, sweet organic raisins, cinnamon, vanilla, and a generous swirl of melting brown sugar and vegan butter. I have also added some healthy, potassium-rich bananas, selenium-rich Brazil nuts, and healthy-fat walnuts (or pecans). Serve with some toast and jam—dunking the toast in the silky cereal is the way to go!

SERVES 4

1. Bring 2½ cups of the almond milk and 2 cups water to a boil in a medium saucepan. Add the Cream of Wheat and salt. Bring to a strong boil, stirring gently and continuously, for 30 seconds, then reduce the heat to medium and simmer, stirring to prevent lumps, until the cereal thickens, 4 to 5 minutes. The cereal is done when it has a thick yet hydrated consistency (like thick applesauce).

2. Stir in the raisins, 2 tablespoons of the brown sugar, the cinnamon, and vanilla and continue to simmer until the raisins have softened, 1 minute more. If you desire a thinner cereal, add additional almond milk.

3. Turn off the heat and divide the cereal among four bowls. Top with the nuts, banana, remaining 2 tablespoons brown sugar, and the vegan buttery spread. Season the remaining 1 cup almond milk with cinnamon and serve it alongside the porridge, adding splashes to taste.

3½ cups plain almond milk, plus more as needed

¾ cup plain unsweetened Cream of Wheat or Cream of Rice cereal

¾ teaspoon sea salt

½ cup raisins

¼ cup brown sugar

¾ teaspoon ground cinnamon, plus more as needed

¼ teaspoon pure vanilla extract

4 tablespoons chopped pecans or walnuts

6 Brazil nuts, chopped

1 banana, sliced

2 teaspoons vegan buttery spread

NUTRITION FACTS
(per serving–325g)

Calories: 290; Fat: 13g; Carbs: 43g; Protein: 4g; Fiber: 4g

Vitamin C: 5%; Iron: 18%; Calcium: 31%; Vitamin A: 9%

GENERAL RULES FOR **COOKING OATMEAL**

1 cup rolled oats to 2 cups water plus a pinch of sea salt

1 cup steel-cut oats to 3 cups water plus a pinch of sea salt

Combine the oats, salt, and water in a saucepan and bring to a simmer over medium heat. Simmer until the oats are tender, 7 to 10 minutes for rolled oats and 20 to 30 minutes for steel-cut oats. When the oats are nearly done you can begin folding in spices, add-in ingredients, and sweeteners.

CHOCOLATE-COVERED STRAWBERRY OATMEAL

One of my favorite breakfasts is oatmeal. I love it with berries and banana on top. One day, when prepping some melted dark chocolate for my husband's soy mocha, I decided to drizzle some of the melted chocolate over my berry oatmeal. This soon became my favorite way to eat oatmeal: berries, banana, rustic oats, and a small splash of chocolate! You only need a touch to get a totally craveable chocolate accent. For this recipe, I added a spoonful of chia seeds, too. They help thicken the oatmeal and add nutrients like fiber and healthy fats. Chocolate and berries for a healthy breakfast—let's do that! Double the recipe below to serve two.

SERVES 1

---

1 Cook the oats according to your favorite stovetop method, or follow this simple method for cooking them in the microwave: Place the oats, cinnamon, salt, vanilla, and 1 cup water in a microwave-safe serving bowl. Microwave on high until the oats are near boiling, 1 to 3 minutes. Stir and microwave for 1 minute more.

2 Fold the almond milk and chia seeds into the cooked oats. Set the oats aside to thicken and set.

3 Place the chocolate chips, coconut oil, and agave in a small microwave-safe cup and microwave for 20 seconds. Stir briskly with a spoon until the chocolate mixture is silky and combine. If the chips are not fully melted, microwave for another few seconds until they are. When the chocolate mixture is thin and silky, it is ready to pour.

4 If you'd like, rewarm the oats for a few seconds in the microwave right before serving. Top with the berries, banana, and walnuts. Drizzle a swirl of the chocolate sauce over the fruit. Garnish with fresh mint.

½ cup rolled oats or steel-cut oats

⅛ teaspoon ground cinnamon

⅛ teaspoon sea salt

2 drops of pure vanilla extract

¼ cup vanilla almond milk

½ teaspoon chia seeds or flaxseeds

2 teaspoons vegan semisweet chocolate chips

1 teaspoon virgin coconut oil

1 teaspoon agave syrup

¾ cup sliced fresh strawberries

½ banana, sliced

1 tablespoon chopped walnuts

Fresh mint, for garnish

NUTRITION FACTS
(per serving–585g)

Calories: 488; Fat: 20g; Carbs: 68g; Protein: 13g; Fiber: 14g

Vitamin C: 126%; Iron: 30%; Calcium: 28%; Vitamin A: 3%

CRANBERRY-NUT FARRO PORRIDGE

I first tried farro porridge for breakfast at a cafe in New York City. They had a delicious holiday breakfast bowl featuring warm farro, pecans, and cranberries. I would sip a spicy soy chai latte alongside the bowl and pour some of the chai right in the cereal. The flavor combination of chai and farro porridge was something I grew to crave! So I created this farro porridge to make at home. The chai tea bag is actually optional, but do try it if you love spiced flavors. Farro is a low-gluten, nutrient-dense wheat alternative. It is higher in protein than most traditional grains.

SERVES 4

1 cup whole-grain farro (you can use cracked farro for faster cooking)

1 chai tea bag

¾ cup plain nondairy milk, plus more as needed

Few pinches of sea salt

1 cup fresh cranberries, or ½ cup dried cranberries

2 tablespoons grade B maple syrup

¾ teaspoon ground cinnamon

Freshly grated orange zest (optional)

1 banana, sliced

¼ cup chopped pecans or walnuts

4 sprigs fresh mint

1 Place the farro in a medium saucepan. Toast the grains over high heat for about a minute, tossing them a bit. Turn off the heat and set aside.

2 Warm 2 cups water in the microwave for about 2 minutes and then add the chai tea bag. Let steep until the water is light caramel in color, just a minute or so.

3 Remove the chai tea bag and add the tea and the nondairy milk to the pot with the farro. Add the salt and bring the mixture to a boil. Reduce the heat to low, cover, and simmer for 20 to 40 minutes. The longer you simmer the farro, the softer it will become, so cook it according to the texture you desire. I usually do about 35 minutes of simmering.

4 In a separate saucepan, warm the fresh cranberries over medium heat just until they burst and soften a bit, 2 to 4 minutes. The berries will pop when they warm, so be sure to cover the pot with a lid to prevent splattering. (You could also warm them in the microwave just until tender, about 1 minute.)

5 Fold the cranberries, maple syrup, cinnamon, and orange zest (if using) into the farro. Simmer for 1 or 2 minutes more. Add more nondairy milk if you want the texture a bit moister.

6 Divide the farro among four serving bowls and top with the banana, pecans, and a splash of nondairy milk. Garnish with the mint.

Tip: For a faster cooking time, soak the farro overnight before cooking or use cracked farro, which cooks in about 15 minutes.

NUTRITION FACTS
(per serving–266g)

Calories: 323; Fat: 7g; Carbs: 56g; Protein: 9g; Fiber: 10g

Vitamin C: 27%; Iron: 13%; Calcium: 10%; Vitamin A: 2%

PEANUT BUTTER TOASTED COCONUT OATMEAL BARS

These tender oatmeal-infused bars are perfect when you need to grab something fast in the morning but still want to stick to your "oatmeal morning" routine. These bars are made using silken tofu and homemade oat flour so they have a sponge cake–like texture that is fluffy yet moist. The best part is that you can fold a napkin around one and eat it as a handheld breakfast! No spoon required. Toasted coconut mingles with the bold nut butter, cinnamon, and vanilla bean flavors. Toss these bars in the freezer and reheat in the microwave as you crave them. Perfect for busy weekday mornings. Try them with a maple drizzle for a sweeter treat.

SERVES 12

Virgin coconut oil, for the pan

⅔ cup plus 2 to 3 tablespoons shredded unsweetened coconut, toasted

1 cup homemade oat flour (from rolled oats; see Sidebar, page 38)

¼ cup rolled oats

1 tablespoon ground flaxseeds

2 teaspoons baking powder

1 teaspoon ground cinnamon

½ teaspoon sea salt

12 ounces silken tofu

1 large very ripe banana

⅔ cup ceamy peanut or almond butter, melted

⅓ cup brown sugar

¼ cup sugar (any variety)

ingredients continue

1 Preheat the oven to 375°F. Grease a 9-inch square or round baking pan with coconut oil.

2 In a large bowl, combine ⅔ cup of the shredded coconut, the oat flour, rolled oats, flaxseeds, baking powder, cinnamon, and salt. In a blender or food processor, combine the tofu, banana, peanut butter, sugars, coconut oil, vinegar, and vanilla and blend until smooth. Fold the tofu mixture into the oat mixture.

3 Pour the batter into the prepared pan and top with the remaining 2 to 3 tablespoons coconut. Bake until the edges are crispy and the bars appear slightly browned, about 35 minutes.

4 Let cool slightly in the pan, then slice into squares while still warm. Let cool completely before removing from the pan. For faster cooling and easier handling, you can place the warm pan in the freezer for 10 to 15 minutes.

5 If adding the maple drizzle, combine the maple syrup and vegan buttery spread in a small bowl and microwave until bubbling, about 30 seconds. Let cool in the freezer until the mixture has a caramel consistency, 5 to 7 minutes. If the caramel becomes too hard, let stand at room temperature until it warms up to a drizzleable state. Drizzle the maple mixture over the bars while they are still in the pan or after you have sliced and removed them from the pan. The bars can be served warm or cooled. If you are serving the bars warm, the caramel will melt a bit once poured. If you are serving the bars cool, the caramel should retain its sticky texture upon drizzling over the top.

ingredients continued

1½ tablespoons virgin coconut oil, melted

½ teaspoon apple cider vinegar

¼ teaspoon pure vanilla extract

1 tablespoon grade B maple syrup (optional)

1 tablespoon vegan buttery spread (optional)

NUTRITION FACTS
(per serving–81g)

Calories: 217; Fat: 12g; Carbs: 22g; Protein: 8g; Fiber: 3g

Vitamin C: 2%; Iron: 10%; Calcium: 6%; Vitamin A: 0%

PUMPKIN BUTTER BREAKFAST SANDWICH, A.K.A. "THE JACK-O'-PUMPKIN"

This is my favorite breakfast sandwich recipe ever. It combines the salty-savory protein-rich flavor of vegan veggie sausage with creamy, sweet, spiced pumpkin butter, savory peppered mushrooms, and a bit of melty vegan cheese. This hearty handheld breakfast is a must-try during fall and winter pumpkin seasons. I even keep some pumpkin puree around the house year-round just for this recipe! It's also rich in protein and a good source of vitamin A from the pumpkin.

— SERVES 1 —

PUMPKIN BUTTER

¼ cup canned unsweetened pumpkin puree

1 teaspoon grade B maple syrup

1 teaspoon melted virgin coconut oil

¼ teaspoon pumpkin pie spice

BREAKFAST SANDWICH

1 whole-grain English muffin (I like spelt or sprouted grain varieties)

1 teaspoon extra-virgin olive oil, plus more as needed

¼ cup chopped onions

¼ cup sliced mushrooms

Pinch of sea salt and freshly ground black pepper

1 tablespoon vegan cheese shreds

⅓ cup vegan sausage (see Note)

¼ cup chopped arugula, kale, or fresh spinach

1. **For the Pumpkin Butter:** In a small bowl, whisk together the pumpkin butter ingredients. Cover and refrigerate until needed.

2. **For the Breakfast Sandwich:** Toast the English muffin and set aside.

3. In a skillet, heat the oil over high heat. Add the onions, mushrooms, salt, and pepper and cook, stirring, until the onions are translucent and the mushrooms are soft, 3 to 4 minutes. Push the veggies to one side of the skillet and sprinkle the cheese shreds over the top so that they melt into the veggies.

4. Add some oil to the empty portion of the pan if it looks dry. Form the vegan sausage into a patty and place it in the hot skillet. Cook the patty for about 1 minute on each side, meanwhile tossing the veggies a bit on the side so they do not burn. The sausage cooks very quickly and browns quite nicely.

5 **To Assemble:** Slather pumpkin butter thickly on both cut sides of the English muffin. Top one half with the sausage patty followed by the cheesy mushrooms and onions. Top with the arugula and close the sandwich with the other half of the muffin, pumpkin butter–side down. Slice in half and serve warm. If you are not eating the sandwich right away, wrap it tightly in foil and serve within an hour. Alternatively, place the wrapped sandwich in the fridge and reheat in the oven when ready to eat.

Note: Lightlife Gimme Lean brand vegan sausage is suggested.

NUTRITION FACTS (per serving–268g)	Calories: 374; Fat: 13g; Carbs: 50g; Protein: 16g; Fiber: 9g	Vitamin C: 14%; Iron: 26%; Calcium: 18%; Vitamin A: 193%

SMOKY TEMPEH BACON

Better than the real thing (because it is delicious and cruelty free!), this smoky-sweet tempeh-based "facon" is so easy to make. Try it as a breakfast side, layer it on sandwiches, or snack on it straight from the skillet! Seek out a bottle of vegan liquid smoke specifically for use in this recipe. That smoky flavor is what gives the tempeh its true bacon-y appeal.

SERVES 3

8 ounces tempeh

1 tablespoon grade B maple syrup

1 teaspoon tamari

½ to 1 teaspoon vegan liquid smoke

Pinch of cumin and/or cayenne

2 to 3 teaspoons safflower or virgin coconut oil

Freshly ground black pepper

Sea salt (optional)

Note: Make Facon Bits! Simply chop the tempeh bacon into tiny bits and use as vegan bacon bits in salads, soups, and more.

1 Slice the tempeh as thin as you can into short slices or long, skinny slices; either way works, depending on what you will be using the tempeh for. Longer slices can sometimes be easier to add to sandwiches, but the skinny, small slices tend to be a bit crispier around the edges.

2 In a shallow dish, combine the maple syrup, tamari, liquid smoke, and spices of your choice. Add the tempeh and let soak in the marinade for at least 30 minutes; overnight is best. If you are in a big hurry, tempeh that is marinated for only 1 to 2 minutes will still be quite delicious, but will have less flavor infused.

3 Set a sauté pan over high heat and add enough oil to coat the pan. As you sauté the tempeh you can adjust the pan oil as desired. Less oil will produce a drier tempeh bacon and more oil will crisp up the edges a bit more. Lay the tempeh flat in the skillet in a single layer with no overlapping pieces. Let cook for 2 minutes, then flip the tempeh and add a drizzle of the marinade. It should be sizzling a lot now. Cook until the tempeh is thoroughly blackened, 1 to 2 minutes more. You want both sides to become browned and crispy or blackened on the edges.

4 Lay the cooked tempeh on parchment paper or a plate to cool. Sprinkle with freshly ground black pepper to taste. The tamari should be enough to salt the tempeh, but add a few pinches of salt if needed.

Cheesy garlic variation: Add 1 tablespoon nutritional yeast flakes and a few pinches of garlic powder to the cooked tempeh just before removing it from the pan.

Note: You can also bake the tempeh bacon on a lightly greased baking sheet in a 400°F oven, until crisp, about 15 minutes. This will not produce the nice crispy edges you'll get from frying, but is still very delicious and flavorful.

NUTRITION FACTS (per serving–88g)	Calories: 191; Fat: 11g; Carbs: 12g; Protein: 15g; Fiber: 7g	Vitamin C: 0%; Iron: 12%; Calcium: 9%; Vitamin A: 0%

CINNAMON MAPLE CITRUS SWEET POTATO HOME FRIES

In this recipe, home fries get a sweet potato spin, infused with citrus, maple, and cinnamon. Plus sweet potatoes are rich in vitamin A. If you love sweet potatoes as much as me, you will be overjoyed to add them to your breakfast or brunch table.

SERVES 2

2 cups diced peeled sweet potato

2 teaspoons grade B maple syrup

1 teaspoon ground cinnamon

½ to 1 teaspoon freshly grated orange zest, plus more as needed

1 tablespoon virgin coconut oil

Coarse salt

Tip: For "lighter" home fries, reduce the oil by half. Use splashes of water to moisten the pan, if needed.

1 Bring a large pot of water to a boil. Add the sweet potatoes and boil lightly just until tender, 6 to 10 minutes. Do not overboil or the home fries will be very soft.

2 Drain the potatoes and pat dry with paper towels. Place the potatoes in a large bowl and add the maple syrup, cinnamon, and orange zest to taste. Toss gently to combine.

3 In a skillet, heat the coconut oil over high heat. Add the potatoes and cook, stirring, until the edges are brown and crisp, about 5 minutes. Do not move the potatoes around in the pan too much to avoid mushing them up.

4 Sprinkle with coarse salt and another pinch of fresh orange zest before serving.

NUTRITION FACTS (per serving–215g) Calories: 259; Fat: 7g; Carbs: 47g; Protein: 4g; Fiber: 7g Vitamin C: 65%; Iron: 9%; Calcium: 9%; Vitamin A: 769%

EASY CHEEZY HASH BROWNS

Hash browns are a potato lover's treat as a breakfast side. Toasty, crispy, and browned, hash brown potatoes pair well with tofu scrambles, omelets, pancakes, or waffles. I add a "cheezy" spin on my hash browns by adding (not cheese) but nutritional yeast and spices. Easy, cheezy, amazin'. After creating this recipe, I simply cannot eat hash browns without nutritional yeast now!

SERVES 2

---

1. In a skillet, heat the oil over high heat. You want the pan to be very hot when you add the potatoes.

2. Using paper towels, squeeze as much moisture as you can out of the grated potato. Place the potato in a small bowl and toss with the nutritional yeast, pepper, garlic powder, and any optional spices desired.

3. Add the potatoes to the hot pan in a very thin layer, covering the bottom of the pan. Allow the potatoes to sizzle and cook until they are clearly getting browned and crispy, 2 to 4 minutes. Sprinkle another few pinches of nutritional yeast and spices over the exposed side of the hash browns if you'd like, as this also helps absorb excess moisture. Before flipping, make sure the underside of the potatoes have browned to a crispy golden state. If not, a few more minutes should do it. Flip the potatoes in large sections using a large spatula. Cook until golden brown on the bottom, 3 to 5 minutes more. Try not to move the potatoes around too much in the pan; this will make them more mushy and less crispy.

4. Divide the hash browns between two serving plates. Sprinkle with the salt and any additional spices you'd like. A sprinkle of pepper and finely chopped parsley is a nice touch, too.

1 tablespoon safflower oil

1 large russet potato, peeled and grated

⅓ cup nutritional yeast, plus more as needed

¼ teaspoon freshly ground black pepper, plus more as needed

⅛ teaspoon garlic powder

Optional spices: smoked paprika, cumin, ground turmeric, cayenne (add a few pinches of one or more)

¼ teaspoon sea salt

Finely chopped fresh flat-leaf parsley (optional)

Tip: Before flipping the hash browns, spray the exposed side with cooking spray if you are worried about them sticking to the pan.

Sweeten the Deal! Substitute the white potato with grated sweet potato to add plenty of sweetness and vitamin A. Substitute 1 teaspoon cinnamon for the nutritional yeast.

NUTRITION FACTS (per serving–102g) Calories: 196; Fat: 8g; Carbs: 21g; Protein: 11g; Fiber: 5g Vitamin C: 23%; Iron: 17%; Calcium: 2%; Vitamin A: 0%

EASY VEGAN GRANOLA AND VARIATIONS

Granola is easier to make at home than most people think. The steps are pretty simple: Just toss the ingredients, spread on greased or parchment paper–lined baking sheets, and bake until the oats and nuts toast, crisp, and become crunchy and flavor infused. Plus, the best part about baking granola is the way it makes your entire kitchen—your entire house, even— smell like vanilla, spice, and everything nice. The other best part is how easy it is to modify the recipe based on whatever ingredients you have on hand. Here are a few recipes to get you started.

Basic Granola Directions:

1 Preheat the oven to 300°F. Lightly grease a baking sheet (or two) with oil, or line with parchment paper.

2 In a large bowl, combine all the ingredients and toss very well for a few minutes.

3 Spread the granola on the baking sheet(s) in a thin, even layer. Bake until crisp and browned, 20 to 25 minutes, tossing the granola every 10 minutes. The granola will crisp up even more as it cools.

4 Let the granola cool and firm up in the pan for about an hour before serving or transferring to containers or baggies for storage. Storing the granola before it has cooled should be avoided, because the steamy moisture from the heat would soften the texture of the granola.

BASIC GRANOLA

Follow the directions on page 66 to prepare the granola.

Virgin coconut oil or parchment paper, for the pan

2½ cups rolled oats

1½ to 2 cups chopped nuts, seeds, dried fruit, or coconut (Add more of these accents for a heartier, more textured granola.)

⅓ to ½ cup grade B maple syrup (Add only ⅓ cup for a less sweet granola.)

3 to 4 tablespoons oil, vegan buttery spread, or melted nut butter. (The more you add the richer your granola will taste. I love virgin coconut oil for homemade granola!)

1 tablespoon ground cinnamon

Sea salt

Spices, such as vanilla bean powder, nutmeg, turmeric, cayenne, cardamom, ginger powder, and cacao powder

NUTRITION FACTS
(per serving–47g)

Calories: 178; Fat: 6g; Carbs: 28g; Protein: 6g; Fiber: 3g

Vitamin C: 0%; Iron: 11%; Calcium: 2%; Vitamin A: 0%

SERVES 8

COCONUT ORANGE SPICE GRANOLA

Follow the directions on page 66 to prepare the granola.

Virgin coconut oil or parchment paper, for the pan

2 cups rolled oats

½ cup raw buckwheat groats or more rolled oats

½ cup chopped walnuts or pecans

½ cup grade B maple syrup

½ cup shredded unsweetened coconut

¼ cup roughly chopped Brazil nuts

4 tablespoons virgin coconut oil, melted

1 tablespoon ground cinnamon

1 teaspoon freshly grated orange zest

1 teaspoon pure vanilla extract

½ teaspoon sea salt

NUTRITION FACTS
(per serving–70g)

Calories: 286; Fat: 15g; Carbs: 35g; Protein: 7g; Fiber: 5g

Vitamin C: 1%; Iron: 13%; Calcium: 4%; Vitamin A: 0%

SERVES 8

PUMPKIN SPICE GRANOLA

Follow the directions on page 66 to prepare the granola.

Virgin coconut oil or parchment paper, for the pan

3 cups rolled oats

1 cup chopped pecans or walnuts

⅓ cup canned unsweetened pumpkin puree, warmed to soften

½ cup grade B maple syrup

2 tablespoons fresh orange juice

1 tablespoon pumpkin pie spice

1 teaspoon pure vanilla extract

1 teaspoon freshly grated orange zest

½ teaspoon sea salt

NUTRITION FACTS
(per serving–82g)

Calories: 286; Fat: 11g; Carbs: 43g; Protein: 7g; Fiber: 5g

Vitamin C: 7%; Iron: 13%; Calcium: 4%; Vitamin A: 32%

SERVES 8

PEANUT BUTTER DOUBLE CACAO GRANOLA

Follow the directions on page 66 to prepare the granola.

Virgin coconut oil or parchment paper, for the pan

2½ cups rolled oats

½ cup chopped nuts (any variety)

½ cup grade B maple syrup

⅓ cup vegan chocolate chips or cacao nibs

3 tablespoons peanut or almond butter, melted

2 tablespoons virgin coconut oil, melted

1 tablespoon cacao powder

1 teaspoon ground cinnamon

½ teaspoon pure vanilla extract

Pinch of sea salt

NUTRITION FACTS
(per serving–67g)

Calories: 294; Fat: 14g; Carbs: 40g; Protein: 7g; Fiber: 4g

Vitamin C: 0%; Iron: 4%; Calcium: 3%; Vitamin A: 0%

SERVES 8

POWER-UP BAKED ALMOND PROTEIN BARS

Grab one of these protein-rich bars on a busy morning! Skip the store-bought bars and discover how easy and fun it can be to make your own at home. Feel free to get creative by trying your own crafty flavors and ingredient tweaks.

SERVES 8

1. Preheat the oven to 350°F. Grease a rimmed baking sheet with coconut oil or line with parchment paper.

2. Heat a skillet over high heat. Add the coconut and lightly toast just until the edges are browned, 2 to 3 minutes. Transfer to a large bowl.

3. Add the oats, sweetener, almonds, almond butter, protein powder, coconut oil, flaxseeds, vanilla, cinnamon, and salt. Fold well until the oats soften a bit.

4. Spread the oat mixture in a thick layer (about ¾ inch thick) on the prepared baking sheet and press down firmly to pack the oats. (Thinner bars will be crispier and less chewy, thicker bars, more chewy.)

5. Bake until the edges brown a bit, 20 to 25 minutes. Let cool slightly in the pan before slicing into bars. Let the bars cool completely before removing from the pan. Place the pan in the freezer for 10 minutes to speed up the cooling process.

6. If adding the chocolate drizzle, place the sliced bars in the freezer. Combine the chips and oil in a small bowl and microwave for 40 to 60 seconds to create a chocolate liquid. Stir until smooth and well combined. Microwave the mixture for a few seconds more if chocolate lumps remain.

Virgin coconut oil, for the pan

½ cup shredded unsweetened coconut or unsweetened puffed rice or puffed kamut cereal

2 cups rolled oats

½ cup liquid sweetener, such as coconut nectar syrup or brown rice syrup

½ cup chopped almonds

3 tablespoons salted almond butter, softened

1 tablespoon vanilla-flavored or plain vegan protein powder

2 teaspoons virgin coconut oil, melted

2 teaspoons ground flaxseeds

¼ teaspoon pure vanilla extract

½ teaspoon ground cinnamon

¼ teaspoon sea salt

ingredients continue

recipe continues

continued

CHOCOLATE DRIZZLE (OPTIONAL)

⅓ cup vegan chocolate chips

1 tablespoon virgin coconut oil

NUTRITION FACTS
(per serving-64g)

Calories: 251; Fat: 11g; Carbs: 33g; Protein: 9g; Fiber: 4g

Vitamin C: 1%; Iron: 11%; Calcium: 5%; Vitamin A: 0%

7 Pull the bars from the freezer. They should be hard and cold when you pour the drizzle over them. Drizzle the warm chocolate over the bars—it will firm up on contact.

8 Store the bars in an airtight container in the refrigerator for up to a week. These are delicious served chilled or at room temperature as they are, or try them crumbled into granola topping or cereal.

NO-BAKE CHEWY ENERGY BARS OR BALLS

For quickie snacks or a light morning nibble, these energy bars are perfect! Packed with goodies like seeds, nuts, and dried fruit, these guilt-free treats will provide an instant burst of plant-based energy. This easy no-bake recipe is a keeper!

MAKES 8 BARS OR 20 BALLS

½ cup raw sunflower seeds

¼ cup raw pumpkin seeds

½ cup walnuts

¼ cup raisins or pitted dates

2½ tablespoons brown rice syrup

3 tablespoons almond butter, softened

1 tablespoon virgin coconut oil

1 teaspoon maca powder (optional)

½ teaspoon ground cinnamon

¼ teaspoon pure vanilla extract

1 Line a rimmed baking sheet with parchment paper.

2 Place the sunflower seeds, pumpkin seeds, and walnuts in a food processor and process until crumbly. Do not overprocess. Transfer to a bowl and set aside.

3 Place the raisins in the food processor and process for a few seconds until roughly chopped. Add to the bowl with the seed mixture.

4   In a small microwave-safe bowl, combine the brown rice syrup, almond butter, and coconut oil and microwave for 30 seconds. Stir briskly until silky smooth and well combined. If lumps remain, microwave for 15 seconds more.

5   Fold the almond butter mixture into the bowl with the seed mixture. Fold in the maca, if desired, cinnamon, and vanilla. Stir well to combine. Place the bowl in the freezer for 2 to 4 minutes to firm up just a bit.

6   Using your hands, form the mixture into balls or shape into bars and place them on the prepared baking sheet. (If you want perfectly rectangular bars, spread the mixture on the prepared baking sheet, place in the freezer to firm up, and slice into bars.) Place the baking sheet in the freezer to firm the balls or bars, about 15 minutes.

7   Serve the balls or bars chilled. I like to allow them to warm up just slightly (a bit colder than room temperature). Store any leftovers in an airtight container in the refrigerator or freezer. They will stay delicious for a good month in the freezer, since they are high in healthy fats from the nuts and high-fat foods usually freeze quite well. In the fridge, they'll keep for up to a week.

NUTRITION FACTS
(per serving–34g)

Calories: 175; Fat: 14g; Carbs: 12g; Protein: 6g; Fiber: 2g

Vitamin C: 1%; Iron: 37%; Calcium: 2%; Vitamin A: 0%

"SAVE THE DAY" TOAST!

I make this grilled banana morning toast for my husband at least once a week. It "saves the day" on those busy mornings when you are dreading walking out the door with an empty stomach, but you are short on time. Healthy almond butter mingles with swoon-worthy grilled bananas and superfood sprinkles. And yes, if you are in a super hurry, you can always leave the banana raw!

SERVES 1

1 teaspoon virgin coconut oil

1 banana, cut lengthwise into long strips

1 teaspoon grade B maple syrup

Pinch of ground cinnamon

1 slice whole-grain or sprouted grain bread

1 tablespoon almond butter, softened

½ teaspoon chia seeds

Generous sprinkle of cacao nibs

1 In a skillet, heat the coconut oil over medium-high heat. Add the banana slices, laying them flat against the skillet, and cook for 1 to 2 minutes. Add the maple syrup and cinnamon, flip the banana slices, and cook for 1 to 2 minutes more. Remove from the heat and set aside in the pan.

2 Toast the bread and slather with the almond butter.

3 Lay the banana over the almond butter. Sprinkle the chia seeds and cacao nibs over the top. Slice in half and serve.

Boost It! Add a sprinkle of goji berries, chopped dates, flaxseeds, or golden mulberries.

NUTRITION FACTS (per serving–204g) — Calories: 372; Fat: 15g; Carbs: 54g; Protein: 10g; Fiber: 11g — Vitamin C: 17%; Iron: 15%; Calcium: 12%; Vitamin A: 2%

BAKERY

MUFFINS, BISCUITS, BREADS, AND MORE

Turn up your oven and start baking! Muffins, breads, and biscuits are some of my favorite things to bake at home. The dreamy aromas that will fill your kitchen, combined with the deliciousness of freshly baked goodies, will leave you feeling calm and cozy.

MAPLE BAR BAKED DONUTS

My favorite donuts as a kid were those long, sticky maple bars with glossy caramel-colored frosting. Here are all those flavors made into a vegan baked donut. Sprinkles optional.

SERVES 4 TO 5

1 **For the Donut Batter:** Preheat the oven to 400°F. Grease a donut pan with coconut oil.

2 In a small bowl, combine the banana, flour, nondairy milk, sugar, coconut oil, flaxseeds, vanilla, and cinnamon. Stir well to combine. Pour the batter into the prepared pan.

3 Bake for about 18 minutes, until the donuts are fluffy and lightly browned. Let cool in the pan on a wire rack.

4 **For the Maple Frosting:** In a small bowl, whisk together the sugar, coconut oil, and syrup. For a fluffier frosting, whisk in the vegan buttery spread. Place the frosting in the fridge to chill until the donuts have cooled.

5 Either dip the donuts in the frosting, warm up the frosting a bit to room temperature and drizzle over the top of the donuts like a glaze, or spread it on top. Top with vegan sprinkles, if desired.

DONUT BATTER

Virgin coconut oil, for the pan

½ ripe banana, mashed

½ cup oat, whole wheat, or spelt flour

⅓ cup plain nondairy milk

2 tablespoons vegan sugar

2 teaspoons virgin coconut oil, melted

2 teaspoons ground flaxseeds

¼ teaspoon pure vanilla extract

¼ teaspoon ground cinnamon

MAPLE FROSTING

¼ cup confectioners' sugar

1 tablespoon virgin coconut oil, melted

1 tablespoon grade B maple syrup

1 tablespoon vegan buttery spread (optional)

Vegan sprinkles (optional)

NUTRITION FACTS
(per serving–72g)

Calories: 181; Fat: 7g;
Carbs: 30g; Protein: 2g;
Fiber: 2g

Vitamin C: 2%;
Iron: 4%; Calcium: 5%;
Vitamin A: 1%

COCONUT OIL BLUEBERRY MUFFINS

These muffins are rich and fluffy, with blueberries in every bite. A generous amount of coconut oil makes these muffins quite memorable. Because the muffins bake at a high temperature to start, the coconut oil–greased edges and the coconut-infused muffin tops become brown and toasty. I like to call these "bed-and-breakfast" muffins because they remind me of the rich and fluffy muffins you find served at cozy vacation spots—only these gems are vegan, too! You can use a variety of flours, but if you do not mind gluten and want to indulge, try using "00" flour (it's what I've used in the photo). The texture is pretty amazing. Otherwise, try healthy flours like oat flour, spelt, whole wheat, etc. The texture will vary a bit based on which flour you choose.

SERVES 12

Virgin coconut oil, for the pan

2 cups all-purpose white flour, preferably "00" flour (a whole-grain flour like spelt, whole wheat, or oat can be substituted), plus more as needed

1 tablespoon baking powder

2 teaspoons ground flaxseeds

¾ teaspoon sea salt

12 ounces pureed silken tofu

½ cup plus 2 teaspoons virgin coconut oil, melted

½ cup plus 1 tablespoon raw turbinado sugar, plus more for sprinkling

2 tablespoons fresh lemon juice

1 teaspoon freshly grated lemon zest

½ teaspoon pure vanilla extract

1 Preheat the oven to 410°F. Grease a standard 12-cup muffin tin with a generous amount of coconut oil. Glob it on with your finger so that you can see the opaque white oil coating the tins.

2 In a large bowl, combine the flour, baking powder, flaxseeds, and salt. In a blender, combine the tofu, coconut oil, sugar, lemon juice, lemon zest, and vanilla and puree until silky-smooth and well combined.

3 Add the tofu mixture to the flour mixture and fold well. The batter should be nice and fluffy. If the batter feels a bit wet, add a few more spoonfuls of flour. Fold in the shredded coconut, if desired. Last, fold in the frozen blueberries. The clumpy texture of the batter makes for more textured muffin tops.

4 Fill the wells of the prepared muffin tin evenly with the batter. Sprinkle a pinch of shredded coconut and sugar over each muffin before baking.

5 Bake until the edges of the muffins have browned and the tops have risen, about 10 minutes, then reduce the oven temperature to 375°F and bake for 8 to 12 minutes more. Let cool in the tin on a wire rack for about 20 minutes before removing the muffins from the tin—they will be very delicate right out of the oven due to the high coconut oil content.

6 Serve warm. These are best the same day they're baked. Store any leftover muffins in an airtight container in the refrigerator for 1 to 2 days or in the freezer for 2 to 3 months. Rewarm the muffins for 30 seconds in the microwave or toast before serving.

3 tablespoons shredded coconut, sweetened or unsweetened (optional)

1 cup frozen wild blueberries (or fresh blueberries, frozen; see Note)

Toasted or untoasted shredded coconut, for sprinkling

Note: Frozen blueberries are less likely to sink to the bottom of the batter before being baked, giving you better berry distribution in your muffins! If you have fresh berries, freeze them until firm before mixing them into the batter.

| NUTRITION FACTS (per serving–93g) | Calories: 235; Fat: 11g; Carbs: 30g; Protein: 5g; Fiber: 2g | Vitamin C: 7%; Iron: 10%; Calcium: 8%; Vitamin A: 1% |

ORANGE GLOW MUFFINS

Wake up to a warm glow humming from your kitchen via these energizing muffins! They are sunny and inviting. Muffin lovers, give these citrus-and-spice-infused muffins a try for a perky start to your day.

SERVES 12

Virgin coconut oil, for the pan

1½ cups all-purpose white, spelt, or homemade oat flour (from rolled oats; see Sidebar, page 38)

½ cup rolled oats

1 tablespoon baking powder

1 teaspoon ground cinnamon

½ teaspoon sea salt

⅛ teaspoon cayenne

1 cup canned butternut squash, pumpkin, or sweet potato puree

½ cup grade B maple syrup

½ cup almond milk

⅓ cup fresh orange juice

2 tablespoons virgin coconut oil, softened

1½ teaspoons freshly grated orange zest, plus more for sprinkling

½ cup chopped walnuts

⅓ cup peeled and diced seedless orange or tangerine

1 teaspoon grated peeled fresh ginger

Pinch of raw sugar

NUTRITION FACTS
(per serving–84g)

Calories: 183; Fat: 6g; Carbs: 28g; Protein: 4g; Fiber: 4g

Vitamin C: 14%; Iron: 7%; Calcium: 9%; Vitamin A: 52%

1 Preheat the oven to 410°F. Grease a standard 12-cup muffin tin with a generous amount of coconut oil. Glob it on with your finger so that you can see the opaque white oil coating the wells.

2 In a large bowl, combine the flour, oats, baking powder, cinnamon, salt, and cayenne.

3 In a small bowl, combine the squash puree, maple syrup, almond milk, orange juice, coconut oil, and orange zest. Stir briskly until smooth. You may need to warm the mixture in the microwave to help soften it. Fold this wet mixture into the flour mixture.

4 Fold the walnuts, oranges, and ginger into the batter.

5 Fill the wells of the prepared muffin tin with the batter. Sprinkle orange zest and sugar on top of each muffin.

6 Bake for 10 minutes, then reduce the oven temperature to 375°F and bake for 10 to 15 minutes more. The tops should turn golden brown on the edges when done. Let cool in the tin on a wire rack for 5 to 10 minutes before removing the muffins from the tin.

7 Serve warm. These are best the same day they're baked. Store any leftover muffins in an airtight container in the refrigerator for 1 to 2 days or in the freezer for 2 to 3 months. Rewarm the muffins for 30 seconds in the microwave or toast before serving.

APPLE-BRAN MUFFINS

I have always loved bran muffins, that sticky-sweet blackstrap molasses flavor accenting the bumpy bran flour base. And these bran muffins are classic with an apple-cinnamon spin! Start your day with one of these fiber-rich muffins.

SERVES 12

1. Preheat the oven to 375°F. Grease a standard 12-cup muffin tin with a generous amount of coconut oil.

2. In a large bowl, combine the flour, wheat bran, wheat gluten, baking powder, cinnamon, and salt.

3. In a small bowl, combine the applesauce, nondairy milk, coconut sugar, coconut oil, molasses, and vanilla. Stir until smooth.

4. Fold or beat the liquid mixture into the flour mixture until a smooth batter forms.

5. In a small bowl, combine the apples, raisins (if using), lemon juice, and a dash of cinnamon. Fold the apple mixture and walnuts into the batter.

6. Fill the wells of the prepared muffin tin.

7. Bake for about 25 minutes, until the muffin tops have slightly crisp edges and are dark brown in color. Let cool in the tin on a wire rack for at least 20 minutes before removing the muffins from the tin.

8. Serve warm. These are best the same day they're baked. Store any leftover muffins in an airtight container in the refrigerator for 1 to 2 days or in the freezer for 2 to 3 months. Rewarm the muffins for 30 seconds in the microwave or toast before serving.

Virgin coconut oil, for the pan

1 cup all-purpose white flour

¾ cup wheat bran

2 tablespoons vital wheat gluten or more wheat bran

2 teaspoons baking powder

1 teaspoon ground cinnamon, plus more as needed

½ teaspoon sea salt

1 cup applesauce, at room temperature

½ cup plain nondairy milk, warmed

½ cup coconut sugar or any dry vegan sugar

⅓ cup virgin coconut oil, softened

2 tablespoons blackstrap molasses

1 teaspoon pure vanilla extract

1 cup chopped apple

⅓ cup raisins (optional)

1 teaspoon fresh lemon juice

¼ cup chopped walnuts

NUTRITION FACTS
(per serving–65g)

Calories: 156; Fat: 7g; Carbs: 25g; Protein: 3g; Fiber: 3g

Vitamin C: 0%; Iron: 7%; Calcium: 7%; Vitamin A: 1%

GINGER PEACH STRAWBERRY SPELT MUFFINS

Spicy ginger and cinnamon, soothing sweet peach, and nutty spelt flour make this a muffin to crave. Pair with a steamy hot tea or latte for instant breakfast bliss.

SERVES 12

Virgin coconut oil, for the pan

1¾ cups spelt flour

¼ cup rolled oats or homemade oat flour (from rolled oats; see Sidebar, page 38)

1 tablespoon ground flaxseeds

2 teaspoons baking powder

½ teaspoon ground cinnamon

½ teaspoon ground ginger

¼ teaspoon sea salt

Pinch of cayenne

1 large ripe banana, mashed

1 cup silken tofu, blended until smooth, or plain nondairy milk

½ cup vegan buttery spread, melted

½ cup grade B maple syrup

1 tablespoon fresh lemon juice

1 teaspoon pure vanilla extract

1 teaspoon grated peeled fresh ginger

1 cup diced fresh peaches

½ cup strawberries, quartered, or more peaches

NUTRITION FACTS
(per serving–97g)

Calories: 195; Fat: 8g; Carbs: 28g; Protein: 4g; Fiber: 4g

Vitamin C: 11%; Iron: 6%; Calcium: 9%; Vitamin A: 2%

1 Preheat the oven to 400°F. Grease a standard 12-cup muffin tin with a generous amount of coconut oil. Glob it on with your finger so that you can see the opaque white oil coating the wells.

2 In a large bowl, combine the flour, oats, flaxseeds, baking powder, cinnamon, ground ginger, salt, and cayenne.

3 In a small bowl, combine the banana, tofu, vegan buttery spread, maple syrup, lemon juice, vanilla, and fresh ginger. Stir until smooth. If needed, warm the mixture in the microwave for a minute to soften.

4 Fold or beat the liquid mixture into the flour mixture until a smooth batter forms. Fold the peaches and strawberries into the batter.

5 Fill the wells of the prepared muffin tin.

6 Bake for 10 minutes, then reduce the oven temperature to 375°F and bake for 8 to 10 minutes more. The muffin tops will be slightly browned on the edges when done and the fruit will be cooked and sticky around the edges. Let cool in the tin on a wire rack for at least 20 minutes before removing the muffins from the tin.

7 Serve warm. These are best the same day they're baked. Store any leftover muffins in an airtight container in the refrigerator for 1 to 2 days or in the freezer for 2 to 3 months. Rewarm the muffins for 30 seconds in the microwave or toast before serving.

SWEET POTATO BISCUITS

Fluffy biscuits infused with vitamin A–rich sweet potatoes and cinnamon, maple, and coconut accents are perfect paired with soups, stews, brunches—just about anything really!

SERVES 12

1. Preheat the oven to 400°F. Lightly grease a baking sheet with coconut oil.

2. Poke a few holes in the sweet potato using a fork. Bake the sweet potato for about 1 hour, until easily pierced with a fork. Remove the sweet potato and raise the oven temperature to 415°F.

3. Remove the skin from the potato and mash the flesh in a large bowl. Mash in the almond milk, coconut oil, maple syrup, salt, orange juice, cinnamon, and orange zest. Fold in the flour and baking powder until a warm dough forms.

4. Dust your work surface with flour. Turn out the dough and knead it by hand for a few minutes. If the dough feels too wet, add a few more pinches of flour. Return the dough to the bowl and place in the fridge for about 10 minutes. This makes the dough easier to handle.

5. Roll out the chilled dough to a 1-inch thickness. Cut out biscuit rounds using a round cookie cutter, biscuit cutter, or a round glass, if you're desperate. Keep gathering the scraps and rerolling until all the dough is used. Transfer the dough rounds to the prepared baking sheet.

6. Bake for 15 minutes. The biscuits will have lightly browned tops and be lightly puffy in appearance when done. Let cool on the pan for 2 to 3 minutes before transferring the biscuits to a wire rack.

7. Serve warm. These biscuits are best served same day, but can be stored in the freezer for 2 to 3 months.

Virgin coconut oil, for the pan

1 medium sweet potato

½ cup plain almond milk

⅓ cup virgin coconut oil

2 tablespoons grade B maple syrup

1 teaspoon sea salt

1 teaspoon fresh orange juice

½ teaspoon ground cinnamon

Pinch of freshly grated orange zest

2 cups spelt flour, plus more as needed

1 tablespoon baking powder

NUTRITION FACTS
(per serving–68g)

Calories: 165; Fat: 7g; Carbs: 25g; Protein: 3g; Fiber: 2g

Vitamin C: 9%; Iron: 7%; Calcium: 9%; Vitamin A: 97%

SWEET SPOONABLE CORNBREAD

I remember eating at a few Mexican restaurants as a kid that served this sweet scoop of cornbread on the side of the plate. I always asked for an extra scoop! So I wanted to re-create this memorable sweet side with plant-based ingredients. This spoonable cornbread is soft and silky with rich corn flavor. The secret ingredient is the masa harina, which adds a very smooth corn texture and lovely corn flavor. It is the same ingredient used to make homemade tortillas and tamales.

SERVES 20

5 tablespoons vegan buttery spread, plus more for the pan

2 large ears corn, kernels removed (about 1½ cups kernels)

1⅔ cups masa harina

¾ cup agave syrup

3 tablespoons cornmeal

1 teaspoon baking powder

¼ teaspoon sea salt

⅛ teaspoon freshly ground black pepper

1 cup full-fat coconut milk

2 teaspoons apple cider vinegar

¼ cup drained and chopped canned green chiles

1 Preheat the oven to 350°F. Grease a loaf pan or 9-inch round cake pan with vegan buttery spread.

2 In a blender or food processor, pulse the vegan buttery spread with 1 cup of the corn kernels.

3 Pour the corn mixture into a large bowl. Stir in the masa harina, agave, cornmeal, baking powder, salt, and pepper. Mix well.

4 Stir in the coconut milk and the vinegar. Fold in the remaining corn kernels and the chiles. Mix well until all the flour is incorporated and any clumps are broken up. The batter should be fairly thin.

5 Pour the batter into the prepared pan. Bake for 35 to 40 minutes if using a loaf pan or 25 to 30 minutes if using a cake pan. The cornbread will have a moist yet firm consistency when done. The top should be soft yet firm and the insides cooked yet moist, perfect for spooning to serve.

6 Allow to cool in the pan slightly before serving, but serve warm, scooped directly from the pan with a spoon or ice cream scooper. Store any leftovers in an airtight container in the refrigerator for 2 to 3 days. Leftovers can be served cool or warmed. Reheat in a 350°F oven for 15 minutes.

NUTRITION FACTS
(per serving–48g)

Calories: 163; Fat: 6g; Carbs: 25g; Protein: 2g; Fiber: 2g

Vitamin C: 1%; Iron: 9%; Calcium: 4%; Vitamin A: 3%

YEAST-FREE CRUSTY BROWN BREAD WITH CITRUS AND PUMPKIN SEEDS

Homemade bread leads to a homey sort of kitchen bliss that I can't even describe. You will feel it when you slide your loaf out of the oven and hold its plump, crusty-topped self in your hands. Slicing homemade bread makes you feel like you can do anything in the kitchen! This brown bread is yeast free and accented with citrus and pumpkin seeds.

SERVES 9

1. Preheat the oven to 415°F. Grease a 9x5-inch loaf pan with coconut oil spray.

2. In a large bowl, combine the flour, wheat bran, baking powder, flaxseeds and/or vital wheat gluten, salt, and cinnamon.

3. In a blender or food processor, combine the applesauce, orange zest, orange, agave, molasses, and coconut oil.

4. Pour the liquid mixture into the bowl with the flour mixture and fold until everything is combined and a light and fluffy dough forms. Fold in ⅓ cup of the pumpkin seeds. If you like working with a drier dough, add another few spoonfuls of flour, one at a time, until the desired consistency is reached.

5. Lightly spray the top of the dough with coconut oil spray. Sprinkle the remaining 1 tablespoon pumpkin seeds on top.

6. Form the dough into a log and set it in the prepared loaf pan.

recipe continues

Coconut oil spray

2½ cups plus 1 tablespoon sprouted spelt flour (see Note, page 84), plus more as needed

1 cup plus 1 tablespoon wheat bran

1 tablespoon baking powder

1 teaspoon ground flaxseeds, or 1 tablespoon vital wheat gluten (use both for an even sturdier bread)

½ teaspoon sea salt

⅛ teaspoon ground cinnamon

1 cup applesauce (homemade recommended; see Sidebar, page 84)

Pinch of freshly grated orange zest

1 medium juicy orange, peeled

¼ cup agave syrup or grade B maple syrup

1 tablespoon blackstrap molasses

1 tablespoon virgin coconut oil, melted

⅓ cup plus 1 tablespoon raw salted and sprouted pumpkin seeds

continued

Note: Substitute 1 tablespoon vital wheat gluten in place of 1 tablespoon of flour. This adds some additional binding and improves the bread texture by adding gluten.

7 Bake for 20 minutes, then reduce the oven temperature to 350°F and bake for 30 minutes more. The bread will be lightly browned on the top with crisp crevices and texture. The insides will be moist but cooked through. Let cool in the pan for at least 15 minutes. Slicing is easier if you let the bread cool for at least 30 minutes after removing it from the oven.

8 This bread is best served slightly warm or toasted the same day it is baked. Leftovers can be wrapped in plastic wrap and stored on the counter for up to 1 day, or in the fridge for 2 to 3 days. Reheat the bread by toasting slices in a toaster or warming them in a 350°F oven until browned and toasty, 3 to 10 minutes depending on the thickness of the slice.

Note: You can try a spelt, wheat, or gluten-free variety of all-purpose flour. Whole-grain or sprouted grain flour is advised for this bread.

TO MAKE HOMEMADE APPLESAUCE

In a blender, combine 2 cored and roughly chopped apples, a few teaspoons fresh lemon juice, and 1 to 3 tablespoons water. Blend, adding more water as needed to help blend, then add a pinch of cinnamon and pulse to combine. You should end up with around 2 cups.

NUTRITION FACTS (per serving–96g) — Calories: 126; Fat: 4g; Carbs: 22g; Protein: 4g; Fiber: 5g — Vitamin C: 17%; Iron: 11%; Calcium: 9%; Vitamin A: 1%

HARVEST PUMPKIN LOAF

Pumpkin is one of those flavors that you crave during the fall and winter months, but I could easily eat pumpkin loaf year-round. The autumn flavor of pumpkin and spice is perfect paired with afternoon tea. Plus pumpkin is rich in vitamin A and fiber! I sweeten this loaf with maple syrup and add plenty of pumpkin pie spice.

MAKES 1 LOAF; SERVES 9

1. Preheat the oven to 400°F. Grease a loaf pan with coconut oil.

2. In a large bowl, combine the flour, baking powder, pumpkin pie spice, flaxseeds, salt, and cayenne and stir well.

3. In a blender or food processor, combine the pumpkin, maple syrup, coconut oil, vegan buttery spread, orange juice, orange zest, and vanilla. Process on low until smooth. Fold the pumpkin mixture into the flour mixture and stir well.

4. Pour the batter into the loaf pan and top with the pumpkin seeds and sugar.

5. Bake for 10 minutes, then reduce the oven temperature to 350°F and bake for 45 minutes more. The bread will be bronzed-orange in color and fluffy yet firm in texture when done. Cool the bread in the pan at least 15 minutes before transferring to a breadboard or plate for slicing. Serve warm or chilled. Store any leftovers, covered, in the fridge.

Note: Fold in ⅓ cup dried or fresh cranberries or pomegranate seeds for more harvest flair.

Virgin coconut oil, for the pan

2 cups whole wheat, spelt, or homemade oat flour (from rolled oats; see Sidebar, page 38)

1 tablespoon baking powder

1½ teaspoons pumpkin pie spice

1 teaspoon ground flaxseeds

½ teaspoon sea salt

Pinch of cayenne

1½ cups canned unsweetened pumpkin puree

½ cup grade B maple syrup

¼ cup virgin coconut oil, melted

¼ cup vegan buttery spread

1 tablespoon fresh orange juice

Pinch of freshly grated orange zest

1 teaspoon pure vanilla extract

Pinch of pumpkin seeds

Pinch of vegan sugar

NUTRITION FACTS (per serving–107g)   Calories: 280; Fat: 14g; Carbs: 36g; Protein: 6g; Fiber: 5g   Vitamin C: 5%; Iron: 16%; Calcium: 11%; Vitamin A: 128%

BANANA BREAD BLISS LOAF

Banana bread is a must for any at-home baker. Master this recipe and you will never again fear a fruit bowl filled with black-spotted bananas! This cozy loaf does not disappoint. The vital wheat gluten is optional but really adds an extra level of binding. That is also why I use the silken tofu. I do not like my banana bread crumbly—I like it very sturdy, thickly sliced, and with heaps of banana flavor in every bite.

MAKES I LOAF; SERVES 9

Virgin coconut oil, for the pan

1 cup whole wheat flour (or more oat flour)

1 cup homemade oat flour (from rolled oats; see Sidebar, page 38)

1 tablespoon vital wheat gluten (optional)

1 tablespoon baking powder

1 teaspoon ground cinnamon

½ teaspoon sea salt

12 ounces silken tofu, at room temperature

½ teaspoon pure vanilla extract

⅓ cup grade B maple syrup

¼ cup virgin coconut oil, melted

¼ cup vegan buttery spread

1 tablespoon fresh orange juice

Pinch of freshly grated orange zest

½ cup chopped walnuts

2 large very ripe bananas, mashed

1 tablespoon rolled oats

½ firm banana, sliced

Note: Also delicious for banana bread: dark chocolate chips! Just a small sprinkle can go a long way in creating decadence.

1 Preheat the oven to 400°F. Grease a loaf pan with coconut oil.

2 In a large bowl, combine the flours, wheat gluten, baking powder, cinnamon, and salt and stir well.

3 In a blender or food processor, combine the tofu, vanilla, maple syrup, coconut oil, vegan buttery spread, orange juice, and orange zest, and blend on low until smooth. Fold the tofu mixture into the flour mixture, stir well, then fold in the walnuts and mashed bananas.

4 Pour the batter into the loaf pan and top with the oats and sliced banana.

5 Bake for 10 minutes, then reduce the oven temperature to 350°F and bake for 45 minutes more. The bread will be slightly browned when done. Cool the bread for at least 10 minutes in the pan before transferring to a breadboard or plate for slicing. This bread is delicious served warm or chilled. Store any leftovers, covered, in the fridge.

Tip: If desired, substitute the tofu with another large, ripe banana and reduce the flour by ½ cup.

NUTRITION FACTS (per serving–118g) Calories: 272; Fat: 14g; Carbs: 31g; Protein: 6g; Fiber: 4g   Vitamin C: 7%; Iron: 10%; Calcium: 11%; Vitamin A: 7%

SANDWICHES

I am a sandwich lover. I remember riding my bike to the local deli every day after school to get a veggie sandwich. Sourdough bread, stacks of veggies, and layers of buttery avocado. And plenty of sprouts, too! Sandwiches are anytime meals for me—lunches, dinner, snacks, and even breakfast! Sandwiches and wraps can be infused with just about any flavors you crave. For the best sandwiches ever, find fresh breads that you love or make a loaf yourself! And P.S.: Sandwiches are perfect for sharing, so find a pal and show them some vegan love.

PHILLY CHEESE SANDWICH

Confession, I have never had a non-vegan Philly cheese sandwich. But this recipe request came from my husband who, after giving up meat, had a craving. So my "veganize this" task was in play! I did my research and came up with this stunning vegan sandwich replica. Sizzling bell peppers? Check. Melty orange cheese? Check. Peppered, hot slices of seitan (a.k.a. wheat meat)? Check. Hoagie roll? Check. This sandwich passed his taste test with flying colors.

─────────── SERVES 1 ───────────

1. Preheat the oven to 350°F. Slice the bread down the center and toast it in the oven for about 5 minutes.

2. Heat a sauté pan over high heat. Add the oil, bell pepper, onion, and chiles (if using), along with the seitan. Cook, stirring, until the edges of the seitan and onion begin to blacken, 3 to 5 minutes. Add the garlic powder, salt, and black pepper toward the end of the cooking process to avoid burning them.

3. Add the cheese so it melts over the mixture. Transfer the filling to the roll. Garnish with the cilantro. Serve warm.

Note: Use the cheese sauce recipe from my Favorite Vegan Mac and Cheese recipe on page 224 for homemade orange melty cheese. Thicken the recipe up by adding less liquid and more nutritional yeast.

Gluten-Free Version: Choose gluten-free bread and substitute finely sliced portobello mushrooms for the seitan.

1 vegan hoagie roll or long slice of French bread (see Note)

1 to 2 teaspoons oil, such as safflower or extra-virgin olive oil

½ large red or green bell pepper, thinly sliced into strips

½ medium sweet onion, sliced

1 tablespoon canned diced fire-roasted hatch chiles (optional)

½ cup seitan strips

Few pinches of garlic powder

Sea salt and freshly ground black pepper

2 tablespoons vegan cheddar cheese (I like Teese brand for this recipe, but Daiya cheese shreds will also work; see Note)

1 tablespoon finely chopped fresh cilantro, for garnish

Note: Add a few pinches of cayenne or sliced fresh jalapeño for extra spiciness.

Note: I like brushing olive oil on the inside and outside of the roll before toasting it.

NUTRITION FACTS (per serving–365g) Calories: 467; Fat: 12g; Carbs: 52g; Protein: 39g; Fiber: 7g   Vitamin C: 201%; Iron: 24%; Calcium: 12%; Vitamin A: 53%

THE CALIFORNIAN: SPROUT AVOCADO SANDWICH

This is the sandwich I grew up eating. California avocados, toasted sourdough or sprouted grain bread, a giant handful of crunchy alfalfa sprouts, juicy tomato, thin red onion, and a thick slathering of hummus. Vegan mayo or Dijon mustard optional. If you want a taste of sunshine, California-style, make this sandwich and serve with a tall glass of lemon iced tea. Eat it while sitting in the sunshine and you'll almost be able to hear a few waves crashing in the distance.

SERVES 1

1 teaspoon fresh lemon juice

1 small avocado, or ½ large avocado, sliced

2 slices sprouted grain or sourdough bread

1 tablespoon Classic Hummus Dip (page 197)

1 teaspoon vegan mayonnaise and/or Dijon mustard

2 to 3 slices tomato

1 to 2 thin slices red onion

2 tablespoons shredded carrots

½ cup sprouts (any variety)

Sea salt and freshly ground black pepper

1 Sprinkle the lemon juice over the avocado.

2 Toast the bread and slather the hummus on one slice. Spread the vegan mayo and/or mustard on the other slice.

3 Layer the sandwich by adding the avocado, tomato, onion, and carrots and top with the fluffy sprouts. Sprinkle some salt and pepper over the top. Slice to serve.

NUTRITION FACTS (per serving–372g)

Calories: 496; Fat: 30g; Carbs: 38g; Protein: 14g; Fiber: 15g

Vitamin C: 34%; Iron: 17%; Calcium: 3%; Vitamin A: 100%

TEMPEH REUBEN

This veganized Reuben sandwich is warm and toasty with smoky tempeh bacon, rye bread, and a generous layer of warmed sauerkraut. I love this as a dinner sandwich, served with a small soup or salad on the side.

— SERVES 1 —

EASY VEGAN RUSSIAN DRESSING (SEE NOTE)

1 tablespoon vegan mayonnaise

1 teaspoon grade B maple syrup

Pinch of Spanish paprika

Pinch of garlic powder

Pinch of freshly ground black pepper

MAPLE TEMPEH

4 ounces tempeh

Vegetable oil

2 teaspoons grade B maple syrup

1 teaspoon tamari

Few splashes of vegan liquid smoke (optional)

Freshly ground black pepper

⅓ cup sauerkraut

2 slices vegan rye bread

2 slices tomato

3 rings thinly sliced red onion

Lettuce or leafy greens (optional)

1. **For the Easy Vegan Russian Dressing:** In a small bowl, whip together the dressing ingredients. Cover and refrigerate until ready to use.

2. **For the Maple Tempeh:** Slice the tempeh in half, then down the center to make thin square slices. Heat a skillet over medium-high heat. Add a tiny splash of oil to the pan and then add the sliced tempeh. Add the maple, tamari, and liquid smoke (if using). Cook the tempeh for about 2 minutes on each side. The edges should be blackened when finished. Add some pepper over the top. Push the tempeh to the side of the pan and add the sauerkraut to the warm pan. Sprinkle some pepper over the kraut. Flip the kraut once so both sides warm from the pan; about 30 seconds on each side will properly warm the kraut. Cook longer if you like the kraut more wilted and warm.

3. Assemble the sandwich. Toast the bread and spread the Russian dressing on both slices. Pile on the tempeh, tomato, onion, and sauerkraut. Add additional lettuce or leafy greens, if desired. Slice and serve warm.

Note: If you'd prefer, make a vegan version of classic Russian dressing by stirring together 2 tablespoons vegan mayonnaise, 2 teaspoons ketchup, 1½ teaspoons pickle relish, 2 teaspoons fresh lemon juice, ½ teaspoon vegan Worcestershire sauce, and a pinch of cayenne, if you'd prefer a spicier version.

NUTRITION FACTS
(per serving—308g)

Calories: 487; Fat: 16g; Carbs: 60g; Protein: 30g; Fiber: 8g

Vitamin C: 21%; Iron: 33%; Calcium: 15%; Vitamin A: 8%

CHIPOTLE TOFU SANDWICH

Crispy-edged tofu steaks meet all your favorite sandwich toppings, with a rich drizzle of spicy chipotle sauce bringing everything together in this lovable, protein-rich sandwich.

SERVES 1

1 **For the Blackened Tofu:** Slice the tofu into thick rectangular planks. Press it dry with a few paper towels. Press out as much liquid as possible to keep the tofu surface dry. This helps with the crispy tofu edges.

2 In a skillet, heat the safflower oil over high heat. Add the tofu and cook for 1 minute. Add the tamari, maple syrup, and liquid smoke (if using) and sprinkle the nutritional yeast (if using), pepper, and garlic powder over the top. Flip the tofu and cook for another minute. Flip one more time and cook until the edges have clearly started to blacken and crisp. Total cooking time is 3 to 4 minutes, depending on how firm you like your tofu. The tofu firms up the longer you cook it, as it loses moisture from the cooking process. Remove from the heat.

3 **For the Smoky Chipotle Sauce:** Combine all the sauce ingredients in a blender and blend until smooth and creamy. Slather a generous amount of the sauce on both pieces of toast. Top one piece with the tofu and add another spoonful of sauce right over the tofu. Top the tofu with the onion, tomato, and lettuce. Place the second piece of toast on top to close the sandwich, slice, and serve with the leftover chipotle sauce on the side.

Boost It!! Make this a club sandwich by adding avocado and adding another slice of toasted bread to the stack. A club serves two, easily.

BLACKENED TOFU

6 ounces firm tofu

½ teaspoon safflower oil

2 teaspoons tamari

2 teaspoons grade B maple syrup

½ teaspoon vegan liquid smoke (optional)

1 teaspoon nutritional yeast (optional)

Few pinches of freshly ground black pepper

Pinch of garlic powder

SMOKY CHIPOTLE SAUCE

1 heaping tablespoon vegan mayonnaise

½ canned chipotle pepper, carefully chopped (see Note)

2 teaspoons grade B maple syrup

1 teaspoon adobo sauce from chipotle can

Few drops of vegan liquid smoke

Pinch of freshly ground black pepper

2 slices bread, toasted

1 to 2 slices sweet onion

1 to 2 slices tomato

2 to 3 romaine lettuce leaves

Note: Use chipotle powder, to taste, in place of chipotle in adobo.

NUTRITION FACTS
(per serving–492g) Calories: 531; Fat: 20g; Carbs: 70g; Protein: 26g; Fiber: 7g   Vitamin C: 135%; Iron: 39%; Calcium: 42%; Vitamin A: 26%

SAUTÉING TOFU

Tofu right out of the package is wet, lifeless, soft, and bland. Okay, so once in a while I actually enjoy cold, unseasoned tofu in soups and salads, but most of the time I want it seared in a skillet so that the edges become crisp and the surfaces browned. Here are a few key tips:

- **Low moisture:** Remove as much moisture as possible from the tofu before placing it in the pan to cook. Firmly press or squeeze the wet tofu with a few paper towels to soak up the moisture, or use a tofu press. No matter what, make sure that the surfaces of the tofu are free of moisture before placing it in the pan. If you are in a rush, even a quick blotting of the surfaces with a few paper towels will help. Dry tofu will help you achieve those crisp, seared edges.

- **High heat:** The pan must be very hot when the tofu first goes in so it will properly sear and those pretty golden colors start to form. Make sure the pan is well heated over medium to high heat. Add a splash of oil. You do not need a lot of oil—just a teaspoon or less can help a lot. I like safflower oil the best for a crisp tofu sauté. Extra-virgin olive oil and virgin coconut oil are also great.

- **Timing:** Do not move the tofu around in the pan excessively. The tofu should sit in one spot for about a minute to really achieve that dark sear along the sides and edges.

- **Moist pan:** A wet pan can lead to soggy tofu, but a dry pan can lead to a cooking disaster by burning your pan. You do not want your pan to get too hot and dry—a happy medium is desired. Use broth, fresh juice, oil, or even water to add a bit of moisture to the pan. A trick is to spoon the hot pan liquid over the tofu while it is in the pan, this helps bathe the tofu in flavorful liquid, while cooking it faster. But you do want the tofu to be pulled from a dry pan. When the cooking liquid is absorbed or steamed away and the tofu is seared nicely, pull the tofu to serve!

- **Seasoning:** Tofu, in its basic form, is very bland. It needs salt and seasoning or marinades to give it life. Dry spices, dry salts, tamari, citrus juices, vinegar, sweeteners, and marinades can all infuse some flavor appeal into tofu.

EGGLESS SALAD SANDWICH

Picnic perfect and easy to make, this egg-free "egg salad" sandwich has savory spiced flavors from the turmeric, Dijon, and spices. The celery and onion add a welcoming crunchy accent to the marinated tofu base, and the salad is rich in protein and wonderful served on toast or as a side.

SERVES 4

1 Place the veggies in a large bowl. Drain the tofu and pat dry. Cube or crumble the tofu into the bowl.

2 **For the Dressing:** In a small bowl, whisk together the dressing ingredients. Pour the dressing over the veggies and tofu and toss very well. You want the dressing to coat all the tofu. Taste and adjust the spices and salt to taste. Add more seasoning for bolder flavors.

3 Chill for at least an hour before serving to allow the flavors to marinate and the tofu to chill.

4 Top four slices of the toast with the salad, add a second piece of toast to close, slice, and serve.

Tip: If you like the tofu a bit more "cooked" in taste and texture, steam, bake, or cook the tofu, stirring occasionally, before cubing or crumbling to mix with the veggies and dressing.

½ cup chopped scallions

½ cup chopped celery

12 ounces firm or extra-firm tofu

DRESSING

¼ cup vegan mayonnaise

¼ cup Dijon mustard

3 tablespoons nutritional yeast, plus more as needed

1 teaspoon celery seeds

1 teaspoon ground turmeric

1 teaspoon grade B maple syrup

½ teaspoon garlic powder

¼ teaspoon freshly ground black pepper

⅛ teaspoon cayenne

Sea salt

8 slices sprouted grain bread or pita pocket halves, toasted

NUTRITION FACTS (per serving–215g) Calories: 278; Fat: 7g; Carbs: 39g; Protein: 20g; Fiber: 10g Vitamin C: 6%; Iron: 29%; Calcium: 21%; Vitamin A: 5%

AVOCADO TOAST

Avocados are one of my favorite foods not only because they taste amazing, but because they are incredibly healthy. Avocados are loaded with healthy fats and are a vegan source of vitamin E, folate, potassium, fiber, and magnesium. If you are not already an avocado toast superfan like me, just make it a few times and you will see how addictive this easy recipe can be. I always keep avocados on hand just in case an avocado toast craving strikes! This base recipe is fun to customize and add to as well—see variation ideas below.

SERVES 2

1 avocado, peeled, pitted, and diced

2 to 3 teaspoons fresh lemon juice

Few pinches of garlic powder

Pinch of sea salt and freshly ground black pepper

2 slices Yeast-Free Crusty Brown Bread with Citrus and Pumpkin Seeds (page 83) or any variety of bread, toasted

1 tomato, diced (optional)

Pinch of red pepper flakes

1 Place the avocado, lemon juice, garlic powder, salt, and black pepper in a small bowl. Mash well.

2 Slather the mashed avocado on each slice of bread and top with the tomato (if using) and red pepper flakes. Slice each sandwich in half and serve open-face.

VARIATIONS

Add sunflower seeds and diced tomato.

Add cooked chickpeas and a drizzle of pesto sauce.

Add thinly sliced citrus or mango for a fruity twist.

Add tempeh bacon and micro greens.

Add thinly sliced radishes and carrots with a drizzle of extra-virgin olive oil.

NUTRITION FACTS
(per serving–153g)

Calories: 282; Fat: 20g; Carbs: 16g; Protein: 7g; Fiber: 10g

Vitamin C: 29%; Iron: 8%; Calcium: 3%; Vitamin A: 37%

BIG BEAUTIFUL KALE WRAP

Oh, kale, how you enchant me so. So much so that I built an entire vegan wrap sandwich around you. This big beautiful wrap is stuffed to overflowing with marinated kale. I have basically taken my favorite kale salad and stuffed it into a handheld wrap. For a grain-free version, substitute brown rice paper wraps for the grain wrap. The rice paper wraps will be smaller, but you can still stuff them to the brim with lovely leafy greens.

SERVES 1

1 Chop the kale into small pieces and place in a large bowl. Add the carrots, apple, and hemp seeds.

2 Heat a skillet over high heat. Toast the walnuts in the skillet for a quick minute, just to bring out their nutty flavor. (You could also just leave them raw, if preferred.) Add them to the bowl with the kale.

3 Pour the dressing into the kale bowl and toss very well. You can simply use a large spoon or you can massage the kale with your hands to wilt it even further.

4 Heat a skillet over medium heat. Place the wrap in the pan and warm until the wrap softens and browns a bit, 1 to 3 minutes. (Alternatively, a quick method using a gas burner is to place the wrap directly on the burner over low heat for 2 to 5 seconds on each side. You can also warm the wrap in the microwave for 15 to 30 seconds to soften.) Make sure the wrap is nice and pliable when you begin to fill it.

5 Slather the hummus and mayo (if desired, for a creamier wrap) inside the wrap, add the avocado, and fill with as much of the dressed kale as the wrap will hold. Sprinkle bacon bits over the kale, if desired. Carefully smash the kale into the wrap as you fold it into a burrito shape. Slice and serve.

3 heaping cups raw kale leaves

⅓ cup shredded carrots

⅓ cup diced apple

2 teaspoons raw hemp seeds

1 to 2 tablespoons walnuts or pumpkin seeds

Tahini Maple Dressing (page 178)

1 extra-large whole wheat flour tortilla wrap, brown rice paper wraps, or steamed giant collard leaf

1 to 2 tablespoons Classic Hummus Dip (page 197)

1 teaspoon vegan mayonnaise (optional)

¼ avocado, diced

2 tablespoons chopped Tempeh Bacon Bits (page 62; optional)

NUTRITION FACTS
(per serving–362g)

Calories: 558; Fat: 22g; Carbs: 75g; Protein: 21g; Fiber: 12g

Vitamin C: 423%; Iron: 39%; Calcium: 35%; Vitamin A: 742%

SMOKY TEMPEH WRAP

Smoky tempeh strikes again! So flavorful and rich in protein, tempeh is a go-to protein source for vegans. This is my favorite tempeh sandwich recipe. The smoky-spicy flavor of the tempeh logs mingles with the creamy avocado and crunchy carrots, tossed in a touch of vegan mayo. I also love to pair the tempeh with leftover 5-Step Raw Kale Salad (pg 153) for a super-easy wrap recipe.

SERVES 1

CARROT-CITRUS SLAW

½ cup shredded carrots

1 Satsuma tangerine, or ½ orange, peeled and diced

1 to 2 teaspoons vegan mayonnaise or tahini

1 teaspoon apple cider vinegar

Pinch of freshly grated orange zest

Pinch of paprika

Pinch of freshly ground black pepper

OR

Leftover 5-Step Raw Kale Salad (page 153) mixed with 1 teaspoon vegan mayonnaise

SMOKY TEMPEH LOGS

1 teaspoon safflower oil

4 ounces tempeh, sliced into logs

2 teaspoons tamari

2 teaspoons grade B maple syrup

Few drops of vegan liquid smoke

Pinch of freshly ground black pepper

Pinch of cayenne

1 large wrap, warmed

1 **For the Carrot-Citrus Slaw:** If making the slaw to add to the wrap, mix together the slaw ingredients in a big bowl. Smash some of the citrus so that it becomes soft and juicy, marinating the carrots. Cover and refrigerate.

2 **For the Smoky Tempeh Logs:** Heat a sauté pan over high heat. Add the oil and tempeh logs. Cook, stirring occasionally, for a few minutes to blacken the edges of the tempeh, then drizzle in the tamari, maple syrup, liquid smoke, pepper, and cayenne to finish. When the liquid is absorbed and edges are blackened, 2 to 4 minutes, remove the logs from the pan and transfer to the warmed wrap.

3 Top the wrap with the carrot slaw or leftover kale salad.

4 Roll up the wrap like a burrito, slice in half, and serve.

Tip: If you plan ahead, you can marinate the tempeh for a while in the spices, tamari, liquid smoke, and maple syrup to infuse the flavor further.

NUTRITION FACTS (per serving–373g) — Calories: 513; Fat: 20g; Carbs: 60g; Protein: 24g; Fiber: 5g — Vitamin C: 65%; Iron: 25%; Calcium: 18%; Vitamin A: 296%

KATHY'S THANKSGIVING SWEET POTATO POCKETS

This is one of my first signature recipes that I made before starting my blog. I would bring these pockets to family holiday dinners where I knew there would be only a few vegan options. I wanted all my favorite flavors of Thanksgiving and the holidays in one tiny pita pocket. The tender, flavorful filling is delicious beneath a crisp, oven-toasted pita exterior. Sweet potatoes, creamy garlic hummus, and sweet-tart cranberry sauce in every festive bite! I make these every year for Thanksgiving, and I hope you can try these and start your own sweet potato pocket tradition! Tip: You can also use this recipe to use up leftovers the day after the feast.

SERVES 4

1 Preheat the oven to 400°F.

2 Rub the pita quarters with oil. Place them directly on the oven rack to lightly toast the outsides. Do not over-toast, since you still want to be able to open the pita pocket—it should be pliable but toasted enough so that it doesn't get mushy when you add the filling. Reduce the oven temperature to 200°F.

3 Fill each pita quarter with 1 to 2 teaspoons of the hummus, 1 teaspoon of the cranberry sauce, and 1 to 2 tablespoons of the sweet potato mash. Add a generous pinch of the leafy greens and parsley. Press the pitas closed at the tips with your fingertips. Place the stuffed pitas on an oven-safe serving tray.

4 Place the stuffed pitas in the oven for 15 minutes to warm the filling. Sprinkle some parsley over the pitas just before serving to add color. Store leftover pitas in the fridge and reheat for 10 minutes in a 400°F oven.

2 whole wheat pita pockets, quartered

Extra-virgin olive oil

½ cup Classic Hummus Dip (page 197)

⅓ cup cranberry sauce, store-bought

1½ cups Kathy's Famous Sweet Potato Mash (page 127), warmed

1 cup finely chopped leafy greens (any variety)

2 teaspoons finely chopped fresh flat-leaf parsley, plus more for garnish

NUTRITION FACTS
(per serving–150g)

Calories: 175; Fat: 5g; Carbs: 30g; Protein: 6g; Fiber: 4g

Vitamin C: 21%; Iron: 6%; Calcium: 5%; Vitamin A: 192%

APPLE-JACK PANINI ON CINNA-RAISIN BREAD

Okay, so the next rainy day that comes along, I want you to promise me that you will pop a movie into your DVD player, or rent one on your tablet device, sit close to the window so you can hear the rain, and make either a bowl of Rainy Day Tomato Soup (page 258) or *this* sandwich recipe. It is the ultimate savory-sweet comfort food grilled cheese sandwich. Sweet crunchy apples meet melty vegan Monterey Jack cheese on raisin-speckled cinnamon-swirl toast, with buttery crispy edges and warm savory-sweet insides. You can easily make this on a panini press, but in a skillet also works.

─────────────── SERVES 1 ───────────────

½ teaspoon vegan buttery spread

2 slices cinnamon-raisin bread (try the sprouted grain variety)

1 very thin slice red or sweet onion (optional)

½ medium green apple, thinly sliced

⅓ cup vegan Monterey Jack flavor cheese

1 Spread the vegan buttery spread on each of the bread slices.

2 Heat a skillet over medium heat or warm a panini press. Place the onion (if using) and apple slices directly on the skillet or panini press. If using a skillet, heat for 2 to 3 minutes, flipping once, to warm and soften the onion and apple. If using a press, close for a minute to lightly grill. Transfer them to one slice of the bread on the unbuttered side. Layer the cheese on top of the apple and onion. Top with the second slice of bread, buttered side up, and transfer to the hot skillet or panini press.

3 Cook or press until the cheese has melted and the bread is toasted and browned, 2 to 3 minutes on each side.

Note: A panini press works best for fast grilled cheese sandwiches, but a skillet will also work. To help speed up the melting cheese process, cover the sandwich with either a grill press or a lid. This helps heat the inside of the sandwich. Medium heat under the skillet works best so the outside of the bread doesn't toast too quickly and burn.

NUTRITION FACTS (per serving-196g)

Calories: 308; Fat: 10g; Carbs: 53g; Protein: 8g; Fiber: 12g

Vitamin C: 7%; Iron: 7%; Calcium: 10%; Vitamin A: 3%

CURRIED QUINOA PITAS

A touch of curry spice brings quinoa to a whole new level of deliciousness. Sweet golden raisins and alluring mint mingle with toasty cashews, colorful veggies, and creamy warmed hummus in these delightful, hearty pita pockets. Dinner approved!

SERVES 4

3 whole wheat pita pockets, rubbed with extra-virgin olive oil

6 tablespoons Classic Hummus Dip (page 197)

2 cups Fluffy Quinoa (page 189)

2 tablespoons golden raisins

1 tablespoon sweet curry powder

1 tablespoon chopped fresh mint

½ teaspoon sea salt

¼ teaspoon freshly ground black pepper

CASHEW VEGGIES

2 teaspoons extra-virgin olive oil

½ cup frozen peas

½ cup broccoli florets

¼ cup chopped sweet onion

¼ cup raw cashews

2 tablespoons fresh orange juice

2 tablespoons chopped Candied Orange Peel (see Sidebar, page 45; optional)

1 tablespoon tahini

1 tablespoon grade B maple syrup

1 teaspoon freshly grated orange zest

ON THE SIDE

Hot sauce or harissa

1 Preheat the oven to 250°F. Toast the pitas in the oven until lightly browned, about 5 minutes. Turn the oven off but leave the pitas in the warm oven until needed. Place the hummus in an oven-safe bowl and set in the oven to warm as well.

2 Pour the quinoa into a large bowl and toss with the raisins, curry powder, mint, salt, and pepper to taste (if using).

3 **For the Cashew Veggies:** In a skillet, heat 1 teaspoon of the olive oil over high heat. Add the peas, broccoli, and onion. Cook, stirring, until the peas are fully warmed and the onions have begun to caramelize, 3 to 5 minutes. Add the cashews, orange juice, candied orange peel (if using), tahini, maple syrup, and orange zest. Continue to cook, stirring, until the liquid has been absorbed into the veggies, 2 to 4 minutes.

4 Fold the cashew veggies into the bowl with the quinoa and fluff with a fork.

5 Start filling the pitas with the oven-warmed hummus and the quinoa-veggie-cashew mixture. Add shredded cabbage, if desired. Drizzle lemon-tahini sauce over the top, if desired, and serve. You can also serve with hot sauce or harissa.

NUTRITION FACTS (per serving–266g)

Calories: 480; Fat: 20g; Carbs: 61g; Protein: 14g; Fiber: 10g

Vitamin C: 57%; Iron: 28%; Calcium: 8%; Vitamin A: 8%

AVOCADO-CHIMICHURRI SEITAN SUB

Avocado, bright green and garlicky chimichurri sauce, and savory peppered seitan meet inside a toasty roll, for a vegan sandwich to crave! Hot, lively, and steamy, this sub will impress. Not that hungry? Share this with a friend. Gluten-free version: Use sliced portobellos in place of seitan.

━━━━━━━━━━━━ SERVES 1 ━━━━━━━━━━━━

1. **For the Avocado-Chimichurri Sauce:** In a blender or food processor, process the chimichurri ingredients until smooth.

2. In a skillet, heat a drizzle of oil over high heat. Add the onions and cook, stirring, until translucent, 3 to 5 minutes. Add the seitan and pepper and cook, stirring occasionally, until the edges of the seitan begin to brown, 3 to 5 minutes. Since seitan is precooked, you are really just warming it and blackening the edges.

3. Slice the roll down the center, leaving a bit attached to hold the halves together and drizzle some of the chimichurri sauce inside. Fill with the seitan sauté, top with a generous drizzle of the remaining sauce, and sprinkle with the cilantro and crushed peanuts, if desired.

AVOCADO-CHIMICHURRI SAUCE

½ cup diced avocado

⅓ cup chopped fresh cilantro

1 to 2 cloves garlic

2 tablespoons fresh lemon juice

1 tablespoon chopped fresh flat-leaf parsley

2 teaspoons extra-virgin olive oil

¼ teaspoon fresh or dried oregano

⅛ teaspoon sea salt

⅛ teaspoon freshly ground black pepper

Cooking oil (extra-virgin olive oil, sunflower oil, or safflower oil)

¼ cup chopped onion

1 cup seitan strips

½ teaspoon freshly ground black pepper

1 large whole wheat sub roll, warmed or toasted

1 teaspoon finely chopped fresh cilantro (optional)

1 teaspoon crushed peanuts (optional)

NUTRITION FACTS
(per serving–228g)

Calories: 572; Fat: 27g; Carbs: 47g; Protein: 32g; Fiber: 11g

Vitamin C: 48%; Iron: 6%; Calcium: 3%; Vitamin A: 16%

EASY HUMMUS SPIRAL WRAPS

This fun little hummus and veggie wrap is fun to serve on a big party platter or as a snack for easy vegan finger food. I use fluffy lavash bread as the wrap, since it is light and flavorful and lower in calories than most tortillas. These pretty spirals can also be packed in a lunchbox or nibbled deskside for lunch. I like to think of these bites as sandwich sushi. No chopsticks required.

SERVES 1

1 whole wheat lavash wrap or large flour tortilla

Coconut oil spray (optional)

¼ cup Classic Hummus Dip (page 197)

¼ cup frozen edamame, steamed, boiled, or warmed in the microwave

¼ cup chopped fresh spinach

1 roasted red pepper, thinly sliced, or ½ cup shredded carrots

¼ cup chopped onion

1 teaspoon fresh lemon juice

Sea salt and freshly ground black pepper

1. In a dry sauté pan, heat the lavash wrap over high heat for a few seconds, or warm it in the microwave for 20 to 40 seconds or in a 350°F oven for 2 minutes. You can spray it with a bit of coconut oil spray to soften, if desired.

2. Spread the hummus evenly over one side of the warmed lavash wrap. Arrange the edamame, spinach, red pepper, and onion evenly over the hummus. Add the lemon juice over the top and sprinkle with salt and pepper to taste. Roll the lavash wrap up in a tight spiral, as if you were wrapping veggie sushi or cinnamon rolls.

3. Slice crosswise into 1½-inch-thick rounds to serve. The wraps can be made and sliced ahead of time and left to chill in the fridge, covered, until ready to serve.

Change It Up! You can also switch out the hummus for cashew cheese spread or vegan cream cheese. Add a variety of fruit and veggie ingredients to make this spiral wrap hundreds of different ways!

NUTRITION FACTS (per serving–242g)

Calories: 257; Fat: 18g; Carbs: 90g; Protein: 21g; Fiber: 11g

Vitamin C: 231%; Iron: 38%; Calcium: 9%; Vitamin A: 59%

TOASTY TUXEDO GRILLED CHEESE

Black and white and cheesy all over. This two-toned grilled cheese sandwich is somewhat sophisticated and elegant. Black olive tapenade meets white melty vegan cheese, spicy horseradish, and sassy sweet black balsamic. Black-tie optional.

SERVES 1

1. Spread the cashew cheese and horseradish on one slice of the bread (or, alternatively, stir the cheese shreds into the horseradish and spread on one slice of the bread).

2. In a blender or food processor, combine the black olive tapenade ingredients and blend until smooth but still slightly chunky.

3. Spread 1 to 2 tablespoons of the olive tapenade on the other slice of bread and drizzle the vinegar over the tapenade. Reserve the remaining tapenade for another use. Close up the sandwich by placing the black and white sides together.

4. In a skillet over high heat, melt the vegan buttery spread. Place the sandwich in the pan and cook for about 1 minute on each side to crisp and brown the bread. You could also prepare this sandwich using a panini press. Slice and serve warm.

1 to 2 tablespoons Vegan Cashew Ricotta (page 223) or vegan mozzarella cheese shreds

1 teaspoon prepared horseradish

2 slices sourdough bread or another white bread

1 to 2 tablespoons Black Olive Tapenade (below)

½ teaspoon balsamic vinegar

½ teaspoon vegan buttery spread or veggie oil

BLACK OLIVE TAPENADE

2 cups kalamata olives, pitted

½ cup drained and rinsed canned white beans

2 to 3 tablespoons chopped fresh flat-leaf parsley

2 tablespoons extra-virgin olive oil

⅛ teaspoon freshly ground black pepper

Pinch of fresh rosemary or thyme (optional)

NUTRITION FACTS (per serving–59g) Calories: 218; Fat: 16g; Carbs: 15g; Protein: 4g; Fiber: 2g   Vitamin C: 4%; Iron: 9%; Calcium: 3%; Vitamin A: 4%

TOWERING TEMPEH KALE SKILLET SANDWICHES WITH SPICY PUMPKIN SEED PESTO

When you truly want to make your sandwich into a hearty meal, serve up these skillet-based sandwiches. Overflowing leaves of crispy yet wilted kale top Cajun-spiced slabs of tempeh. Spicy pumpkin seeds add a buttery, nutty accent. Make an extra portion of kale and let your sandwich truly overflow on your plate for a hearty, healthy meal.

SERVES 2

2 sprouted grain or whole wheat buns

SPICY PUMPKIN SEED PESTO

1 cup fresh basil leaves

2 tablespoons pumpkin seeds

2 tablespoons fresh lemon juice

2 cloves garlic

1 tablespoon extra-virgin olive oil

Pinch of sea salt and freshly ground black pepper

6 ounces tempeh, sliced into 2 square pieces

1 teaspoon virgin coconut oil

1 teaspoon Cajun spice mix

Sea salt and freshly ground black pepper

2 teaspoons grade B maple syrup

1 cup torn kale leaves

2 teaspoons pumpkin seeds

1 tablespoon nutritional yeast

1 Preheat the oven to 200°F. Toast the buns in the oven for about 5 minutes. Turn off the oven but leave the buns in the oven to keep warm.

2 **For the Spicy Pumpkin Seed Pesto:** In a blender or food processor, combine the pesto ingredients and blend until smooth and creamy. Pour into a small bowl, cover, and refrigerate until needed.

3 Heat a dry skillet over high heat. Place the tempeh in the hot pan and add a spoonful of cold water. Cover the pan immediately and allow the steam to soften the tempeh for a minute or so. Uncover and add the coconut oil. Toss the tempeh in the oil, then sprinkle the Cajun spice, salt, and pepper over the tempeh. Cook for 1 minute. Flip the tempeh, drizzle the maple syrup over the top, and cook for 1 to 2 minutes more. You want the tempeh to be nice and blackened when you are finished.

4 Reduce the heat to low and push the tempeh to one side of the pan. Add the kale, pumpkin seeds, and nutritional yeast to the empty portion of the pan. Using a spatula, spread the kale around in the hot pan so that it soaks up the excess oil and spices from the tempeh sauté. This will also wilt the kale just enough to be tender. Cook the kale until it is lightly wilted and delicately coated in the excess seasonings, 1 to 3 minutes.

5 Pull the toasted buns from the oven and split them. Spread the pesto on both inside sides of the buns and top with the tempeh, wilted kale, and pumpkin seeds. Add additional toppings, if desired. Slice and serve warm.

OPTIONAL TOPPINGS

Red onion

Shredded carrots

Tomato

Dijon mustard

Vegan mayonnaise

NUTRITION FACTS
(per serving–280g)
Calories: 540; Fat: 42g; Carbs: 59g; Protein: 33g; Fiber: 10g
Vitamin C: 151%; Iron: 43%; Calcium: 22%; Vitamin A: 220%

DAD'S TOASTED BLT

This classic-gone-vegan sandwich is simple and just right—just like Dad. Toasted sourdough or whole-grain bread, a generous layer of smoky tempeh bacon, thick slices of juicy tomato, and some crunchy romaine leaves. There is a reason why a BLT is such a popular sandwich. Now try the vegan version!

SERVES 1

1. Spread the vegan mayonnaise and mustard (if using) on one side of each slice of bread.

2. Layer the tomato, lettuce, avocado (if using), and tempeh bacon on one slice of bread. Add pepper to taste. Close the sandwich with the second slice of bread. Slice and serve.

1 teaspoon vegan mayonnaise and/or 1 teaspoon Dijon mustard

2 slices whole-grain or sourdough bread, toasted

2 to 3 slices tomato

2 leaves romaine or green leaf lettuce

Thin slices of avocado (optional)

5 to 6 slices Smoky Tempeh Bacon (page 62)

Freshly ground black pepper

NUTRITION FACTS
(per serving–199g)

Calories: 325; Fat: 4g; Carbs: 53g; Protein: 20g; Fiber: 7g

Vitamin C: 10%; Iron: 26%; Calcium: 11%; Vitamin A: 40%

MUSHROOM MARINARA SANDWICH

Slow-simmering marinara sauce isn't just for pasta. Pair it with tender portobello mushrooms for this hot sandwich meal.

—— **SERVES 1** ——

¼ cup 15-Minute Marinara Sauce (page 226)

1 teaspoon extra-virgin olive oil

1 portobello mushroom, sliced

1 teaspoon balsamic vinegar

Few pinches of sea salt and freshly ground black pepper

2 slices soft wheat bread, toasted

½ cup sprouts, shredded kale leaves, or romaine lettuce

1 In a small saucepan, heat the marinara sauce until lightly boiling, or place in a microwave-safe bowl and microwave for 1 to 2 minutes until hot. Set aside.

2 In a skillet, heat the oil over high heat. Add the mushrooms and cook, stirring, for 3 to 5 minutes. Finish off with a splash of balsamic vinegar and a few pinches of salt and pepper.

3 Slather a bit of the marinara sauce to wet one side of each slice of the toasted bread. Top one slice with the mushrooms then top the mushrooms with a generous few spoonfuls of the additional marinara sauce. Place the sprouts over the marinara mushrooms and cover with the top half of the sandwich bread, marinara-side down. Slice and serve warm.

Tip: This works great as a "next day" sandwich if you have leftover marinara sauce from last night's pasta!

NUTRITION FACTS (per serving–215g)

Calories: 258; Fat: 8g; Carbs: 34g; Protein: 11g; Fiber: 6g

Vitamin C: 6%; Iron: 15%; Calcium: 8%; Vitamin A: 8%

BBQ TEMPEH SAUTÉ PITAS WITH RED SLAW

I am a sucker for barbecue sauce—you too? For these warm, hearty pitas, sweet, sticky sauce coats protein-rich tempeh, rounded out with a crunchy accent of red slaw. Serve this pita with a baked sweet potato or some potato salad for a tasty Southern-style meal.

SERVES 3

1. **For the Easy Red Slaw:** In a large bowl, toss together the slaw ingredients, cover, and refrigerate until ready to use.

2. **For the Tempeh:** Dice the tempeh into small cubes or crumble with your hands.

3. In a skillet, heat the oil over high heat. Add the tempeh and cook for 3 to 4 minutes, flipping the tempeh every minute or so. (For more tender tempeh, steam-cook the tempeh by adding a tiny splash of cold water and covering the pan. This steaming process will also remove some of the tempeh's bitterness.)

4. Reduce the heat to medium and pour the barbecue sauce over the tempeh. Sprinkle the pepper over the top. Cook for about 2 minutes more and flip the tempeh a bit to smother all sides in the sauce. Remove from the heat and let cool in the pan for a few minutes.

5. Toast the pita pocket halves and open them to fill. Spread the mayo (if using) inside the pocket, then add 1 or 2 generous scoops of the BBQ tempeh, followed by about ½ cup of the slaw. Serve right away for that hot and cold contrast in each bite.

EASY RED SLAW

1½ cups shredded red cabbage

¼ cup diced onion (optional)

2 teaspoons vegan mayonnaise

2 teaspoons apple cider vinegar

1 teaspoon agave syrup

¼ teaspoon Spanish or spicy paprika or chipotle powder

⅛ teaspoon freshly ground black pepper

TEMPEH

8 ounces tempeh

1 teaspoon safflower oil

2 tablespoons Vegan Barbecue Sauce (page 244) or store-bought vegan barbecue sauce

¼ teaspoon freshly ground black pepper

3 whole wheat pita pocket halves

3 teaspoons vegan mayonnaise (optional)

NUTRITION FACTS
(per serving–175g)

Calories: 306; Fat: 12g; Carbs: 34g; Protein: 18g; Fiber: 2g

Vitamin C: 23%; Iron: 13%; Calcium: 16%; Vitamin A: 1%

VEGAN TUNA SALAD SANDWICHES

This tuna-free tuna salad is simply amazing. Rustic, nutty, mashed chickpeas act as the base, while lively lemon and spices lead the flavor profile. Crunchy celery adds texture and lightness. Serve this salad between toasted bread slices or over a bed of greens. This go-to sandwich is one of my lunch-hour favorites. Delicious with a tall glass of iced tea!

— SERVES 2 —

1½ cups drained and rinsed canned chickpeas

2 to 3 tablespoons Classic Hummus Dip (page 197)

Pinch of freshly grated lemon zest

Juice of 1 lemon

Sea salt and freshly ground black pepper

1¼ cups chopped celery

1 teaspoon crushed nori sheets or kelp sprinkle (optional)

Pinch of cayenne (optional)

1 to 2 tablespoons nutritional yeast (optional)

2 teaspoons vegan mayonnaise (optional)

4 slices crusty bread

1 Place the chickpeas in a large bowl and mash well with a fork.

2 Add the hummus, lemon zest, lemon juice, and a few pinches of salt and pepper. Toss well and taste. Adjust the seasoning as desired. Fold in the celery and if desired, add the nori, cayenne, nutritional yeast, and mayo.

3 Cover and refrigerate until ready to serve—at least 30 minutes is best.

4 Top two slices of the bread with half of the tuna salad each, and close with the remaining two slices of bread. You can also serve the tuna salad as a topping for a salad, or serve it with crackers as a dip.

NUTRITION FACTS (per serving-299g) — Calories: 340; Fat: 8g; Carbs: 47g; Protein: 18g; Fiber: 13g — Vitamin C: 30%; Iron: 10%; Calcium: 10%; Vitamin A: 7%

VEGGIE-LOADED BEAN TOASTS

I whipped up this recipe one day and have loved it ever since. It takes the basic mashed bean salad idea found in recipes like my tuna-less salad and infuses it with avocado and tons of veggies. Serve this salad mixture piled high on toasted bread or English muffins for an open-faced, healthy, stacked sandwich meal.

SERVES 2

---

1 Place the beans and avocado in a large bowl. Mash well with a fork until thick and chunky yet creamy, like a chunky guacamole or hummus.

2 Fold the veggies into the avocado-bean mixture.

3 In a small bowl, whisk together the white miso paste (if using—otherwise, use salt to taste), lemon juice, orange juice, nutritional yeast, and orange zest. Fold this liquid into the veggie-bean mixture until well combined and the veggies begin to soak up the liquid. Fold in the hemp seeds.

4 Cover and refrigerate for 10 to 15 minutes before serving. This salad should be served the same day it is made.

5 Toast the English muffins and top with large, towering scoops of the bean salad. Top with the harissa and chives, if desired. Serve open-faced.

Change It Up! Feel free to change up some of the veggie ingredients or add others! Celery, green apple, kale, bell pepper, candied or raw nuts, and more can all be optional add-ins or substitutes.

1½ cups drained and rinsed canned cannellini beans (see Note)

1 small avocado, pitted, peeled, and diced

⅓ cup diced sweet onion

1 small carrot, chopped

½ cup chopped fresh spinach

2 teaspoons white miso paste (optional)

Sea salt (optional)

Juice of 1 small lemon

2 tablespoons fresh orange juice

2 tablespoons nutritional yeast

Pinch of freshly grated orange zest

1 tablespoon hemp, pumpkin, or sunflower seeds

2 sprouted grain or whole wheat English muffins

1 teaspoon smoky harissa (optional)

Fresh chives (optional)

Note: As an alternative, use half cannellini beans and half chickpeas.

Tip: To help soften canned beans for mashing, rinse them in hot water.

NUTRITION FACTS
(per serving–409g)

Calories: 460; Fat: 23g; Carbs: 48g; Protein: 19g; Fiber: 22g

Vitamin C: 73%; Iron: 30%; Calcium: 11%; Vitamin A: 101%

AVOCADO CAPRESE SANDWICH

Vegan cheese, basil, and tomato, flavors reminiscent of a classic Caprese, are molded into a tasty sub sandwich with an accent of avocado. If there is one thing you learn from this chapter, know this: Avocados make just about any sandwich better!

SERVES 4

PUMPKIN SEED CASHEW CHEESE

¾ cup raw cashews

Sea salt

½ cup plain almond milk (add to taste for cheese thickness and texture)

⅓ cup raw salted pumpkin seeds

2 tablespoons extra-virgin olive oil

⅛ to ¼ teaspoon pink salt

⅛ teaspoon freshly ground black pepper

ITALIAN HERB-MARINATED TOMATO SALAD

2 medium tomatoes, sliced into rounds

¼ cup sliced onion

1 tablespoon extra-virgin olive oil

1 clove garlic, minced

1 tablespoon fresh lemon juice

1 tablespoon chopped fresh basil

½ teaspoon dried Italian seasoning

Pinch of sea salt and freshly ground black pepper

1. **For the Pumpkin Seed Cashew Cheese:** Soak the cashews in very hot water with a pinch of salt for at least 30 minutes. This cashew cheese is a bit nutty and textured when blended, so you do not need to soak it overnight like you would for making almond milk. Drain and rinse the cashews.

2. Combine the soaked cashews with the remaining cashew cheese ingredients, except the pink salt and pepper, in a blender or food processor and blend until smooth, yet still nutty in texture. Add a splash more liquid if needed to blend. You want a very thick consistency, kind of like hummus. Season to taste with the salt and pepper. You can use this cheese as a spread either raw or warmed. If warmed, pour the mixture into an oven-safe bowl and bake in a 350°F oven until a thin, lightly crisp crust appears on top and the mixture darkens slightly, 15 to 20 minutes. If raw, pour into a bowl, cover, and refrigerate for at least 15 to 20 minutes before spreading on the bread.

3 **For the Italian Herb–Marinated Tomato Salad:** In a large bowl, toss the tomatoes and onion with the oil, garlic, lemon juice, basil, Italian seasoning, and salt and pepper. Cover and refrigerate for at least 15 to 20 minutes. The longer you marinate the salad, the more flavorful the tomatoes and onions will be. Marinate overnight, if desired. Both the cheese and salad can be prepared ahead of time and stored in the fridge until ready to be used.

4 Toast the bread or rolls. Slice down the center to fill. Add a generous slathering of the cashew cheese followed by the tomato salad. Thinly slice the avocado, rub it with the lemon juice, and add to the sandwich. Finish things off with a big handful of chopped fresh basil. Add a drizzle of oil over the top, if desired. Serve while the bread is still toasty warm.

Serving Tip: If you place the assembled sandwiches in a warm oven for 5 to 10 minutes, they become toasty subs!

4 sandwich rolls or baguettes

1 avocado

1 tablespoon fresh lemon juice

¼ cup chopped fresh basil, or ⅓ cup fresh micro basil sprouts

Extra-virgin olive oil, optional

Lighten It Up: To lighten up these sandwiches, simply use less cashew cheese per sandwich or omit the avocado.

NUTRITION FACTS (per serving–300g)	Calories: 546; Fat: 39g; Carbs: 35g; Protein: 15g; Fiber: 10g	Vitamin C: 47%; Iron: 34%; Calcium: 14%; Vitamin A: 18%

BURGERS

Ah, the veggie burger. Lovely, plump, exploding with flavor, and just as good as any non-vegan burger out there. I am a huge fan of having a weekly veggie burger night in my house. Veggie burgers are delicious paired with salads and veggie sides of all sorts. So toast up some buns and slice up some burger toppings—veggie burger heaven is just a cooking session away.

TURMERIC HEMP
WHITE BEAN BURGER PATTIES

Golden turmeric accents these hemp and white bean patties. Savory nutritional yeast adds a cheesy accent while maple adds a hint of sweetness. These cheerful burgers are a delicious way to add some healthy turmeric spice to your meals.

SERVES 5

1. If baking the patties, preheat the oven to 400°F and grease a baking sheet with the coconut oil. (Otherwise, proceed to step 2, reserving the coconut oil.)

2. In a large bowl, mash together all the ingredients except for the coconut oil. Cover and refrigerate for a few minutes to make the mixture easier to shape.

3. Form the mixture into 5 patties and place them on the prepared baking sheet. Bake until the edges are slightly crisped and lightly browned and darkened on the outside, about 20 minutes. Alternatively, in a skillet, melt the coconut oil over medium-high heat. Add the patties (working in batches, if necessary) and cook for about 3 minutes on each side. Serve warm with any desired toppings.

2 teaspoons virgin coconut oil

1½ cups drained and rinsed canned white beans

½ cup chopped white onion

3 to 6 tablespoons nutritional yeast

¼ cup hemp seeds

1 tablespoon tahini

2 teaspoons ground turmeric

2 teaspoons grade B maple syrup

⅛ teaspoon sea salt

TOPPINGS

Lettuce or sprouts

Tomato

Onion

Shredded carrots

Dijon mustard or barbecue sauce

NUTRITION FACTS
(per patty–106g)   Calories: 154; Fat: 6g; Carbs: 17g; Protein: 10g; Fiber: 5g   Vitamin C: 2%; Iron: 19%; Calcium: 5%; Vitamin A: 0%

BBQ PEANUT BURGERS

These Southern-style burgers include sassy barbecue sauce, sweet potato, mashed white beans, and nutty ground peanuts.

SERVES 6

---

1 small sweet potato

Coconut oil spray (optional)

½ cup roasted salted peanuts

1½ cups drained and rinsed canned cannellini beans (rinse in hot water to soften)

½ cup cooked short-grain brown rice

¼ cup diced onion

2 tablespoons finely chopped fresh flat-leaf parsley

2 tablespoons vegan barbecue sauce, plus more for serving

1 tablespoon dry barbecue spice blend

Sea salt

Safflower or virgin coconut oil (optional)

6 buns, toasted

TOPPINGS

Red onion

Coleslaw

Avocado

Tomato

Vegan mayonnaise

1 Before preparing the burgers, poke a few holes in the sweet potato using a fork and bake in a 400°F oven for about 45 minutes or until tender. If baking the patties, preheat the oven to 400°F and coat a baking sheet with coconut oil spray. (Otherwise, proceed to step 2.)

2 In a food processor, process the peanuts until fine and powdery with a few crumbly pieces, too. Do not overprocess into nut butter.

3 Place the peanut powder in a large bowl and add the beans, sweet potato, rice, onion, parsley, barbecue sauce, spice blend, and salt to taste. Mash until the mixture is thick and moist. Cover and refrigerate for about 10 minutes.

4 Form the mixture into 6 patties and place them on the prepared baking sheet. Bake until the edges are brown, about 15 minutes. I like my patties on the softer side so I always undercook them a bit. Alternatively, in a sauté pan, heat a splash of oil over medium-high heat. Add the patties and cook for 2 to 4 minutes on each side. The patties will bind and firm up a bit as they cool.

5 Serve on the toasted buns with additional barbecue sauce and toppings of your choice.

NUTRITION FACTS (per patty–148g) — Calories: 193; Fat: 7g; Carbs: 27g; Protein: 8g; Fiber: 5g; Vitamin C: 7%; Iron: 13%; Calcium: 6%; Vitamin A: 77%

VEGGIE BURGER PATTIES

Veggie burger recipes are incredibly easy to improvise once you know the basics. Some tips and components to watch for when crafting a veggie burger recipe:

- **Start with a moist, bindable base:** This ingredient will have a nice amount of moisture to help seal in all the other ingredients. My favorite ingredient for this includes mashed canned beans (like cannellini beans) and lentils. Also try mashed potatoes or mashed sweet potato. These thick, dense, and clingy ingredients offer a perfect veggie burger base.

- **The technique:** The main technique involves placing all the ingredients in a large bowl and mashing them well with a fork so that they become sticky enough to form into patties. For ease, chill the mashed mixture in the fridge before forming it into patties.

- **Something with texture:** Textured ingredients like chopped veggies, seeds, whole grains, and more will give the burger some texture and also help bring substance to your base binding ingredient.

- **Something sticky:** To further aid the binding of the burger, add items that can become sticky, like flour, nutritional yeast, tahini, nut butters, nut flour, finely ground seeds (like flax and chia!), or nuts.

- **Seasoning:** Every burger will need some salt, pepper, and spices. These can vary greatly, from simple garlic powder, salt, and pepper, to spice blends and more. This is where you will give your veggie burger some personality. I love dry spices for veggie burgers since they can sink into the moist base

so easily, but wet seasonings like sauces and purees can work, too. Fresh herbs like parsley and cilantro are also wonderful for flavor. As always, taste as you go.

- **Something sweet:** Adding a touch of sweetness is optional, but a spoonful of maple or agave syrup may be right for some recipes!

- **How to cook:** I love both baking and sauté methods for veggie burgers. When baking, I usually bake for 15 to 20 minutes at 350°F and allow the veggie burgers 15 minutes to cool and bind. The burgers will have slightly crisped edges and be lightly browned and darkened on the outer layer when done. When sautéing, I make sure to use ingredients that are already completely cooked and then I simply do a quick 2- to 3-minute sauté on each side to crisp the edges and warm the burger. I love sautéing veggie burgers in safflower or coconut oil best.

- **To serve:** Veggie burger patties do not have to be served on a traditional bun. They are so flavorful and delicious you can serve them as solo side patties, over salads, or on open-face sandwiches.

- **Ingredient ideas:** Start experimenting! Try: grains like rice and farro, diced carrots, mashed potatoes, mashed beans and lentils, chopped onions, chopped mushrooms, spices, chopped fresh herbs, shredded beets, chopped greens, TVP, crumbled tempeh or processed tofu, quinoa, chopped or finely processed nuts and seeds, tahini, nut butters, citrus juices and zest, artichoke hearts and hearts of palm . . . The list goes on!

SWEET POTATO VEGGIE BURGER
WITH AVOCADO

This recipe was a big hit on my blog. People just loved it. And so do I! The simple combination of sweet potato and mashed white beans with some creamy tahini and spices is made amazing when you coat each patty in panko bread crumbs for a quick skillet sauté. Add the most amazing fresh veggie toppings and thick slices of creamy avocado. If you are a sweet potato lover like me, give this recipe a try and make it a household specialty. And keep in mind that this burger patty is very moist and loose—it does sort of fall apart as you eat it, but for some reason that turns out to be part of the appeal! If you want to add more binding, toss in a handful of ground flaxseeds, a few spoonfuls of brown rice, or a bit more flour.

SERVES 5

1 medium sweet potato

1½ cups drained and rinsed canned cannellini beans

2 to 3 tablespoons oat or wheat flour

1 tablespoon tahini or nut butter, softened

1 teaspoon grade B maple syrup

¼ teaspoon garlic powder or spice blend (like Cajun, lemon pepper, or other)

Sea salt

Pinch of freshly ground black pepper

Pinch of cayenne (optional)

1 tablespoon nutritional yeast, plus more as needed (optional)

½ to 1 teaspoon additional spice of your choice (I like Cajun spice blend or chipotle powder; optional)

ingredients continue

1. Preheat the oven to 400°F. Poke a few holes in the potato using a fork. Bake the sweet potato until sticky-sweet and super tender, about 1 hour. Remove the skin and place the flesh in a large bowl.

2. Add the drained beans to the bowl and using a fork, mash the beans with the potato.

3. Mash in the flour, tahini, maple syrup, and all the spices and seasonings, adding the optional seasonings as desired. The mixture will be quite soft and moist, but you should be able to form it into a patty. Cover and refrigerate until the mixture firms up enough to be easily handled, 15 to 20 minutes.

recipe continues

continued

1 to 3 teaspoons safflower or virgin coconut oil

½ cup panko bread crumbs (optional)

5 whole-grain buns, toasted

TOPPINGS

Tomato

Vegan mayonnaise

Romaine lettuce

Onion

Avocado

Dijon mustard

Olive oil

Freshly ground black pepper

Baking option: If baking the patties, omit the panko and add ¼ cup cooked brown rice for added texture. Bake at 350°F on a greased baking sheet for about 20 minutes. The burgers will be lightly browned and toasty on the edges, but still moist on the insides when done.

Tip: Fold an additional ¼ to ½ cup panko bread crumbs into the patty mixture if you want a drier mixture to work with, or if the mixture is too wet. Potatoes can vary in moisture content, so this is a good trick. For more binding, add 1 tablespoon ground flaxseeds.

4 In a sauté pan, heat 1 tablespoon of the oil over high heat. Form the potato-bean mixture into 5 patties and coat them on all sides in the panko, if desired—make sure the panko coating is thick. Place the patties in the hot pan, working in batches if needed, and cook until browned, 2 to 3 minutes on each side. (Alternatively, fry the patties in an oven-safe skillet until browned, then place the skillet directly in a preheated 350°F oven to bake for about 10 minutes. I find this firms up the patty just a bit more.) The patties will be done when they have crisp, lightly browned edges. The patties will still be very tender on the inside with a toasty outer crust.

5 Transfer the cooked patties to a paper towel and let cool for a few minutes. Serve warm on a toasted bun with toppings of your choice.

Tips:

* Add more flour or a scoop of bread crumbs or uncooked rice to thicken the mixture, if needed.

* Place the mixture in the fridge to chill for at least 20 minutes for easier handling.

NUTRITION FACTS (per patty–142g)

Calories: 176; Fat: 4g; Carbs: 30g; Protein: 7g; Fiber: 5g

Vitamin C: 4%; Iron: 13%; Calcium: 7%; Vitamin A: 90%

SOUTHERN BURGERS: BLACK-EYED PEA COLLARD GREEN PATTIES

These Southern-inspired veggie burgers include some favorite flavors of mine, like black-eyed peas, Cajun spice, and collard greens. Serve with a side of red slaw, sweet potato home fries, or sassy wilted kale. This is a delicious way to enjoy healthy black-eyed peas.

SERVES 4

1 Preheat the oven to 400°F. Poke a few holes in the sweet potato using a fork. Bake the sweet potato until tender, 40 minutes. When cool enough to handle, remove the skin and place the potato flesh in a large bowl. Mash the potato with a fork. You should end up with about 1 cup mashed sweet potato.

2 Place the black-eyed peas in a microwave-safe bowl and microwave for 2 to 3 minutes, or heat in a saucepan until tender, 3 to 5 minutes.

3 Place the peas, mashed sweet potato, greens, onion, tahini, nutritional yeast, seasoning, and salt in a large bowl and mash well to combine. Cover and refrigerate until needed, if desired, or start forming into patties immediately. Form the mixture into 4 patties.

4 In a skillet, heat the oil over high heat. Place the patties in the pan and cook for 2 to 3 minutes on each side. (You could also bake the patties in the oven at 350°F until they are lightly crisp on the outside, about 20 minutes.)

5 Serve on warmed buns with any toppings you'd like.

1 small sweet potato

1½ cups frozen black-eyed peas

½ cup finely chopped collard greens

¼ cup diced sweet onion

1 tablespoon tahini

1 tablespoon nutritional yeast

1 teaspoon Cajun seasoning

½ teaspoon sea salt

1 to 2 teaspoons sunflower, safflower, or extra-virgin olive oil

4 buns, warmed

TOPPINGS

Summer Slaw (page 141)

Sweet mustard

Barbecue sauce

Red onion

Sliced peaches

Shredded carrots

NUTRITION FACTS (per patty–178g) — Calories: 196; Fat: 4g; Carbs: 43g; Protein: 11g; Fiber: 7g — Vitamin C: 20%; Iron: 22%; Calcium: 10%; Vitamin A: 196%

AZTEC TEMPEH BURGERS WITH SWEET POTATO SECRET SAUCE

A taste of the Southwest! These thickly spiced tempeh patties are topped with delicious toppings like red onion, avocado, and crisp romaine. Spicy vegan mayo and a sweet potato secret sauce seal the deal.

— SERVES 2 —

SWEET POTATO SECRET SAUCE

1 small sweet potato, baked (see steps 1 and 2 on page 81) and still warm

1 teaspoon agave syrup

1 teaspoon virgin coconut oil

Pinch of sea salt

Freshly ground black pepper

Garlic powder

Cayenne

TEMPEH

Safflower or virgin coconut oil

8 ounces tempeh, sliced into 2 large planks

Spices: chili powder, freshly ground black pepper, sea salt, cayenne, garlic powder, onion powder

1 teaspoon agave syrup

2 slices red onion

2 sprouted grain burger buns

2 tablespoons vegan mayonnaise

Splash of hot sauce

2 large romaine leaves

½ cup Summer Slaw (page 141)

¼ cup sliced avocado

1 **For the Sweet Potato Secret Sauce:** Mash the sweet potato; you should have about ½ to ¾ cup. Mash in the agave, coconut oil, and spices to taste. Set aside.

2 **For the Tempeh:** In a skillet, heat a drizzle of the oil over high heat. Add the tempeh and cook for 2 to 3 minutes. Add a plentiful coating of spices (I use a Southwest spice blend) and a drizzle of the agave to the exposed side. Flip the tempeh and add another coating of spices and drizzle of agave. Cook until the edges blacken, 2 to 3 minutes more. Remove from the pan and set aside to rest on a plate.

3 Add the onions to the hot pan and cook, stirring, until they soak up the excess spices and oil, 1 to 2 minutes.

4 Toast the buns. You can even wet the inside of the buns with some of the excess oil from the pan by dragging the sliced buns across the pan after or before toasting them in a warm oven.

5 In a small bowl, whisk the vegan mayo with the hot sauce. Spread the spicy vegan mayo over the bottom half of the warmed buns. Top with the tempeh and warmed onions. Add the lettuce, some slaw, and avocado. Spread a generous layer of the sweet potato sauce on the top bun and close the burger. Slice and serve warm.

NUTRITION FACTS (per burger-356g)
Calories: 566; Fat: 23g; Carbs: 63g; Protein: 33g; Fiber: 10g
Vitamin C: 23%; Iron: 31%; Calcium: 16%; Vitamin A: 198%

SPICY CHILI BEAN BURGERS

Red rice and beans in a sassy veggie burger with chipotle mayo on top. Add toppings like tomato, crisp green lettuce or coleslaw, and onion to serve.

_____ SERVES 4 _____

1 Preheat the oven to 200°F. Warm the buns in the oven while you prepare the sauce and the patties.

2 **For the Chipotle Mayo (optional):** In a small bowl, whisk together the chipotle mayo ingredients, cover, and refrigerate until ready to use.

3 **For the Patties:** In a large bowl, mash together all the patty ingredients in a large bowl. The beans should be about 75 percent mashed—leave a few whole for texture. Cover and refrigerate for about 15 minutes.

4 Form the chilled bean mixture into 4 patties. In a sauté pan, heat a drizzle of oil over medium-high heat. Add the patties and cook for 2 to 3 minutes on each side. (You could also bake the patties on a greased baking sheet for 15 to 20 minutes.) The burgers will be textured and toasty, with slightly browned edges when done.

5 Place the patties in the warmed buns, and add toppings. If desired, spread the chipotle mayo on the inside of the bun to serve.

4 buns

CHIPOTLE MAYO (OPTIONAL)

1 tablespoon vegan mayonnaise

1 teaspoon agave syrup

¼ teaspoon chipotle powder

PATTIES

1½ cups drained and rinsed canned kidney beans

1½ cups cooked short-grain brown rice

½ cup finely chopped kale or fresh spinach

½ cup diced spicy veggie sausage (optional)

¼ cup diced red onion

2 cloves garlic, finely chopped

3 to 4 tablespoons nutritional yeast

2 teaspoons hemp seeds or homemade oat flour (from rolled oats; see Sidebar, page 38) (optional)

1 teaspoon apple cider vinegar

1 teaspoon salt-free chili powder

¾ teaspoon Spanish paprika

½ teaspoon vegan liquid smoke

¼ teaspoon sea salt

Pinch of freshly ground black pepper

Extra-virgin olive or safflower oil

Lettuce and tomato, for topping

NUTRITION FACTS
(per patty–178g)
Calories: 205; Fat: 2g; Carbs: 36g; Protein: 12g; Fiber: 9g
Vitamin C: 6%; Iron: 17%; Calcium: 4%; Vitamin A: 7%

VEGGIE SIDES

Vegetable sides, both super simple and elegantly complex, are wonderful for most meals. I sometimes build entire meals out of veggie sides because vegetables are truly *that* delicious if you give them time and effort in your cooking prep and method. These are a few of my favorite veggie sides.

KATHY'S FAMOUS SWEET POTATO MASH

This is an old recipe that I started making around the holidays when I was in college. I used this mash to stuff my Thanksgiving Sweet Potato Pockets (page 99) but it is delicious on its own as well! I serve it as a side dish or I glam it up by adding cooked grains or beans, veggie proteins, or even fruit (sliced apples taste amazing folded into this mash!). Garlic hummus makes the potato extra creamy and rich, while onions, parsley, and carrots add loads of texture and flavor.

SERVES 6

1. Preheat the oven to 400°F. Poke a few holes in the potato using a fork. Bake the sweet potato until sticky-sweet and very tender, 55 to 60 minutes. Reduce the oven temperature to 200°F.

2. In a large bowl, mash all the ingredients together. Pour the mixture into an oven-safe serving bowl and warm in the oven until ready to serve or use in recipes.

1 large or 2 small sweet potatoes

1 large carrot, chopped

½ cup chopped sweet onion

½ cup garlic hummus

½ cup chopped fresh flat-leaf parsley

1 tablespoon grade B maple syrup

Pinch of sea salt and freshly ground black pepper

Pinch of cayenne or chipotle powder (optional)

NUTRITION FACTS
(per serving–135g)

Calories: 145; Fat: 3g; Carbs: 28g; Protein: 4g; Fiber: 4g

Vitamin C: 21%; Iron: 11%; Calcium: 5%; Vitamin A: 196%

ROASTED BEETS WITH GINGER AND CITRUS

Some simple pink beets are made divine by the addition of stimulating ginger and sweet citrus and by roasting them in a hot oven until sticky-sweet and tender. Roasted beets are dreamy and rich in healthy phytochemicals.

SERVES 4

Olive oil, for the pan

2 large or 3 medium beets

1 apple

2 tablespoons grade B maple syrup

2 tablespoons extra-virgin olive oil

2 tablespoons fresh orange juice

1 teaspoon grated peeled fresh ginger, plus more for garnish

½ teaspoon freshly grated orange zest

Coarse pink sea salt

Freshly ground black pepper

3 tablespoons raw pumpkin seeds

1 tablespoon finely chopped fresh flat-leaf parsley

For extra-sweet beets: Add a sprinkling of brown or coconut sugar over the beets just before placing them in the oven.

1 Preheat the oven to 400°F. Grease a baking sheet with oil.

2 Wash and scrub the beets, removing any the rough spots and the stems if they are attached. Chop the beets into large odd-shaped cubes. Wash and core the apple, and then chop it into cubes the same size as the beets.

3 Place the beets, apples, maple syrup, extra-virgin olive oil, orange juice, ginger, orange zest, salt, and pepper to taste in a large bowl and toss until the beets and apples are coated. Transfer the mixture to the prepared baking sheet and pour any excess liquid and spices from the bowl over the top. Scrape the bowl for any seasoning and make sure it gets on the beets.

4 Bake for 25 minutes. Flip and toss the beets and apples a bit. Continue to bake until a beet is tender when stuck with a fork, 5 to 15 minutes depending on the size of the cubes. Roast longer for softer, more caramelized beets. Finish the cooking by turning the oven to broil and broiling the beets and apples until blackened edges form, 1 to 3 minutes.

5 Heat a dry skillet over medium heat. Lightly toast the pumpkin seeds for 1 to 2 minutes.

6 Transfer the beet mixture to serving platter. Sprinkle the pumpkin seeds around the edge, and add the parsley and more fresh ginger to garnish. Serve warm or chilled.

NUTRITION FACTS
(per serving–248g)

Calories: 224; Fat: 10g; Carbs: 32g; Protein: 5g; Fiber: 5g

Vitamin C: 27%; Iron: 15%; Calcium: 4%; Vitamin A: 4%

SASSY GARLIC WILTED GREENS

This quickie wilted greens recipe makes for a craveable go-to side dish. The extra-virgin olive oil adds a silky texture to the greens, while the garlic and vinegar add some sassy flavor.

SERVES 4

1. In a sauté pan, heat the oil over medium heat. Add the garlic and cook, stirring, until the garlic starts to soften, 1 to 2 minutes (do not allow it to burn). Reduce the heat to low.

2. Add the greens and vinegar. Quickly cover the pan and let the greens steam to soften them. Leave the greens covered for about 1 minute.

3. Remove the lid and stir the greens around in the hot pan. Add a sprinkle of salt and pepper (and any other spices you'd like) and serve warm.

Note: Add more or less vinegar or lemon based on how sassy you want the flavor.

1 tablespoon extra-virgin olive oil

4 cloves garlic, finely chopped

5 cups mixed shredded kale and chard leaves

1 to 2 tablespoons apple cider vinegar or fresh lemon juice (see Note)

Pinch of sea salt and freshly ground black pepper

NUTRITION FACTS (per serving-94g) Calories: 77; Fat: 4g; Carbs: 9g; Protein: 3g; Fiber: 2g   Vitamin C: 169%; Iron: 8%; Calcium: 12%; Vitamin A: 258%

MAPLE CITRUS ROASTED CARROTS

Sticky-sweet and velvety in texture, these maple and citrus roasted carrots taste more like candy than veggies! Be sure to roast them long enough so that they become very tender; larger carrots will take longer to roast. These carrots provide a delicious boost of vitamin A. I also love using roasted carrots in blended soups, so be sure to check those recipes in my soups section (pages 254–272)!

SERVES 4

7 to 8 medium rainbow carrots

1 Satsuma tangerine, or ½ juicy orange, peeled and thinly sliced

2 tablespoons plus 1 teaspoon grade B maple syrup

2 tablespoons fresh orange juice

3 to 4 teaspoons extra-virgin olive oil

⅛ teaspoon freshly ground black pepper

Pinch of freshly grated orange zest

¼ teaspoon coarse salt

¼ cup pecans

Pinch of cayenne

Sea salt

1. Preheat the oven to 410°F.

2. Wash and scrub the carrots. Remove any stems and halve the carrots lengthwise. (Extra-large carrots can be sliced into quarters; skinny carrots may be kept whole.)

3. In a bowl, toss the citrus slices with 1 teaspoon of the maple syrup and set aside.

4. Place the carrots in a rectangular or square casserole dish and add the maple-tossed citrus slices, remaining 2 tablespoons maple syrup, the orange juice, oil, pepper, and orange zest. Toss the carrots well so the coating is evenly distributed. Arrange the carrots in a single layer.

5. Bake for 10 minutes, then turn the oven to broil and broil for 2 minutes. Flip the carrots and reduce the oven temperature back to 410°F. Bake until the carrots are soft, super tender, and caramelized, 10 to 20 minutes more. Finish with another minute under the broiler to blacken the other side of the carrots. The citrus should be candied as well.

6. Remove the carrots from oven, sprinkle with the salt, and transfer to a serving platter. Pour the excess liquid from the baking dish over the carrots, and arrange the candied citrus around the edges of the platter.

7 Allow the carrots to rest while you lightly toast the pecans in a dry skillet over high heat—just a minute or two should do it. Toss the pecans with the cayenne and salt and add them to the carrot platter. Serve warm.

Note: You can salt the carrots before or after cooking, but I prefer to salt them after, when the carrots are still hot and only slightly dissolve the coarse salt.

NUTRITION FACTS
(per serving–175g)

Calories: 171; Fat: 9g; Carbs: 25g; Protein: 2g; Fiber: 5g

Vitamin C: 43%; Iron: 4%; Calcium: 6%; Vitamin A: 409%

EASY MASHED POTATOES

Mashed potatoes are a must-make recipe for any comfort-loving cook (like me!). So whip out the potato peeler and start mashing to create your own perfect, fluffy bowl of homemade mashed potatoes. Do not forget the melting vegan buttery spread on top!

SERVES 7

2½ pounds russet potatoes or mini white potatoes

5 cloves garlic

Sea salt

1⅓ cups plain nondairy milk

2 to 3 tablespoons vegan buttery spread, softened, or substitute your favorite healthy oil, such as walnut, coconut, or extra-virgin olive oil

Freshly ground black pepper

1   Scrub the potatoes and chop them into rough cubes. Toss the chopped potatoes, garlic, and a few pinches of salt in a large soup pot and fill with water to cover the potatoes by about 1 inch. Bring to a boil and cook until the potatoes are tender enough to slice with a fork, 15 minutes or a few minutes longer.

2   Drain the potatoes and place them in a large bowl. Add 1 cup of the nondairy milk, 2 tablespoons of the vegan buttery spread, and a pinch of salt and pepper.

3   Using a handheld mixer, with the mixer off, mash the potatoes as much as possible. Then start blending on the lowest setting. (If you have a fancy potato-mashing tool for the mixer you can use that too. But an ordinary beater will work.) While blending, slowly add the remaining ⅓ cup nondairy milk.

4   Blend until the clumps are gone or mostly softened and the potatoes are silky smooth. Taste and adjust the seasoning, adding more vegan buttery spread, if desired.

5   Fold in the spices as desired (see Variations).

6   Serve warm or reheat in a 350°F oven for about 15 minutes. If the potatoes are in the fridge a bit too long before serving, blend again with an added splash of nondairy milk before reheating and serving.

VARIATIONS

BUTTERY CHIVE: Top with chopped fresh chives and extra vegan buttery spread.

CHEESY HEMP: Fold in ½ cup nutritional yeast, an added ⅓ cup nondairy milk or creamer, and raw hemp seeds.

GOLDEN TURMERIC: Fold in ground turmeric to taste (I add about ½ teaspoon per 1½ cups potatoes).

SMOKY PAPRIKA: Fold in Spanish-style smoky paprika to taste (I add about ½ teaspoon per 2 cups of potatoes).

ULTRA CREAMY: Substitute half of the nondairy milk with unsweetened soy creamer.

SUPER SAVORY: Substitute half of the nondairy milk with veggie broth. Monitor the added salt closely since most broths contain sodium.

FULLY LOADED: Top with vegan cheese shreds and vegan tempeh bacon bits. Warm in the oven to melt the cheese and serve topped with vegan sour cream and chopped fresh chives.

NUTRITION FACTS (per serving–214g)	Calories: 163; Fat: 3g; Carbs: 30g; Protein: 5g; Fiber: 3g	Vitamin C: 83%; Iron: 38%; Calcium: 9%; Vitamin A: 5%

EASY CHEEZY ROASTED BROCCOLI

This is my go-to way to prepare broccoli: roasted, with ultra-cheesy flavor from nutritional yeast. This veggie dish is one your whole family will come to crave! Craving veggies? Broccoli? Oh yes!

SERVES 2

Extra-virgin olive oil, for the pan

2 cups broccoli florets

1 tablespoon extra-virgin olive oil (see Note)

3 to 4 tablespoons nutritional yeast, plus more as needed

1 tablespoon fresh lemon juice (optional)

Sea salt and freshly ground black pepper

Cayenne (optional)

Garlic powder (optional)

1 Preheat the oven to 400°F. Lightly grease a baking sheet with extra-virgin olive oil.

2 Toss the broccoli florets with the oil, 3 tablespoons of the nutritional yeast, and the lemon juice (if using).

3 Spread the broccoli in a thin layer on the prepared baking sheet. Sprinkle the remaining nutritional yeast over the broccoli.

4 Bake until tender, 15 to 20 minutes.

5 Remove the broccoli from the pan and season with salt and pepper and additional nutritional yeast and cayenne and/or garlic powder, if desired. Serve warm.

Note: Replace 2 teaspoons of the oil with fresh lemon juice for a lighter roast.

NUTRITION FACTS (per serving–117g) Calories: 170; Fat: 9g; Carbs: 15g; Protein: 13g; Fiber: 8g   Vitamin C: 131%; Iron: 9%; Calcium: 4%; Vitamin A: 11%

SIMPLE SALT-AND-PEPPER SHIITAKES

Peppery and savory, healthy shiitakes can be served as a side, over top an entrée salad, or added to veggie burgers!

—— SERVES 2 ——

1 In a skillet, heat the oil over high heat. Add the mushrooms and cook, stirring, until the edges begin to brown, 2 to 3 minutes. Add a few pinches of the pepper.

2 Reduce the heat to low and pour in the red wine, one spoonful at a time so as not to wilt the mushrooms. Raise the heat to high and continue cooking the mushrooms, shaking the pan around a lot to move the mushrooms and soak up all those spices and flavors. The process takes 2 to 5 minutes to achieve a nice lightly blackened and lightly crisped mushroom.

3 Remove from the heat and toss the mushrooms with the remaining pepper, the parsley, and salt. Serve warm.

1 to 2 teaspoons extra-virgin olive oil

2 cups thinly sliced shiitake mushrooms

½ teaspoon freshly ground black pepper

2 teaspoons red wine, vinegar, or fresh lemon juice

1 tablespoon finely chopped fresh flat-leaf parsley

Pinch of coarse salt

NUTRITION FACTS
(per serving–77g)

Calories: 50; Fat: 1g; Carbs: 10g; Protein: 2g; Fiber: 2g

Vitamin C: 4%; Iron: 2%; Calcium: 0%; Vitamin A: 2%

MAPLE SAGE BUTTERNUT SQUASH

This veggie side dish is simply dreamy. Swirls of maple syrup coat sweet roasted butternut squash cubes, citrus, sage, and cinnamon to accent.

SERVES 4

Virgin coconut oil, for the pan

4 cups butternut squash cubes

3 to 4 fresh sage leaves, shredded, plus whole leaves for garnish

1 tablespoon vegan buttery spread, melted, or melted virgin coconut oil plus a pinch of sea salt

1 tablespoon fresh orange juice

2 teaspoons grade B maple syrup

½ teaspoon freshly grated orange zest

½ teaspoon ground cinnamon

Orange slices, for garnish

1 Preheat the oven to 415°F. Grease a baking sheet or casserole dish with coconut oil.

2 Place the squash in a large bowl and toss with the shredded sage leaves, vegan buttery spread, orange juice, maple syrup, orange zest, and cinnamon. Transfer the squash to the prepared pan.

3 Bake until the squash becomes roasted and tender, about 20 minutes. Baking time will depend on how large you sliced the squash cubes.

4 Transfer the squash to a serving dish and pour the juices from the pan over the top. Garnish with whole sage leaves and orange slices, and serve.

Note: For extra-decadent squash, add another spoonful of coconut oil or vegan buttery spread.

NUTRITION FACTS (per serving–151g) Calories: 95; Fat: 3g; Carbs: 19g; Protein: 1g; Fiber: 5g   Vitamin C: 55%; Iron: 7%; Calcium: 6%; Vitamin A: 220%

SPICY-SWEET CURRIED CARROT RAISIN SLAW

Here is a delicious way to serve raw carrots! This sweet and sassy carrot slaw puts a spicy, sweet curry-infused spin on a classic. Tahini and maple blend with spices and sweet raisins. This carrot slaw is delicious eaten as a side dish or topped with tempeh or tofu cubes.

SERVES 4

1. In a small bowl, whisk together the tahini, lemon juice, maple syrup, curry powder, garlic powder, pepper, and salt.

2. In a large bowl, combine the carrots, raisins, and pumpkin seeds.

3. Pour the dressing mixture over the carrot mixture. Toss until all the carrots are well coated. Pour into a serving bowl, cover, and marinate in the fridge for at least 1 hour.

4. Serve chilled. The slaw can be made a day ahead of time and stored, covered, in the refrigerator until ready to serve.

Note: You can use raw, presprouted pumpkin seeds or lightly pan-toast your own raw pumpkin seeds. If toasting, toast in a sauté pan over high heat for 1 to 2 minutes.

¼ cup tahini

¼ cup fresh lemon juice

2 tablespoons grade B maple syrup

1 to 2 tablespoons Muchi curry powder

½ teaspoon garlic powder

¼ teaspoon fresh ground black pepper

Pinch of sea salt

1¼ cups matchstick carrots (or shredded for a softer texture)

1 cup red or golden raisins

2 tablespoons pumpkin seeds, toasted or raw sprouted (see Note)

NUTRITION FACTS (per serving–150g)   Calories: 267; Fat: 9g; Carbs: 45g; Protein: 5g; Fiber: 5g   Vitamin C: 13%; Iron: 13%; Calcium: 9%; Vitamin A: 0%

OVEN-ROASTED CRISPY TATERS WITH DIPPING SAUCES

This recipe is a favorite of mine for lazy-day television watching. Game day menu approved! Serve these toasty tasters with an array of dips and sauces, and your taste buds will never get bored. The dips are also wonderful paired with veggie sticks, crackers, or toasted bread.

— SERVES 4 —

DIPPING SAUCES

ORANGE-WALNUT PESTO

1 cup leafy greens, such as fresh spinach, arugula, or kale

½ cup walnuts

½ cup fresh basil leaves

½ cup fresh orange juice

3 cloves garlic

¼ cup walnut oil or extra-virgin olive oil

HARISSA-LENTIL

1½ cups drained and rinsed canned black lentils

2 tablespoons fresh lemon juice

1 tablespoon harissa

Sea salt and freshly ground black pepper

SMOKY PAPRIKA BLACK BEAN

1½ cups drained and rinsed canned black beans

2 tablespoons extra-virgin olive oil

2 teaspoons tahini

1 teaspoon Spanish smoky paprika

1. **For the Dipping Sauces:** For each recipe, combine all of the dip ingredients in a food processor or blender and blend until smooth. Transfer to a serving dish, cover, and refrigerate until ready to serve.

2. **For the Crispy Taters:** Preheat the oven to 400°F. Lightly grease a baking sheet with extra-virgin olive oil, sunflower oil, or safflower oil.

3. Scrub the potatoes well and cut them into long skinny halves or quarters. Place the potatoes in a large bowl and toss with the olive oil, nutritional yeast, salt, pepper, and cayenne.

4. Transfer the potatoes to the prepared baking sheet, spreading them in an even layer. Bake until the edges are nice and crispy and the insides are tender, about 20 minutes. Let cool on the baking sheet for a few minutes. The potato skins should be nice and crispy once the potatoes cool. If they are not crispy, return them to the oven for 5 minutes or so more. Sprinkle a fresh layer of nutritional yeast, salt, and pepper over the potatoes after they have cooled a bit. Always salt to taste.

5. Serve the crispy potatoes with the dipping sauces. Potatoes are best served slightly warm. The dipping sauces can be served chilled or warmed, however you'd prefer.

GREEN DREAM DIP

1 avocado

1 cup fresh spinach

½ cup drained and rinsed canned chickpeas

¼ cup fresh lemon juice

1 clove garlic

Pinch of cayenne

SWEET BUTTERNUT

1 cup canned butternut squash puree

½ cup drained and rinsed canned white beans

¾ teaspoon ground cinnamon

1 tablespoon fresh orange juice

2 teaspoons grade B maple syrup

Pinch of sea salt and freshly ground black pepper

Pinch of freshly grated orange zest

MAPLE-DIJON

¼ cup Dijon mustard

2 tablespoons grade B maple syrup

SPICY KETCHUP

¼ cup ketchup

½ teaspoon Spanish paprika

Pinch of cayenne

Pinch of freshly ground black pepper

CRISPY TATERS

Extra-virgin olive oil, sunflower oil, or safflower oil for greasing pan

5 cups small to medium finger potatoes

1 tablespoon extra-virgin olive oil (other options: sunflower or safflower oil)

2 teaspoons nutritional yeast, plus more as needed

½ teaspoon coarse salt, plus more as needed

½ teaspoon freshly ground black pepper, plus more as needed

⅛ teaspoon cayenne or chipotle powder

NUTRITION FACTS (per serving–194g, potatoes only)

Calories: 167; Fat: 4g; Carbs: 30g; Protein: 4g; Fiber: 5g

Vitamin C: 62%; Iron: 6%; Calcium: 2%; Vitamin A: 1%

PICNIC POTATO SALAD

Summertime meals, backyard barbecues, and parkside picnicking all call for a classic potato salad. This delicious recipe contains creamy vegan mayo, spicy mustard, crunchy celery and onion, and an accent of fresh dill, too.

SERVES 6

1 pound mini potatoes or peeled russet potatoes

1 cup chopped celery

1 cup finely chopped fresh dill

¾ cup sweet onion

¼ cup vegan mayonnaise

3 tablespoons apple cider vinegar

2 tablespoons Dijon mustard

2 teaspoons garlic powder

½ teaspoon paprika

Sea salt and freshly ground black pepper

Nutritional yeast (optional)

1 Scrub the potatoes well. Halve and quarter them. Smaller potato bits will cook faster.

2 Bring a pot of salted water to a boil and drop in the potatoes. Cook until tender, 14 to 18 minutes. Do not overcook or you will end up with more of a "mashed" potato salad. Rinse the cooked potatoes in very cold water or dunk them in ice water to halt the cooking.

3 Toss the potatoes in a large bowl with all the remaining ingredients. It is okay if the sauce melts a bit right now— chilling the potatoes will bring everything back to a cool, creamy, and thickened state.

4 Cover and chill the salad until ready to serve.

NUTRITION FACTS (per serving–198g) Calories: 147; Fat: 7g; Carbs: 21g; Protein: 4g; Fiber: 4g — Vitamin C: 15%; Iron: 40%; Calcium: 16%; Vitamin A: 13%

SUMMER SLAW

Cabbage is a wonderful veggie worth embracing. My yummiest way to serve it? Coleslaw! This light and crunchy summer slaw is delicious served as a side salad, or pile it on top of veggie burgers or inside pita pocket sandwiches. Crunchy cabbage, green apple, and onion mingle with tahini, maple, and apple cider vinegar flavors. I actually think this slaw tastes best the day after you make it, because the onions pickle in the fridge and everything becomes very creamy and the cabbage soft yet crunchy.

SERVES 6

1 Place the cabbage, onion, apple, and carrots in a large bowl. Add the remaining ingredients and toss well for a good 1 to 2 minutes so that all the flavors are blended and the cabbage is coated.

2 Place the slaw in a serving dish, cover, and chill for at least 1 hour before serving. This slaw easily keeps in the fridge for 2 days.

Tip: Add some lemon slices to the top of the slaw to help keep it even fresher. Reducing the vinegar amount can also help if you know the cabbage will be served the next day or in a few days as less wilting will occur.

4 cups shredded cabbage

1 small sweet onion, chopped

1 small green apple, diced

1 cup shredded carrots

⅓ cup tahini

⅓ cup grade B maple syrup or agave syrup

⅓ cup apple cider vinegar

⅓ cup hemp seeds, ground pumpkin seeds, chopped nuts, or sesame seeds

2 to 3 tablespoons vegan mayonnaise

Few pinches pf cayenne or paprika

Freshly ground black pepper

Freshly grated lemon zest

NUTRITION FACTS
(per serving–157g)

Calories: 216; Fat: 12g; Carbs: 25g; Protein: 6g; Fiber: 4g

Vitamin C: 34%; Iron: 15%; Calcium: 10%; Vitamin A: 63%

EASY ROASTED CAULIFLOWER

Cauliflower was meant to be served roasted! In my humble opinion, anyways. It becomes caramelized, tender, and sweet when roasted in a hot oven. It soaks in flavors surprisingly well considering its solid texture when going into the oven. I like my roasted cauliflower with a hint of garlic powder, salt, and pepper and a generous dose of nutritional yeast. My husband loves a few pinches of cayenne to spice up the tender florets.

SERVES 4

1 head cauliflower, tough core removed

2 tablespoons extra-virgin olive oil

Garlic powder

Nutritional yeast

Sea salt and freshly ground black pepper

Pinch of cayenne

Drizzle of grade B maple syrup (optional)

1 Preheat the oven to 420°F.

2 Chop the cauliflower into small florets and toss in a large bowl with the oil, spices to taste, and maple syrup (if using). Transfer to a baking dish.

3 Bake until tender, sweet, and caramelized, 25 to 35 minutes.

4 Serve warm and toss with additional seasonings and syrup just before serving. For extra cheesy flavor, add lots of nutritional yeast.

NUTRITION FACTS (per serving–74g) — Calories: 77; Fat: 7g; Carbs: 4g; Protein: 2g; Fiber: 2g — Vitamin C: 51%; Iron: 2%; Calcium: 1%; Vitamin A: 0%

CAKES, BALLS, AND FRITTERS

This section includes a unique set of cakes, balls, and fritters. These appetizer or entrée dishes are filled with flavor and can be served on their own, over the top salads and grain bowls, or even morphed into a veggie burger patty. Hearty and amazing, these simple dishes will win you over at first nibble.

SWEET POTATO–PISTACHIO CAKES

Simple and delicious, these sweet potato cakes are round, golden gems coated with green speckles of pistachio and pumpkin seed. These toasty cakes are a sweet potato lover's dream. Serve them as a side or make them the main event.

— SERVES 4 —

FRITTERS

2 medium sweet potatoes

¼ cup pumpkin seeds

¼ cup pistachios

Pinch of sea salt

Pinch of freshly ground pepper

1 tablespoon virgin coconut oil

CREAMY TAHINI-MAPLE SAUCE

1 tablespoon tahini

2 teaspoons fresh lemon juice

1 teaspoon grade B maple syrup

Sea salt and freshly ground black pepper, to taste

Garlic powder, to taste

CHIPOTLE MAYO SAUCE

1 tablespoon vegan mayonnaise

½ teaspoon agave syrup or grade B maple syrup

⅛ teaspoon chipotle or chili powder

1 **For the Fritters:** Peel and dice the sweet potatoes.

2 In a blender or food processor, process the pumpkin seeds and pistachios until fine, yet still slightly coarsely ground. Do not overprocess into a nut butter. Pour into a wide bowl and set aside.

3 Place the diced potatoes in a wide, deep skillet. Fill the skillet with enough water to cover the potatoes. Bring to a boil over high heat and boil until the potatoes are tender, but not falling apart, 12 to 15 minutes. Fork-tender is perfect.

4 Drain the potatoes and return them to the skillet with a pinch of salt and pepper. Cook over medium heat, stirring, for 1 to 2 minutes just to dry them out a bit and dry out any excess water. The potatoes may stick and brown a bit on the edges, but just scrape them up with a spatula. Turn off the heat after a few minutes and transfer the potatoes to a bowl. They should be quite tender and slightly caramelized now. Very lightly mash the potatoes using a fork. Keep a few cubes intact, but mash about half the cubes. Allow the mashed potatoes to cool for a few minutes before handling.

5 Using your hands, scoop 2 to 3 tablespoons portions of the potatoes and press them into small round, plump fritters. Heavily coat the fritters in the nut-seed mixture, pressing the coating into the fritters. Try not to handle the fritters too much since they are still delicate and soft. A quick dunk

into the nut-seed coating on both side and roll along the sides should do it. Set the uncooked fritters on a plate.

6 Wipe the skillet clean of any potato residue. Add the coconut oil and heat over medium-high heat. Add the fritters to the pan and fry them for a very quick 30 to 60 seconds on each side, then remove them from the pan. You just want to toast and brown the seeded coating since the potato is already cooked and warm.

7 **For the Creamy Tahini-Maple Sauce:** In a small bowl, whip together the sauce ingredients. Set aside.

8 **For the Chipotle Mayo Sauce:** In a small bowl, whip together the sauce ingredients. Set aside.

9 Drizzle the sauces over the fritters to serve or set alongside for dipping. Serve the fritters toasty warm.

NUTRITION FACTS (per serving–304g)

Calories: 356; Fat: 9g; Carbs: 66g; Protein: 5g; Fiber: 5g

Vitamin C: 17%; Iron: 3%; Calcium: 1%; Vitamin A: 441%

GREEN ISLAND FRITTERS

These exotic and savory bean fritters are infused with coconut milk, creamy spinach, nutty chickpeas, and cheesy nutritional yeast. A light coating of panko bread crumbs lets these fritters sauté into crispy warm cakes that are delicious.

MAKES 5 LARGE FRITTERS OR 10 SMALL; SERVES 5

1 cup drained and rinsed canned chickpeas

1 cup drained and rinsed canned cannellini beans

½ cup nutritional yeast

2 tablespoons coconut cream (see page 304)

¼ teaspoon Cajun seasoning, jerk spice, or garlic powder

⅛ teaspoon sea salt

Few pinches of freshly ground black pepper

¾ cup frozen spinach, thawed, or 3 cups fresh spinach, wilted

½ cup plus 2 tablespoons panko bread crumbs

2 tablespoons safflower or virgin coconut oil

1 Place the chickpeas, cannellini beans, nutritional yeast, coconut cream, seasoning, salt, and pepper in a large bowl. Mash until the cannellini beans are all smashed and about half the chickpeas are smashed. Fold in the spinach and ½ cup of the panko.

2 In a skillet, heat 1 tablespoon of the oil over medium-high heat.

3 Form the bean mixture into patties by hand. Roll a patty in the remaining 2 tablespoons panko. Place the patty in the hot pan. Repeat until the pan is filled, spacing the patties about 1 inch apart. Cook the fritters for 2 to 3 minutes. If the patties are thicker in size, cover the pan for a few minutes. When both the sides are browned and crispy and the insides seem firmed, remove from the pan and transfer to a paper plate to cool. They will be delicate upon removing from the pan, so be gentle. Cooling will help bind them. Alternatively, bake the fritters on a lightly greased baking sheet at 375°F until crispy on the outsides and lightly browned, moist and soft on the inside, 15 to 20 minutes.

4 Repeat the process until all the bean mash mixture has been used. Serve warm.

NUTRITION FACTS (per serving–115g) Calories: 180; Fat: 8g; Carbs: 23g; Protein: 7g; Fiber: 5g Vitamin C: 3%; Iron: 13%; Calcium: 5%; Vitamin A: 8%

TOASTY HEMP CHICKPEA PUMPKIN FRITTERS

Come pumpkin season, promise me one thing: you will make these golden fritters! Nutty, silky hemp seeds and plump chickpeas speckle these golden pumpkin rounds.

MAKES 8 SMALL FRITTERS; SERVES 4

1 Place the chickpeas and pumpkin in a large bowl. With a large fork, mash until at least three-quarters of the beans have been mashed together with the pumpkin.

2 Add the hemp seeds, flour, vinegar, maple syrup, garlic powder, salt, pepper, and cayenne. Fold together until a moist mixture forms.

3 In a large skillet, heat a tablespoon of the oil over high heat. When the oil is hot, form the mixture into golf-ball-size balls, flatten them slightly, and roll them in the panko until well covered. Carefully place the fritters in the pan, leaving about 1 inch between them. Continue until the pan is full. Cook for 1 to 2 minutes on each side. Transfer the cooked fritters to a paper towel to cool. Alternatively, omit the panko coating and simply bake the fritters on a well-greased baking sheet in a 350°F oven until the fritters are toasty and lightly browned on the outside, soft and tender on the inside, about 15 minutes.

4 Let cool for just a bit and serve warm.

1 (16 ounce) can chickpeas, drained and rinsed

½ cup canned unsweetened pumpkin puree

¼ cup hemp seeds

1 tablespoon flour (any variety)

1 teaspoon apple cider vinegar

1 teaspoon grade B maple syrup

½ teaspoon garlic powder

¼ teaspoon sea salt

⅛ teaspoon freshly ground black pepper

Pinch of cayenne or chipotle powder

2 tablespoons virgin coconut or safflower oil

½ cup panko bread crumbs (only use if frying)

NUTRITION FACTS
(per serving-173g)

Calories: 262; Fat: 12g; Carbs: 30g; Protein: 11g; Fiber: 7g

Vitamin C: 2%; Iron: 14%; Calcium: 3%; Vitamin A: 70%

FEISTY CORN CAKE BEAN BALLS ON TOMATO MOONS

These colorful, savory-sweet corn cake bites are sunny and cheerful. Each little corn cake ball comes served on a bright red tomato half-moon, with some lime juice to accent. This summery recipe is one to try. Liven up your serving platter!

SERVES 4

2 cups salted crispy rice crackers

1¼ cups canned corn kernels, or 1½ cups fresh corn kernels

1½ cups drained and rinsed canned cannellini beans

3 tablespoons nutritional yeast flakes

4 tablespoons fresh lime juice

1 teaspoon extra-virgin olive oil

1 teaspoon agave syrup

1 teaspoon ground coriander

1 teaspoon ground cumin

¼ teaspoon sea salt

2 to 3 teaspoons oil (any variety)

6 thick tomato slices, cut into half-moons

Pinch of freshly ground black pepper

Few pinches of cayenne or paprika

1. In a blender or food processor, process the rice crackers into a dusty fine flour. Pour into a small bowl and set aside.

2. Warm the corn kernels. In a blender or food processor, combine the beans, corn, nutritional yeast, 2 tablespoons of the lime juice, the olive oil, agave, coriander, cumin, and salt. Pulse until chunky yet smooth. Pour into a large bowl. Add the rice cracker flour and continue folding until the mixture thickens. Cover and refrigerate for at least 10 minutes.

3. Remove the mixture from the fridge and use your hands to form it into 12 balls.

4. In a sauté pan, heat the oil over medium-high heat. Add the balls and cover, and cook for about 2 minutes, then remove the lid and flip the balls. Cook for a few minutes more, gently rolling the balls to crisp and brown them on all sides. Transfer the balls to a paper towel to cool a bit.

5. In a bowl, toss the tomato half-moons with the remaining 2 tablespoons lime juice and some pepper. Top each tomato slice with one ball and a sprinkle of cayenne. Serve warm and toasty from the skillet for the best flavor and texture.

NUTRITION FACTS (per serving–238g) Calories: 293; Fat: 6g; Carbs: 50g; Protein: 16g; Fiber: 11g Vitamin C: 28%; Iron: 38%; Calcium: 11%; Vitamin A: 1%

FRIED RISOTTO BALLS (ARANCINI)

I first made arancini, a.k.a. fried risotto balls, one day when I had leftover risotto in the fridge. I wasn't expecting much—I mean, it's just fried risotto in the shape of a ball, right? But they were delicious! Dreamy, really. I was in blissful heaven at first bite. The crispy coating surrounds a velvety center. And if you really want to party, add a few shreds of vegan cheese to the inside of each ball. Simply form the ball around the cheese, coat as instructed, and get excited about a melty cheese risotto ball coming your way!

SERVES 3

1 Heat 1½ inches of oil in a high-sided pot over medium heat until it registers 375°F on a deep-fry thermometer. Line a rimmed baking sheet with parchment paper.

2 Meanwhile, place the bread crumbs and nutritional yeast in a shallow bowl and mix together.

3 Using your hands, form the chilled risotto into 9 balls. Yes, things will get a little messy. If you'd like, form the balls around some vegan cheese. They do not have to be perfectly stuffed, but try to conceal the cheese inside the ball as best you can.

4 Dredge the balls in the bread crumb mixture, coating them very well on all sides. Place the coated balls on the prepared baking sheet. If desired, place the balls in the fridge to chill for 30 minutes (do this if the balls seem to be a bit crumbly or falling apart).

5 Working in batches, fry the risotto balls in the hot oil for 2 to 3 minutes, turning them gently to evenly fry all sides.

6 Remove the balls from the oil with a slotted spoon or spatula and place on a paper towel–lined plate to drain excess oil. Repeat until all the balls are fried. Serve toasty warm.

Sunflower or virgin coconut oil (I filled my small pot with about 1½ inches of fry oil)

½ cup bread crumbs

1 to 2 tablespoons nutritional yeast

2 cups leftover risotto (1 to 2 days leftover in the fridge), chilled

Vegan cheese shreds (optional)

NUTRITION FACTS
(per serving–50g)

Calories: 234; Fat: 11g; Carbs: 30g; Protein: 5g; Fiber: 2g

Vitamin C: 0%; Iron: 6%; Calcium: 3%; Vitamin A: 0%

ITALIAN MEATLESS MEATBALLS

These meatless balls are perfect for serving over spaghetti for a veganized pasta night. These tender balls and savory and rustic with shiitake mushrooms, parsley, beans, and a hint of red wine.

SERVES 4

1½ cups drained and rinsed canned cannellini or pinto beans (rinse under very hot water)

3 teaspoons extra-virgin olive oil

1 cup finely chopped shiitake mushrooms

¾ cup diced white onion

⅓ cup finely chopped fresh flat-leaf parsley

2 teaspoons chopped garlic

1 teaspoon unsalted dried Italian seasoning

2 tablespoons red wine or fresh lemon juice

½ teaspoon sea salt

¼ teaspoon red pepper flakes

¼ teaspoon freshly ground black pepper

½ cup panko bread crumbs, plus more as needed

¼ cup nutritional yeast, plus more as needed

1 recipe 15-Minute Marinara Sauce (page 226)

Chopped fresh basil or flat-leaf parsley, for garnish

1 Preheat the oven to 375°F.

2 Place the beans in a large bowl and mash very well with a fork.

3 In a large sauté pan, heat 2 teaspoons of the oil over high heat. Add the mushrooms, onion, parsley, and garlic. Add the Italian seasoning. Cook, stirring, for 1 minute, then reduce the heat to medium and cook for 3 to 4 minutes more.

4 When the mixture has reduced in volume quite a bit and the onions are caramelizing, turn off the heat and add the red wine. Return the heat to high for 1 minute more and add the salt, red pepper flakes, and black pepper.

5 Fold the mixture into the beans. Fold in the bread crumbs and nutritional yeast. The mixture should be quite sticky and thick now. Add more yeast or bread crumbs to thicken further if needed. Cover and refrigerate for at least 10 minutes; this will make the mixture easier to handle.

6 Using your hands, form the chilled mixture into 10 to 12 balls. Roll the balls in a thin coating of nutritional yeast or bread crumbs. In a skillet, heat the remaining 1 teaspoon oil over medium-high heat. Add the balls and cook, stirring occasionally, just to brown the outside edges of the balls, 2 to 3 minutes.

7 Fill an oven-safe dish with marinara sauce. Carefully place the balls over the sauce. Bake, uncovered, for at least 20 minutes. When the balls are done, they will be firm and lightly browned on the outside, but still very moist and tender on the inside and where the sauce has soaked into them.

8 Serve the balls warm, with some finely chopped basil over the top. If serving with pasta, see recipe on page 226 for full details.

NUTRITION FACTS
(per serving–163g)

Calories: 217; Fat: 5g; Carbs: 35g; Protein: 9g; Fiber: 9g

Vitamin C: 16%; Iron: 17%; Calcium: 9%; Vitamin A: 8%

SALADS

Salads are a must for vegan meals! Salads can be served as sides or easily be turned into the main event simply by adding a few booster ingredients like beans, tofu, tempeh, grains, nuts, and more. I definitely get big salad cravings for dinner quite often! For the best salads, start with fresh, preferably local and organic produce. A stroll through a farmers' market should be enough to inspire your next salad bowl feast.

5-STEP RAW KALE SALAD

This salad was a big winner on my blog. Everyone fell in love with the ease of the recipe and the deliciousness of the flavors. When you hear about kale salads being trendy and craveable, this is the type of salad that everyone is referring to! Raw kale marinated or massaged with flavors, tahini or nut butter, avocado, veggies, a sweet accent, and something sassy like lemon juice or apple cider vinegar. Make this your go-to raw kale recipe—it only takes five steps!

SERVES 3

1 Wash the kale. Run each thick leaf under warm water and massage any grit away. Tear the leaves away from the thick stalks and place them in a large bowl. Rinse and drain the leaves several times until the kale is adequately clean. Drain the water from the bowl for a final time and squeeze the kale dry with a few paper towels. Remove any large pieces of kale from the bowl and finely chop them into long strips. (If you like large pieces of kale you can skip this last chopping step.) You should have 4 to 6 cups of kale.

2 Place the kale, carrots, diced avocado, optional red pepper, and onion in a large bowl. Reserve the sliced avocado for garnish.

3 **For the Simple Sweet Tahini Dressing:** In a small bowl, whisk the dressing ingredients together.

4 Add the dressing to the bowl of veggies and kale and start tossing. Massage the dressing into the kale with your hands, if you'd like, for more infused flavor. Fluff and toss until the dressing is well absorbed into the greens and veggies. Fold in the seeds, if desired.

recipe continues

1 bunch kale

¾ cups shredded or sliced carrots

1 small avocado, peeled and pitted, one half diced, the other half sliced

½ cup diced sweet onion

SIMPLE SWEET TAHINI DRESSING (SEE NOTE)

3 tablespoons fresh lemon juice (or apple cider vinegar or fresh lime juice)

2 tablespoons tahini or substitute with nut or seed butter

2 tablespoons grade B maple syrup

2 teaspoons extra-virgin olive oil (optional, adds richness)

2 pinches cayenne

Pinch of freshly grated zest

Pinch of sea salt and a few pinches freshly ground black pepper

2 to 3 tablespoons seeds or nuts (optional)

continued

Note: Make a double batch of dressing if you like your greens more heavily dressed.

NUTRITION FACTS
(per serving–235g)

Calories: 259; Fat: 17g; Carbs: 23g; Protein: 5g; Fiber: 8g

Vitamin C: 207%; Iron: 12%; Calcium: 15%; Vitamin A: 369%

5 In a pretty fan design, add the sliced avocado on top of the tossed salad. Serve the salad right away for a fluffy kale mixture, or for a more marinated kale texture, cover and refrigerate the salad for at least 30 minutes for the dressing to sink into the ingredients. You can marinate the salad for 30 minutes to 2 hours for best flavor and texture. This salad is best served the same day you make it.

Tip: If you want to make this salad a day ahead of time, do not add the avocado until right before serving. When ready to serve, simply fold in the diced avocado and garnish with the slices.

Tip: You can easily change up the veggies and other add-ins as desired!

RAW KALE AND CHARD SALADS

Raw salads are delicious, craveable, and easy. The idea is to take greens that you might normally think to cook or wilt to prepare—hearty greens like kale and chard—and massage them until they are softened and marinated with flavor.

I will never forget the first time I saw someone "massage" a giant pile of kale. One of my best blogger friends, Gena, of ChoosingRaw.com, and I were filming a how-to video. Gena was demonstrating how to massage kale. I always thought that "massaging" was just a fancy term for "tossing" the salad with the dressing, but nope. Gena dove hands-first into the kale, dressing, and all the veggies and massaged the heck out of those greens. They were moist and completely flavorful when she was done.

Truth be told, I am not a hands-into-it kale massager. I prefer to use tongs and very vigorously toss the kale and let the dressing and a brief marinating period do the work for me. But choose your own method! The idea is that the oil, salt, spices, and acid from the dressing work to soften and flavor the greens.

SIMPLE SPINACH SALAD WITH CANDIED NUTS

Spinach salad pairs so well with rich toasty, sticky-sweet candied nuts. This is a wonderful salad for a busy weeknight or lunch hour quickie.

SERVES 2

CANDIED SPICED NUTS

¼ cup walnuts

¼ cup raw pumpkin seeds

1 tablespoon grade B maple syrup

Pinch of sea salt

Pinch of Spanish paprika

Pinch of freshly ground black pepper

4 to 5 cups chopped fresh spinach or baby spinach

1 cup oven-roasted fresh corn kernels (optional)

1 tablespoon balsamic vinegar

2 to 3 teaspoons extra-virgin olive oil

½ teaspoon dried Italian seasoning

½ teaspoon freshly grated orange zest

½ avocado, thinly sliced

1 small pear, sliced, or 1 tangerine, diced

4 to 5 slices Baked Cashew Cheese (page 201; optional)

NUTRITION FACTS
(per serving–211g)

Calories: 392; Fat: 31g; Carbs: 19g; Protein: 10g; Fiber: 9g

Vitamin C: 116%; Iron: 16%; Calcium: 20%; Vitamin A: 80%

1. **For the Candied Spiced Nuts:** Heat a small saucepan over high heat. Add the walnuts and pumpkin seeds and toast for 1 to 2 minutes. Add the maple syrup, salt, paprika, and pepper and remove from the heat. Set aside to let the maple syrup thicken and cool over the hot nuts.

2. In a large bowl, toss the spinach with the corn (if using), vinegar, oil, Italian seasoning, and orange zest. Divide the tossed greens between two serving bowls.

3. Top the spinach with the sliced avocado and pear. Sprinkle the candied nuts over the top. If desired, place the cashew cheese slices over the greens.

HOW-TO: CANDIED NUTS IN JUST 1 MINUTE!

- **Toast:** Place the raw nuts and/or seeds in a small saucepan over high heat and toast them for about a minute.

- **Sweeten:** Use 1 teaspoon liquid sweetener for every ⅓ cup nuts and/or seeds.

- **Fold:** Fold the mixture with a small spatula and let the sweetener sizzle for a minute or less. If the pan looks like it is browning, remove it from the heat ASAP. When the nuts are coated in sticky-sweet goodness, remove the pan from the heat.

- **Season:** Sprinkle a few pinches of spices and sea salt over the warm and sticky nuts. I like a pinch of ground cinnamon, a pinch of cayenne, a pinch of pepper, and a few pinches of salt. Toss the nuts and pour them into a small serving bowl.

- **Cool and Serve:** Give the warm nuts 1 to 2 minutes to cool. They will be slightly sticky, yet toasted and crunchy when served. For bolder flavor: Toss cooled nuts in additional spices to taste.

MAPLE-MUSTARD RAW CHARD SALAD

Raw chard salads are simply stunning. But for some reason, they haven't received the amount of buzz that kale salads have garnered. Well, I am giving raw chard its moment to shine with this super craveable mixture of sweet and sassy chard, spicy mustard, and dreamy maple. Apple cider vinegar tones up all those flavors and brightens the greens. Seriously, guys—raw chard. Try it.

SERVES 3

1 Rinse the chard in cold water. Each leaf should be well rinsed to remove any sandy residue. Chop off any brownish ends on the stem. Pat the leaves dry with a paper towel or use a salad spinner dry the leaves once they are chopped.

2 Thinly slice the chard into ribbons and place them in a large serving bowl.

3 **For the Creamy Maple Mustard Dressing:** In a small cup, whisk together the dressing ingredients. Pour over the greens and toss well. Cover and refrigerate for at least 1 hour before serving.

4 Sprinkle lemon zest over the top and serve. The salad should be eaten within a day for the best texture.

Note: Try green chard or my favorite, rainbow chard.

1 bunch Swiss chard (see Note)

CREAMY MAPLE MUSTARD DRESSING

2 teaspoons spicy or whole-grain mustard

2 teaspoons vegan mayonnaise

1 teaspoon grade B maple syrup

1 teaspoon apple cider vinegar or fresh lemon juice

⅛ teaspoon freshly grated orange zest

Pinch of sea salt

Pinch of freshly ground black pepper

Pinch of cayenne

Freshly grated lemon or orange zest, for garnish

NUTRITION FACTS (per serving–201g) Calories: 110; Fat: 9g; Carbs: 6g; Protein: 2g; Fiber: 2g   Vitamin C: 45%; Iron: 9%; Calcium: 5%; Vitamin A: 111%

FARMHOUSE RANCH
CHICKPEA PEACH SALAD

Creamy vegan ranch coats nutty chickpeas and sweet peaches for a salad with summertime in every bite. As you enjoy this friendly salad imagine yourself under a shady tree, birds and blue sky above you. A farmside scene would be the perfect pairing to enjoy this salad bowl.

SERVES 2

CREAMY RANCH BEANS

1½ cups drained and rinsed canned chickpeas

½ cup chopped sweet onion

¼ cup finely chopped fresh flat-leaf parsley

3 tablespoons vegan mayonnaise, plus more as needed

1½ tablespoons apple cider vinegar

1 tablespoon Dijon mustard

1 tablespoon grade B maple syrup

1 teaspoon salt-free mixed dried herbs

⅛ teaspoon freshly ground black pepper

Pinch of sea salt

2 cups chopped romaine lettuce

½ cup shredded carrots

1 tablespoon chopped peanuts

1 chilled peach, pitted and sliced

Fresh lime or lemon juice

1. **For the Creamy Ranch Beans:** Combine the bean ingredients in a large bowl. Toss well until the beans and onion are coated. For extra-creamy ranch flavors, add an extra spoonful of vegan mayo.

2. Cover and refrigerate for at least 20 minutes, or 1 to 2 hours for more marinated flavors.

3. Divide the romaine and carrots between two serving bowls and top with the creamy dressed beans. Top with the peanuts and sliced peaches. Add a squeeze of fresh lime juice over the top.

NUTRITION FACTS
(per serving–305g)

Calories: 383; Fat: 19g; Carbs: 44g; Protein: 11g; Fiber: 11g

Vitamin C: 35%; Iron: 23%; Calcium: 10%; Vitamin A: 206%

POWER TOWER TAHINI SALAD

This was a favorite salad recipe on my blog, and it is easy to see why. It contains all my favorites: avocado, super-greens kale and chard, chickpeas, sweet citrus, and a sassy maple-tahini dressing to finish things off. Give your day a power boost with this super-green power fuel recipe.

SERVES 2

1. Rinse the greens under hot water then in cold water. Spin or pat dry. Slice into thin ribbons and place in a large bowl. Add the dressing and lemon zest and toss.

2. Remove the chickpea skins, if desired. Heat a dry or lightly oiled skillet over medium-high heat and lightly toast the chickpeas for 2 to 3 minutes to bring out the nutty flavor.

3. Halve the avocado. Dice one half and fold it into the greens. Rub the cut sides of the remaining avocado half with lemon juice and set aside to be used as garnish. Fold the chickpeas into the greens.

4. Cover and refrigerate the salad for at least 1 hour before serving. (This step is optional, but intensifies the flavor by marinating the greens with the dressing and chilling to a creamy texture.)

5. Place the greens on a serving plate. Thinly slice the remaining avocado half and arrange it in a fan on top of the salad as a garnish. Add the sliced Satsuma and drizzle the walnut oil over the top, if desired.

½ bunch or 4 whole leaves green chard (about 2 cups)

½ bunch kale (about 2 cups tightly packed)

⅓ cup Tahini-Maple Dressing (page 178)

⅛ teaspoon freshly grated lemon zest

½ cup drained and rinsed canned chickpeas (rinse under hot water then cold water)

Walnut oil (optional)

1 avocado

Fresh lemon juice

1 Satsuma tangerine, peeled and sliced

Drizzle of walnut oil (optional)

NUTRITION FACTS
(per serving–380g)

Calories: 385; Fat: 25g; Carbs: 30g; Protein: 11g; Fiber: 12g

Vitamin C: 218%; Iron: 24%; Calcium: 18%; Vitamin A: 269%

IT'S ALWAYS SUMMER SALAD

This light and lovely chopped salad contains corn, scallion, bell pepper, radish, and chopped leafy greens all tossed with a light and sassy coriander-and-cumin-infused dressing. This salad will brighten up any day. Loads of healthy, fiber-ful veggies make this an excellent detox salad, great for when you want to get your diet back on track.

SERVES 4

2 cups chopped kale leaves or romaine lettuce

3 radishes, thinly sliced

2 large carrots, chopped or grated

1 red bell pepper, diced

1 cup fresh or canned corn kernels

¼ cup chopped scallion

¼ cup finely chopped fresh flat-leaf parsley

2 tablespoons seasoned rice vinegar

2 tablespoons fresh lemon juice

1 tablespoon healthy oil, such as walnut, pumpkin seed, or extra-virgin olive oil

1 teaspoon agave syrup

1 teaspoon ground coriander

1 teaspoon ground cumin

¼ teaspoon freshly ground black pepper, plus more as needed

¼ teaspoon sea salt, plus more as needed

⅛ teaspoon cayenne, plus more as needed

¼ cup sunflower seeds

1. Combine all of the ingredients except the sunflower seeds in a large bowl and toss very well. Cover and refrigerate for at least 1 hour before serving.

2. Right before serving the salad, heat a skillet over high heat and toast the sunflower seeds until browned and toasty, 1 to 2 minutes. Toss the seeds with a few pinches each of pepper, salt, and cayenne. Top the salad with the seeds and serve.

NUTRITION FACTS
(per serving–175g)

Calories: 132; Fat: 5g; Carbs: 20g; Protein: 4g; Fiber: 4g

Vitamin C: 154%; Iron: 13%; Calcium: 7%; Vitamin A: 250%

APPLE EDAMAME SLAW SALAD WITH PEANUT-GINGER DRESSING

Edamame are rich in fiber and protein. They are savory and slightly sweet with a buttery-tender texture. I love pairing them with crunchy sweet apples and this creamy peanut dressing. Pure protein bliss.

───────────────── SERVES 4 ─────────────────

1 **For the Dressing:** Combine the dressing ingredients in a blender and blend until smooth.

2 Place the remaining ingredients in a large bowl, add the dressing, and toss well. Cover and refrigerate for at least 1 hour before serving. Toss again before serving. You can chill the salad overnight for more infused flavor.

DRESSING

3 tablespoons water (or for a richer dressing, try coconut milk)

1½ tablespoons peanut butter, softened

1 tablespoon grade B maple syrup

1 tablespoon apple cider vinegar

1 teaspoon tahini

¼ teaspoon grated peeled fresh ginger

Sea salt and freshly ground black pepper

1 large green apple, thinly sliced

1½ cups broccoli slaw or shredded cabbage

1¼ cup steamed edamame

1 cup matchstick or shredded carrots

¼ cup sunflower seeds, raw and sprouted or lightly toasted

¼ cup finely chopped fresh cilantro

NUTRITION FACTS
(per serving–184g) Calories: 211; Fat: 10g; Carbs: 24g; Protein: 11g; Fiber: 7g   Vitamin C: 67%; Iron: 11%; Calcium: 10%; Vitamin A: 98%

STRAWBERRY AVOCADO MÂCHE SALAD

You simply must try the combination of strawberries and avocado. They pair so well together, buttery with sassy sweet. Tender mâche greens are the perfect cozy bed for this salad. Try this salad with the optional healthy hemp seeds and refreshing mint on top.

SERVES 2

2 cups mâche lettuce

1 to 2 tablespoons fresh lemon juice

1 teaspoon extra-virgin olive oil

½ avocado, diced

1 cup sliced fresh strawberries,

1 teaspoon chopped fresh mint, plus more for garnish

Pinch of freshly grated lemon zest

2 tablespoons raw hemp or sunflower seeds (optional)

Sea salt and freshly ground black pepper

1. Toss the mâche in 1 tablespoon of the lemon juice and the oil. Divide between two serving plates. Gently toss the avocado with the strawberries, mint, and lemon zest. Arrange over the mâche.

2. Sprinkle the hemp seeds over the top, if desired, and garnish with mint and additional lemon juice to taste. Season with salt and freshly ground black pepper to taste.

NUTRITION FACTS
(per serving–251g)
Calories: 203; Fat: 16g; Carbs: 7g; Protein: 6g; Fiber: 5g
Vitamin C: 99%; Iron: 8%; Calcium: 2%; Vitamin A: 2%

AVOCADO DREAMBOAT SALAD WITH HUMMUS CROSTINI

You will look like a dreamboat serving up this avocado salad with a savory, crunchy hummus crostini on the side. I love a salty accent of black olives paired with a mountain of diced avocado. Maple-chili toasted chickpeas add a savory, healthy accent to a crunchy green romaine lettuce base.

=== SERVES 2 ===

CHICKPEAS

2 teaspoons grade B maple syrup

1 teaspoon extra-virgin olive oil

¾ cup drained and rinsed canned chickpeas

¼ teaspoon Spanish paprika

Dash of cayenne

Freshly ground black pepper

1 tablespoon chopped fresh herbs, such as cilantro, basil, or parsley

2 cups chopped romaine lettuce

1 cup fresh baby spinach

¼ cup chopped fresh herbs, such as cilantro, basil, or flat-leaf parsley

½ cup chopped sweet onion

2 tablespoons fresh lemon juice

2 teaspoons extra-virgin olive oil

Sea salt and freshly ground black pepper

2 slices baguette bread

4 tablespoons Classic Hummus Dip (page 197)

1 small tomato, diced

1 small avocado, sliced

2 tablespoons sliced pitted black olives

½ cup diced mango (optional)

1 **For the Chickpeas:** Heat a skillet over high heat. Add the maple syrup, oil, and chickpeas and cook, stirring, for 2 to 3 minutes. Sprinkle the paprika, cayenne, and pepper over the chickpeas and cook, stirring, for another minute. Remove from the heat and toss with the herbs.

2 In a large bowl, combine the lettuce, spinach, herbs, onion, lemon juice, and oil. Season with salt and pepper and toss well to combine.

3 Toast the bread and top each slice with 2 tablespoons of the hummus for crostini.

4 Top the lettuce mixture with the chickpeas, then add the tomato, avocado, and olives. Arrange the mango around the edges, if desired. Serve with the hummus crostini.

NUTRITION FACTS (per serving–400g) Calories: 435; Fat: 25g; Carbs: 37g; Protein: 13g; Fiber: 15g Vitamin C: 58%; Iron: 33%; Calcium: 18%; Vitamin A: 144%

CHILLED PEANUT KALE SALAD

This peanut kale salad with accents of ginger, red onion, and tahini is a creamy, sweet veggie dish that will have you easily devouring an entire bunch of kale.

SERVES 6

1 **For the Spicy Ginger Peanut Sauce:** In a large soup pot, combine all the sauce ingredients and ½ cup water. Heat over medium-high heat, stirring briskly, until melted and well combined. Reduce the heat to medium and simmer, stirring, for about 2 minutes. Reduce the heat to low.

2 Wash the kale well and pull the leaves from the thick stems. Discard the stems. Dry the kale very well and add the leaves to the pot with the sauce. Stir to fold the kale into the sauce. The hot sauce will wilt the kale.

3 Remove the pot from the heat and add the peanuts and red onion. Fold the kale salad well until all the kale has wilted and the leaves and onion mix with the sauce, about a minute. Serve warm or place in the fridge, covered, to chill and serve cold. The salad will keep well in the refrigerator for a few days.

Tip: If you want a thicker dressed salad or the kale bunch is extra large, double the sauce recipe and fold as much as you'd like into the kale.

SPICY GINGER PEANUT SAUCE

2 cloves garlic, finely chopped

2½ tablespoons salted creamy peanut butter

2 tablespoons seasoned rice vinegar

2 tablespoons brown rice syrup

1 tablespoon chopped pickled ginger (optional)

2 teaspoons tahini or additional peanut butter (optional)

2 teaspoons tamari

1 teaspoon sesame oil

1 teaspoon grated peeled fresh ginger

⅛ teaspoon cayenne

⅛ teaspoon freshly ground black pepper

2 large or 3 small bunches kale

½ cup peanuts

1 cup thinly sliced red onion

NUTRITION FACTS
(per serving–186g)
Calories: 211; Fat: 11g; Carbs: 22g; Protein: 10g; Fiber: 5g
Vitamin C: 227%; Iron: 17%; Calcium: 15%; Vitamin A: 343%

FIESTA SALAD WITH PLANTAINS

Sweet and caramelized plantains are sautéed in coconut oil and then added to this feisty fiesta salad featuring black beans, sweet corn, and fresh guacamole on top. Party in a bowl.

— **SERVES 2** —

SALAD

1 cup canned black beans, drained and rinsed

½ cup drained and rinsed canned corn or fresh corn kernels

½ cup finely chopped fresh cilantro

½ cup chopped red onion

Pinch of freshly grated lime zest

3 tablespoons fresh lime juice

2 teaspoons extra-virgin olive oil (optional)

1 teaspoon agave syrup

¾ teaspoon ground coriander

½ teaspoon chipotle powder, or a few pinches of cayenne

⅛ teaspoon freshly ground black pepper

PLANTAINS

1 to 2 teaspoons virgin coconut oil

1 plantain, sliced

Pinch of sea salt

Scoop Sunny Guacamole (page 199)

1 **For the Salad:** In a large bowl, toss together all the salad ingredients. Cover and refrigerate until ready to serve, at least 30 minutes. (The salad can be assembled a day in advance, if desired.)

2 **For the Plantains:** In a skillet, heat the coconut oil over high heat. Add the plantains and salt and cook until the plantains are tender and the edges are blackened, 2 to 3 minutes on each side.

3 Serve the salad topped with the plantains. Top each serving with a scoop of the guacamole.

NUTRITION FACTS (per serving–318g) Calories: 362; Fat: 11g; Carbs: 60g; Protein: 10g; Fiber: 10g | Vitamin C: 53%; Iron: 19%; Calcium: 7%; Vitamin A: 26%

TOFU FETA, WATERMELON, AND BASIL SALAD

For this light and refreshing salad, I have veganized a classic watermelon and feta cheese salad by using tofu! This salad is perfect on a warm day, light and lovely with accents of fresh basil throughout. Hydrating, rich in protein, and delicious.

SERVES 4

1. **For the Tofu:** Drain the tofu and squeeze dry with a paper towel. Slice the tofu into cubes and place them in a large bowl.

2. In a small glass, briskly stir together the lemon juice, miso, oil, and vinegar until the miso paste blends into the liquid. Pour the marinade over the tofu and toss well to coat. Cover and refrigerate for at least an hour to marinate—overnight is best.

3. **For the Salad:** Add the watermelon and basil to the marinated chilled tofu and toss well. Add the cayenne and pepper to taste and the nutritional yeast (if using). Top with additional pepper and some olive oil, if desired, and garnish with fresh basil.

TOFU

18 ounces firm tofu

⅓ cup fresh lemon juice

2 tablespoons white miso paste

1 to 2 tablespoons olive oil

1 tablespoon seasoned rice vinegar

SALAD

2 cups cubed watermelon

1 cup tightly packed fresh basil leaves, shredded (about 1 small bunch whole basil), plus more leaves for garnish

Cayenne

Freshly ground black pepper

2 tablespoons nutritional yeast (optional)

Drizzle of extra-virgin olive oil (optional)

NUTRITION FACTS (per serving–246g) Calories: 165; Fat: 9g; Carbs: 12g; Protein: 12g; Fiber: 2g — Vitamin C: 28%; Iron: 14%; Calcium: 27%; Vitamin A: 15%

MANGO AVOCADO ARUGULA SALAD

Sweet, juicy mango is one of my favorite fruits to slice over salads. This simple salad includes macadamia nuts or pumpkin seeds, spicy arugula greens, healthy-fat-rich avocado, and plenty of antioxidant-infused mango cubes.

— SERVES 4 —

LIGHT "HONEY" MUSTARD DRESSING

¼ cup fresh lemon juice or apple cider vinegar

2 tablespoons olive oil

2 teaspoons Dijon mustard

1 to 3 teaspoons agave syrup

Pinch of garlic powder

Sea salt and freshly ground black pepper

5 cups chopped arugula

½ cup chopped sweet onion (optional)

1 mango, diced

½ avocado, diced

¼ cup macadamia nuts or pumpkin seeds

Sprinkle of smoky paprika or cayenne

1 **For the Light "Honey" Mustard Dressing:** In a large bowl, whisk together the dressing ingredients.

2 Add the arugula to the bowl with the dressing and toss well to coat. Fold in the onion (if using), mango, avocado, and macadamia nuts. Sprinkle with some paprika and serve right away.

NUTRITION FACTS
(per serving–162g)

Calories: 231; Fat: 17g; Carbs: 15g; Protein: 5g; Fiber: 4g

Vitamin C: 49%; Iron: 9%; Calcium: 5%; Vitamin A: 21%

HARVEST SALAD

Bring on fall! And bring on fall salads. Some people think that spring and summer are the "salad seasons," but I truly think salads deserve year-round placement on any dining table. I especially love using fall ingredients like butternut squash, cranberries, and apples in fall salads. Wintery greens like kale are delicious, or stick to something basic, über-healthy, and lovely like spinach.

SERVES 2

1 cup butternut squash cubes

Drizzle of extra-virgin olive oil

Few pinches of sea salt and freshly ground black pepper

MAPLE-CIDER DRESSING

1 tablespoon apple cider vinegar

2 teaspoons grade B maple syrup

1 teaspoon walnut oil

Pinch of sea salt and freshly ground black pepper

Pinch of cayenne

4 cups chopped raw kale or fresh spinach

¼ cup dried cranberries

¼ cup dried apple rings (or use apple slices!)

¼ cup pecans, toasted or candied (see page 156)

1 Preheat the oven to 400°F.

2 In an oven-safe dish, toss the squash with the oil and salt and pepper. Roast until tender, 25 to 30 minutes. Set aside.

3 **For the Maple-Cider Dressing:** In a large bowl, whisk together the dressing ingredients.

4 Add the greens, cranberries, and apple to the bowl with the dressing and toss well to coat.

5 Serve the mixed greens with the squash and pecans over the top.

NUTRITION FACTS
(per serving–475g) Calories: 170; Fat: 11g; Carbs: 18g; Protein: 4g; Fiber: 6g   Vitamin C: 56%; Iron: 15%; Calcium: 11%; Vitamin A: 223%

SMOKY PAPRIKA GREEN BEAN SALAD WITH CANDIED WALNUTS

If you do not consider yourself a fan of green beans, keep reading! Even those who snarl at the classic "holiday green bean casserole" will love the spicy, lively, smoky-sweet flavors of this colorful green bean salad. Candied walnuts, soaked with maple flavor, mingle with crisp golden carrots, a smoky paprika-tahini-maple dressing, and perky boiled green beans. The green beans retain a slightly crisp texture from a quick cooking time. Serve as a veggie-filled lunch or at your next holiday gathering, and watch your guests actually get excited to try the green bean dish!

SERVES 6

4 cups green beans, trimmed and cut into halves or thirds

2 medium carrots, cut into rounds

¼ cup chopped sweet onion

DRESSING

1 small lemon, juiced

2 heaping tablespoons tahini

2 tablespoons grade B maple syrup

1½ teaspoons smoky Spanish paprika

¼ teaspoon sea salt

⅛ teaspoon garlic powder

Few dashes freshly ground black pepper

Few dashes cayenne (optional)

CANDIED WALNUTS

1 cup walnuts

2 tablespoons grade B maple syrup

Coconut oil spray (optional)

1 Rinse the green beans in a large colander under cold water. Set aside.

2 Bring a large pot of salted water to a boil over high heat. Add the beans and boil for about 5 minutes; do not overcook the beans or they will become too soft. For crisper (almost raw!) beans, do a very quick boil of just 1 to 3 minutes. Drain the beans and thoroughly rinse under cold water. Let the beans drain completely.

3 Place the green beans, carrots, and onion in a large bowl. Set aside.

4 **For the Dressing:** In a cup, whisk together the dressing ingredients. Pour the dressing over the veggies and toss until all the veggies are well coated. Pour the salad into a serving bowl and set aside.

5 **For the Candied Walnuts:** Heat a small saucepan over high heat. Add the walnuts and maple syrup and cook for about 1 minute, tossing the walnuts with the maple syrup. (For less sticking, add a spritz of coconut oil spray, if desired, before adding the nuts.) Remove from the heat and let cool for a few minutes.

6 Sprinkle the walnuts over the salad. You may serve this salad right away, but for best flavor, cover and refrigerate for at least 1 hour before serving. You can also make the salad the night before and allow it to marinate overnight in the fridge.

Tip: For toasty warm walnuts, make them right before you plan to serve the salad.

NUTRITION FACTS
(per serving–147g)

Calories: 241; Fat: 16g; Carbs: 20g; Protein: 6g; Fiber: 6g

Vitamin C: 31%; Iron: 12%; Calcium: 8%; Vitamin A: 78%

SUMMER CAESAR
WITH NO-HONEY MUSTARD DRESSING

This is my summery vegan spin on a Caesar salad. I adore this vibrant, sweet and sassy blend of light and crisp romaine lettuce with nutty farro grains, crunchy sunflower seeds, tender edamame, juicy-sweet pink grapefruit, and smoky bits of tempeh bacon. Plus it has sprouted grain "quickie" croutons and creamy No-Honey Mustard Dressing (page 179) over the top and tossed with the greens. No matter what time of year it is, this salad will make you feel like you are in a summertime sunbeam. All warm and happy inside.

SERVES 2

1 Place the romaine in a large bowl and toss with a few spoonfuls of the dressing. Divide the lettuce between two serving bowls.

2 In a small saucepan, combine the farro, ½ cup plus 1 tablespoon water, and the salt. Bring to a boil, then cover, reduce the heat to low, and cook for 35 to 50 minutes, until tender.

3 Sprinkle the cooked farro over the dressed romaine. Add the tempeh bacon and grapefruit slices to the salad. Sprinkle the edamame, sunflower seeds, pepper, and bread cubes over the top. Drizzle the remaining dressing over the top and sprinkle with vegan Parmesan, if desired.

Tip: It is helpful to make a big batch of farro at one time, rather than making it per recipe in small batches. You can store cooked farro in the fridge, covered, for 3 to 4 days for best flavor, so that you can easily pull it from the fridge to prep recipes like this. For 2½ cups cooked farro, use 1 cup dry farro, 2½ cups water, and ¾ teaspoon sea salt.

5 cups chopped romaine lettuce

1 recipe No-Honey Mustard Dressing (Page 179)

¼ cup farro

Pinch of sea salt

3 tablespoons Smoky Tempeh Bacon (page 62), finely diced

6 long slices pink grapefruit, peels and pith removed

2 tablespoons edamame beans, warmed

2 teaspoons sunflower seeds

Few pinches of freshly ground black pepper

½ slice sprouted grain bread, toasted and cubed

Easy Vegan Parmesan (page 226; optional)

NUTRITION FACTS
(per serving–310g)

Calories: 186; Fat: 4g; Carbs: 30g; Protein: 13g; Fiber: 7g

Vitamin C: 36%; Iron: 16%; Calcium: 10%; Vitamin A: 250%

BLUEBERRY FARRO SPINACH SALAD

Blueberries are one of my favorite foods, and since they are so incredibly healthy, I wanted to add them to a salad where they could be the star of the show! Well, blueberries, and some buttery spinach tossed in a ginger-maple dressing, too. Sweet sliced almond clusters, rich in vitamin E, are a healthy and delicious accent.

SERVES 2

5 cups chopped fresh spinach

1 cup cooked farro (see Note)

1 cup blueberries

1 tablespoon fresh lemon juice or balsamic vinegar

2 to 3 teaspoons extra-virgin olive oil

1 teaspoon grade B maple syrup

Pinch of sea salt and freshly ground black pepper

CANDIED ALMOND CLUSTERS

⅓ cup sliced almonds

2 teaspoons grade B maple syrup

Lemon slices, for garnish

⅛ teaspoon grated fresh ginger, for garnish

1. Add the spinach, farro, blueberries, lemon juice, oil, maple syrup, and salt and pepper to a large bowl and toss well.

2. **For the Candied Almond Clusters:** In a small sauce pot, over high heat, lightly toast the sliced almonds for 1 to 2 minutes. Add the maple syrup and toss. Allow the maple to bubble for a few seconds then turn off the heat. Set the pot aside for a minute while the nuts cool and become sticky.

3. Add the salad mix to serving bowls. Scoop the sticky almonds out of the pan and add them in clusters to the salad bowls. Garnish with lemon slices and ginger over the top.

Note: In a saucepan, combine ½ cup farro with 1¼ cups water and a pinch of sea salt. Bring to a boil, then cover and reduce the heat to low. Simmer for 35 to 50 minutes, until the farro is tender.

NUTRITION FACTS (per serving–231g) Calories: 379; Fat: 14g; Carbs: 56g; Protein: 14g; Fiber: 11g   Vitamin C: 53%; Iron: 28%; Calcium: 15%; Vitamin A: 141%

BONUS RECIPES!

14 SALAD DRESSING RECIPES

Here are my favorite homemade salad dressings. Use them to perk up just about any leafy greens, chopped veggies, and more. Simply combine the dressing ingredients in a blender or whisk well in a small cup for dressings with whole food ingredients like fresh herbs or some spices; thick ingredients will need to be blended. Drizzle or toss to serve.

EASY CREAMY RANCH

— **MAKES ½ CUP** —

3 tablespoons vegan mayonnaise

⅛ teaspoon paprika

⅛ teaspoon ground coriander

Pinch of cayenne

Pinch of freshly ground black pepper

⅛ teaspoon fresh dill

Or substitute these spices with 1 teaspoon of a salt-free mixed spice blend (like Mrs. Dash)

Juice of 1 small lemon

1 In a small bowl, combine the vegan mayonnaise along with the spices and herbs. Fold well.

2 Whisk in the lemon juice 1 tablespoon at a time until the dressing is thinned to the desired consistency.

3 Place the dressing in the fridge, covered, until ready to use, or serve right away. For the best flavor, use within 2 days.

   Modify It: To thin the dressing, you can add fresh lemon juice, unsweetened soy milk, or apple cider vinegar to taste.

SWEET SPICY BBQ

— **MAKES ⅓ CUP** —

2 tablespoons barbecue sauce (bottled or homemade)

1 to 2 tablespoons fresh orange juice (or try apple cider vinegar for added zestiness)

1 tablespoon extra-virgin olive oil (or vegan mayonnaise for added creaminess)

1 In a small cup, whisk together all the ingredients until smooth. Add the greater amount of orange juice or apple cider vinegar to thin out the consistency and add vibrancy to the flavor. Using cider vinegar will make the dressing very zesty, while using orange juice will add some sweetness. Substituting vegan mayonnaise for the juice or oil makes this dressing very creamy, rich, and bold in flavor. Serve immediately.

TAHINI MAPLE

—— MAKES ¾ CUP ——

3 to 4 tablespoons fresh lemon juice or 2 tablespoons apple cider vinegar plus 1 tablespoon water

2 tablespoons tahini

2 tablespoons grade B maple syrup

1 to 2 tablespoons vegetable, extra-virgin olive, or safflower oil

Pinch of sea salt (optional)

Spices: garlic powder, freshly ground black pepper, cayenne, any others you'd like

1   In a small bowl, whisk together all the ingredients until smooth, or place in a blender and blend on low until well combined.

2   Serve right away or chill for a thicker dressing. The dressing firms up as the tahini and oils chill. Store, covered, in the refrigerator for up to 2 days.

SWEET CURRY

—— MAKES ¼ CUP ——

1 tablespoon grade B maple syrup (see Note)

1 tablespoon tahini

2 teaspoons fresh lemon juice

1 teaspoon hot curry powder or Muchi curry powder

Few dashes of cayenne

1   In a small bowl, whisk together all the ingredients until combined. Serve immediately.

Note: Add a bit less maple syrup if you do not like your sauce too sweet.

BLENDED GREEN GODDESS

MAKES ¾ CUP

1 Combine all the ingredients in a blender and blend, starting on low speed and increasing to high, until smooth and creamy. Serve immediately.

½ large avocado

3 to 4 tablespoons oil, such as walnut, hemp, extra-virgin olive, or macadamia

Juice of 1 large lemon

Large handful of fresh flat-leaf parsley

⅛ teaspoon garlic powder, or 2 cloves garlic

Sea salt and freshly ground black pepper

Optional: dash of cayenne, 1 tablespoon nuts or seeds, 1 tablespoon vegan mayonnaise

NO-HONEY MUSTARD

MAKES ½ CUP

1 If using the vegan mayo, whisk together all the ingredients, except the salt and pepper, in a small bowl until smooth. If using the silken tofu, place all the ingredients in a blender and blend, starting on low speed and increasing to high, until smooth.

2 Taste and season with salt and pepper as desired. If using vegan mayo, you may not need any additional salt. If using tofu, you will likely need more salt, because tofu is quite bland on its own. This dressing is best served the day it is made, but it can be stored in the fridge, covered tightly, for up to 2 days.

2 tablespoons Dijon or whole-grain mustard

1 to 2 tablespoons vegan mayonnaise, or ¼ cup silken tofu, blended

1 tablespoon grade B maple syrup

1 to 2 teaspoons water or fresh orange juice

Sea salt and freshly ground black pepper

BLENDED CREAMY SPICY PEANUT

MAKES ¼ CUP

2 tablespoons creamy peanut butter

1 tablespoon tamari

2 teaspoons grade B maple syrup

½ teaspoon grated peeled fresh ginger, or 1 clove garlic

Splash of coconut milk or water to thin out dressing as desired (optional)

Pinch of chopped fresh cilantro (optional)

Cayenne

Combine the peanut butter, tamari, maple syrup, and ginger in a blender with ½ cup water and blend, starting on low speed and increasing to high, until smooth. To thin the dressing, add the coconut milk. For added flavor and color, add the cilantro. Taste and add cayenne to taste for a spicier dressing. This dressing is best served the day it is made, but it can be stored in the fridge, covered tightly, for up to 2 days.

BLENDED PINEAPPLE-AVOCADO

MAKES 1½ TO 2 CUPS

1 avocado, pitted and peeled

½ cup fresh orange juice

⅓ cup chopped fresh pineapple

1 tablespoon tahini

2 teaspoons tamari

Sea salt and freshly ground black pepper

Optional: jalapeño or a few pinches of cayenne

Combine all the ingredients in a blender and blend, starting on low speed and increasing to high, until smooth. Start with 1 tablespoon of the oil and add more if desired after doing a taste test. For spicy accents, blend in the jalapeño or cayenne, if desired. This dressing should be used the same day you make it, to prevent browning.

BLENDED AVOCADO DREAM

MAKES 1½ TO 2 CUPS

1. Combine all the ingredients in a blender and blend, starting on low and increasing to high, until smooth. Blend in the herbs for added flavor and color, if desired. Add more or less black pepper to taste. This dressing should be used the same day you make it, to prevent browning.

1 large avocado, pitted and peeled

½ cup fresh orange juice

1 tablespoon tahini

2 teaspoons tamari

2 teaspoons grade B maple syrup (or agave syrup)

1 small jalapeño, seeded (optional)

⅓ cup fresh cilantro or flat-leaf parsley (optional)

Freshly ground black pepper

SIMPLE MAPLE-LEMON

MAKES ½ CUP

1. In a small cup, whisk together all the ingredients. Add variations to taste, adding more maple syrup for a sweeter dressing and more olive oil for a richer dressing. Adding the full 2 tablespoons of maple syrup and olive oil will also tone down the brightness of the lemon. Serve right away.

Make It Spicy: Add a dash of cayenne.

Make It Creamy: Fold in a spoonful of vegan mayonnaise or tahini.

2 tablespoons fresh lemon juice

1 to 2 tablespoons grade B maple syrup

1 to 2 tablespoons extra-virgin olive oil

1 tablespoon apple cider vinegar or more lemon juice

¼ teaspoon chili powder

¼ teaspoon garlic powder

⅛ teaspoon freshly ground black pepper

LEMON PESTO

MAKES 1¾ TO 2 CUPS

1 cup fresh basil leaves (1 large handful)

½ cup walnuts

¼ cup fresh lemon juice

2 tablespoons extra-virgin olive oil

2 teaspoons white miso paste

½ teaspoon chopped raw garlic or roasted garlic

¼ cup warm water (or to taste)

Sea salt and freshly ground black pepper (optional)

Combine all the ingredients, except the salt and pepper, in a blender and blend, starting on low speed and increasing to high, until smooth. Add water as desired to thin and mellow the dressing. Add any optional variation ingredients and blend until smooth. Taste before serving and add salt and pepper, if needed. Serve immediately or store, covered, in the refrigerator for up to 3 days.

Make It Creamy: Add ½ avocado.

Make It Sweet: Add a splash of agave syrup or grade B maple syrup.

Make It Cheesy: Add 1 to 2 tablespoons nutritional yeast.

CREAMY CHIPOTLE

MAKES ABOUT ¼ CUP

3 tablespoons vegan mayonnaise

1 teaspoon agave syrup or grade B maple syrup

¼ to ½ teaspoon chipotle powder

Optional liquid: water, fresh lime juice, or unsweetened nondairy milk

In a small cup, whisk together all the ingredients until combined. For the chipotle powder, add more based on how spicy and bold you want the flavor. Add optional liquid as needed to achieve the desired consistency. Adding water will thin out the consistency and mellow the flavor. Adding lime juice will thin out the consistency and add brightness. Adding non-dairy milk will thin with a creamy tone. Serve immediately or store, covered, in the refrigerator for up to 3 days.

GINGER MISO

Combine all the ingredients in a blender. Use the full amount of oil for a richer dressing, or less for a lighter version. For the tamari, adding the full amount will provide a saltier, bolder intensity of flavor, so use less for a mellower flavor. Blend, starting on low speed and increasing to high, until smooth. Add water as desired, 1 tablespoon at a time, to thin out the consistency and mellow the flavor. Whisk the dressing if needed, but you will want to whisk briskly to ensure the miso is clump-free upon serving. Serve immediately.

2 to 4 tablespoons extra-virgin olive oil

2 tablespoons white miso paste

2 tablespoons seasoned rice vinegar, or juice of 1 lime

1 to 2 tablespoons tamari or soy sauce

1 tablespoon agave syrup, brown rice syrup, or grade B maple syrup

½ teaspoon chopped or grated peeled fresh ginger

Water (optional)

LIME AGAVE

MAKES ¾ CUP

In a small cup, whisk together all the ingredients until combined. If desired, you may use a bit less oil for a lighter dressing. Add the diced jalapeño or cayenne to taste for spiciness, if desired. Serve right away or store, covered, in the refrigerator for up to 3 days.

Juice of 2 large limes

3 tablespoons extra-virgin olive oil

1 tablespoon dark grade agave syrup

1 tablespoon apple cider vinegar

Pinch of freshly ground black pepper

1 teaspoon diced jalapeño or pinch of cayenne (optional)

BOWLS

Bowls. What is a "bowl," anyway? And how is it different from a salad? Bowls are usually heartier than salads, because they may contain both warm and cool ingredients. Bowls usually combine a hearty array of grains, veggies, legumes, and flavorful sauces and dressings. Bowls are kind of like a traditional meal with a variety of ingredients on a plate, but served in a bowl so all those wonderful flavors can combine and mingle. Salads are usually a bit lighter, cooler in temperature, and contain fewer cooked ingredients.

KALE PUMPKIN-RICE BOWL

This bowl takes ordinary brown rice and infuses it with cozy pumpkin flavor. Then I add a variety of healthy ingredients like kale, pistachio, orange, garlic, and onion and jumble everything together so the flavors combine in beautiful pumpkin bliss. The rice goes from plain, nutty, and perky to moist, tender, and flavor infused. Add some crispy maple tofu cubes on top, and you have a meal worth savoring.

SERVES 2

1 In a skillet, heat 1 to 2 teaspoons of the oil over high heat. Add the onion and cook, stirring, for 1 to 2 minutes. Add the pistachios and cook, stirring, until the nuts toast a bit, 1 minute more.

2 Add another ½ to 1 teaspoon of the oil to the skillet and add the rice, kale, pumpkin, garlic (if using), salt, pepper, orange zest, and cayenne (if using). Toss and cook, stirring, so that the pumpkin distributes through the rice as it sizzles and softens.

3 Add the fresh orange juice and cook, stirring, until the liquid has been absorbed, 1 to 2 minutes. Scoop all the rice to one side of the pan in a thick mound. In the empty space in the pan, add ½ teaspoon of the oil and the tofu cubes. Drizzle the maple syrup over the tofu cubes and add a pinch of salt and pepper. Cook over high heat, stirring occasionally, until the edges blacken, 2 to 3 minutes. Add the diced orange and toss all the tofu cubes with the rice in the final minute of cooking.

4 Serve this dish warm with fresh orange slices to garnish, if desired.

2 to 3 teaspoons extra-virgin olive oil

1 small sweet onion, chopped

3 tablespoons pistachios

1¾ cups cooked short-grain brown rice

1½ cups chopped kale

¼ cup canned unsweetened pumpkin puree

1 clove garlic, finely chopped (optional)

⅛ teaspoon sea salt

⅛ teaspoon freshly ground black pepper

Pinch of freshly grated orange zest

Pinch of cayenne or ground turmeric (optional)

Juice of ½ orange

1 cup firm tofu cubes or chickpeas

1 teaspoon grade B maple syrup

½ orange, peeled and diced

Orange slices, for garnish (optional)

NUTRITION FACTS (per serving–325g) Calories: 431; Fat: 14g; Carbs: 36g; Protein: 14g; Fiber: 8g   Vitamin C: 192%; Iron: 21%; Calcium: 21%; Vitamin A: 255%

PESTO CHICKPEA BOWL

This recipe was created, well, by accident. I was planning on making a pesto-infused lasagna, but I was so in love with the pesto sauce that I decided to go very simple and use it to coat some toasted chickpeas and a generous garnish of tomatoes. I added some rice to make this an even heartier bowl. Beans, tomatoes, and pesto: a minimalist pairing that is easy to love.

SERVES 2

1. In a skillet, combine the chickpeas, onion, and oil and cook over high heat, stirring, until the edges of the chickpeas and onion brown. Sprinkle the paprika over the top.

2. Add the rice to the pan and cook, stirring, for about 2 minutes more. Sprinkle in the chopped basil. Divide the rice and bean mixture between two serving bowls.

3. Top with the pesto sauce and arrange the tomato slices around the edges of the bowl. Top each bowl with more fresh basil and 1 tablespoon of the cashew ricotta, if desired.

1 cup drained and rinsed canned chickpeas

¼ cup chopped sweet onion

1 teaspoon extra-virgin olive oil

¼ teaspoon Spanish paprika

1 cup cooked brown or black rice

1 tablespoon chopped fresh basil, plus more for garnish

¾ to 1 cup Pesto Sauce (page 250)

1 large tomato, sliced

2 tablespoons Vegan Cashew Ricotta (page 223; optional)

NUTRITION FACTS
(per serving–242g)

Calories: 289; Fat: 12g; Carbs: 37g; Protein: 9g; Fiber: 6g

Vitamin C: 45%; Iron: 14%; Calcium: 3%; Vitamin A: 32%

GREEK BOWL

Clear blue ocean water, white cube-shaped buildings lining a sunny coast— ah, Greece. Okay, so I have yet to actually travel to Greece, but when I do I will think of this bowl. This is my spin on Greek cuisine: kalamata olives, lemon juice, extra-virgin olive oil, red onions, mint, tofu feta, and quinoa tabouli.

SERVES 4

VEGGIE SALAD

1 cup diced tomatoes

1 cup diced cucumber

½ cup chopped red onions

2 tablespoons pitted kalamata olives, chopped

2 tablespoons fresh lemon juice

1 teaspoon extra-virgin olive oil (try a brand produced in Greece for extra authenticity!)

½ teaspoon dried oregano

Pinch of sea salt and freshly ground black pepper

TOFU FETA

12 ounces firm tofu, cubed

¼ cup fresh lemon juice

1½ tablespoons white miso paste

1 tablespoon seasoned rice vinegar

1 tablespoon extra-virgin olive oil

ingredients continue

1 **For the Veggie Salad:** Combine all the salad ingredients in a large bowl and toss well. Cover and refrigerate for at least 30 minutes.

2 **For the Tofu Feta:** Combine all the tofu feta ingredients in a large bowl and toss to coat the tofu cubes. Cover and refrigerate for at least 30 minutes.

3 **For the Easy Quinoa Tabouli:** Combine all of the tabouli ingredients in a large bowl and toss to combine. Divide the quinoa tabouli among four serving bowls.

4 **For the Tahini-Maple Sauce:** In a small cup, whisk together the sauce ingredients until smooth.

5 **To Serve:** Add the chilled veggie salad alongside the quinoa tabouli and top with the tofu feta. Drizzle the tahini-maple sauce over each bowl. Serve with the hummus, pita triangles, parsley, and lemon wedges for garnish. An additional drizzle of olive oil is encouraged!

NUTRITION FACTS (per serving–298g) Calories: 378; Fat: 16g; Carbs: 43g; Protein: 17g; Fiber: 7g | Vitamin C 65%; Iron: 31%; Calcium: 24%; Vitamin A: 21%

ingredients continued

EASY QUINOA TABOULI

1 cup Fluffy Quinoa (see below), still warm

½ cup finely chopped fresh flat-leaf parsley

¼ cup fresh lemon juice

1 tablespoon finely chopped fresh mint

1 teaspoon extra-virgin olive oil

Pinch of sea salt and freshly ground black pepper

TAHINI-MAPLE SAUCE

2 tablespoons fresh lemon juice

1 tablespoon tahini

2 teaspoons grade B maple syrup

TO SERVE

4 tablespoons Classic Hummus Dip (page 197)

4 small pitas, sliced into triangles and toasted or grilled

Chopped fresh flat-leaf parsley, for garnish

Lemon wedges, for garnish

Extra-virgin olive oil (optional)

HOW-TO: FLUFFY QUINOA

Five easy steps to achieving fluffy quinoa every time:

- **Rinse it:** Rinse the dry quinoa in water before cooking. This removes some of the mush-promoting grit on the grain.

- **Less is more (water):** For fluffy quinoa, less water is more. Most boxes of quinoa say to add 2 cups water for every 1 cup dry quinoa. I say that is too much! And remember: If you are rinsing the quinoa you will be adding a bit more water anyway. I do a ratio of 1 part dry quinoa to 1½ parts water, then I rinse the quinoa and drain as much water as I can.

- **No peeking!:** Once you close that pot lid over the cooking quinoa—no peeking! And no stirring! You don't want to disturb the quinoa fluff factory bubbling inside.

- **Let it sit:** After cooking and before you lift the lid, turn off the stove and, in the words of Kelly Clarkson, "Just Walk Away." Let the quinoa sit for a good 5 to 10 minutes. Again, no peeking!

- **Stick a fork in it:** Fluff the cooked quinoa with a fork. No mush-enhancing spoons allowed.

CAJUN TEMPEH SWEET POTATO BOWL

Sweet potatoes save dinnertime at least once a week in my house. I can easily build a meal around a couple of sticky-sweet baked sweet potatoes. And this bowl recipe comes in handy on a busy night. Healthy kale, spiced tempeh, vegan ranch dressing, and a plump baked sweet potato combine for this comfort food bowl.

SERVES 1

1 small sweet potato

Drizzle of cooking oil

1 cup tempeh cubes

¾ teaspoon Cajun spice blend

Pinch of sea salt and freshly ground black pepper

2 cups chopped kale

1 cup cooked whole grain, such as brown rice, millet, farro, or black rice (optional)

1 tablespoon Easy Creamy Ranch (page 177)

1 tablespoon Vegan Barbecue Sauce (page 244; optional)

1. Preheat the oven to 400°F. Poke a few holes in the potato using a fork. Bake the sweet potato in its skin until tender, about 1 hour. Remove from the oven and let cool for a bit.

2. Heat a skillet over high heat and add the oil. Add the tempeh cubes and sprinkle the Cajun seasoning over the cubes so all the sides are coated. Add the salt and pepper. Cook, stirring occasionally, until the edges begin to blacken, about 5 minutes. Push the tempeh to one side of the pan and add the kale. Allow the kale to soak up the excess pan liquid and flavors as the heat slightly wilts the kale.

3. Transfer the kale to a serving bowl and add the cooked grains (if using). Top with the warm tempeh cubes. Remove the sweet potato skin and slice the potato into thick rounds. Add the sweet potato rounds to the bowl and drizzle the ranch and barbecue sauce (if desired) over the bowl.

NUTRITION FACTS (per serving–377g)

Calories: 434; Fat: 21g; Carbs: 42g; Protein: 25g; Fiber: 6g

Vitamin C 297%; Iron: 28%; Calcium: 31%; Vitamin A: 758%

PINEAPPLE FRIED QUINOA BOWL WITH TAHINI PINEAPPLE DRESSING

This is my spin on "pineapple fried rice." I take sweet and zesty fresh pineapple and cooked quinoa to create a pineapple fried quinoa bowl complete with mint and cashew accents. If you want to get extra fancy, you can even hollow out half of a whole pineapple and serve the quinoa in a pineapple boat. Party perfect.

SERVES 4

1. In a saucepan, combine the pineapple, onion, kale, cashews, nutritional yeast, and coconut oil. Cook over high heat, stirring, for 4 to 5 minutes. Fold in the cooked quinoa and fresh mint and cook, stirring, for 2 to 3 minutes more. Add salt to taste.

2. **For the Tahini Pineapple Dressing:** In a small bowl, whisk together the dressing ingredients.

3. If desired, fill a hollowed-out half of a fresh pineapple with the fried quinoa. Otherwise, use regular serving bowls. Garnish with the diced pineapple and fresh mint. Drizzle the dressing over the quinoa before serving.

1½ cups diced fresh pineapple

½ sweet onion, diced

1 cup shredded kale or collard greens

3 tablespoons raw cashews

2 tablespoons nutritional yeast

2 teaspoons virgin coconut oil

3 cups Fluffy Quinoa (page 189)

2 tablespoons chopped fresh mint

Pinch of sea salt

TAHINI PINEAPPLE DRESSING

3 tablespoons pineapple juice

2 tablespoons tahini

1 teaspoon chopped fresh mint

Pineapple "bowl" (optional)

½ cup finely diced pineapple

Pinch of chopped fresh mint

NUTRITION FACTS (per serving–375g)	Calories: 398; Fat: 12g; Carbs: 64g; Protein: 13g; Fiber: 9g	Vitamin C: 76%; Iron: 30%; Calcium: 12%; Vitamin A: 54%

BLACK RICE PEANUT KALE BOWL WITH PROTEIN

This is a pretty fantastic meal when you crave simple flavors and healthy ingredients that taste amazing. Nutty black rice blends with peanut-dressed kale and a simple maple-pepper tofu or tempeh slice on top. Dinner is done!

SERVES 2

TOFU OR TEMPEH

6 ounces tofu or tempeh

2 teaspoons grade B maple syrup

1 teaspoon tamari

Pinch of freshly ground black pepper

Pinch of cayenne

Pinch of garlic powder

BLACK RICE

¾ cup black rice

Pinch of sea salt

DRESSING

Juice of 1 lime

1 tablespoon creamy peanut butter

2 teaspoons grade B maple syrup, agave, or brown rice syrup

Pinch of sea salt and freshly ground black pepper

Pinch of grated peeled fresh ginger or cayenne (optional)

1. **For the Tofu or Tempeh:** In a bowl, combine the tofu or tempeh, maple syrup, tamari, and spices. Cover and set in the fridge to marinate for at least 10 minutes. Overnight is even better, but not necessary.

2. **For the Black Rice:** In a large saucepan, combine the rice, 1½ cups water, and the salt. Bring to a boil, cover, and reduce the heat to low. Simmer until the rice is tender, 35 to 45 minutes. Drain any excess liquid and fluff the rice with a fork. Cover and refrigerate to set and chill for best texture.

3. **For the Dressing:** Combine the dressing ingredients in a small microwave-safe cup. Warm the dressing in the microwave for about 15 seconds.

4. Place the kale leaves in a large bowl and pour the warmed dressing over the top. Massage the dressing into the kale. The kale should wilt a bit and soften as it becomes marinated with the dressing.

5. Fold in the rice. Toss well. Divide the mixture between 2 serving bowls and set aside.

6 Set a skillet over high heat and add a drizzle of oil. When the oil is hot, add the tofu and pour the excess marinade over the top. Cook for 1 to 2 minutes on each side, just enough time to get a nice blackened sear. Add salt and pepper to taste. Divide the protein between the serving bowls, over the kale and rice. Serve warm.

4 cups torn kale leaves (about ½ large bunch kale)

Drizzle of extra-virgin olive oil

Sea salt and freshly ground black pepper

NUTRITION FACTS
(per serving–334g)
Calories: 300; Fat: 7g; Carbs: 50g; Protein: 15g; Fiber: 6g

Vitamin C: 181%; Iron: 20%; Calcium: 26%; Vitamin A: 178%

COCONUT CLOUD BOWL
WITH COCONUT RICE, TOFU PILLOWS, AND TOASTED CASHEWS

Puffy giant cubes of pillowy tofu top fluffy coconut-infused rice. Accented with toasted cashews, ginger, and cinnamon, this bowl is sweet and soothing, and rich in protein and healthy fats.

SERVES 4

1 cup jasmine rice

Sea salt

¼ cup coconut milk

1 tablespoon grade B maple syrup, plus more for garnish

½ teaspoon ground cinnamon, plus more for garnish

½ teaspoon pure vanilla extract

¼ teaspoon ground ginger or grated peeled fresh ginger

½ cup plus 1 teaspoon shredded unsweetened coconut

1 teaspoon virgin coconut oil

1 cup firm tofu, sliced into large cubes

¼ cup raw unsalted cashews

1 In a large saucepan, combine the rice, 2 cups water, and a pinch of salt. Bring to a boil, then reduce the heat to low, cover, and simmer for 30 minutes. Fluff the rice, then add the coconut milk, maple syrup, cinnamon, vanilla, ginger, and ⅛ teaspoon salt. Raise the heat to medium and simmer until most of the coconut milk has been absorbed but the mixture is still moist, 3 to 5 minutes.

2 In a skillet, toast the coconut over medium heat for 1 to 2 minutes. Fold into the rice mixture, reserving a few spoonfuls for garnish.

3 In the skillet, heat the coconut oil over high heat. Add the tofu and sear for 2 to 3 minutes, to brown on all sides. Add the cashews and cook until they brown a bit, 2 to 3 minutes. Remove from the heat.

4 Fluff the rice and add the tofu and cashews to the pot, right over the rice. Cover the pot, set over low heat, and allow the steam from the rice and subtle heat from the pan to fluff up the tofu cubes. Remove the lid after about 3 minutes.

5 Serve the tofu rice with the reserved toasted coconut, a drizzle of maple syrup, and a dusting of cinnamon over the top.

NUTRITION FACTS (per serving–201g)

Calories: 281; Fat: 14g; Carbs: 31g; Protein: 10g; Fiber: 3g

Vitamin C: 2%; Iron: 20%; Calcium: 13%; Vitamin A: 0%

APPETIZERS, SIDES, SNACKS, AND PARTY PLATTERS

Everything in between! That is what this section encompasses: party dips and appetizer platters to a few snacks and sides for your day of deliciousness. One of my favorite healthy eating tips: If you are hungry, eat! Pretty simple sounding, but it is true! Do not be afraid to eat a snack if you are hungry at an odd hour or nibble in between meals. On the flip side, do not be afraid to skip a meal if you simply are not hungry, then eat when hunger does come. These snacks and nibbles will come in handy for that.

HUMMUS

Learning how to make your own hummus is a must for any vegan cook. I simply blend my hummus ingredients in my high-speed blender. A food processor will also work. One trick when using canned beans is to rinse the beans in very hot water. I find that this makes them easier to blend. It also makes the hummus slightly warm when blended, which is delicious. You can also chill to serve if preferred. Hummus is a very versatile recipe. Once you master a basic hummus recipe, you can get creative and try adding everything from sun-dried tomatoes and garlic to black olives and jalapeño. Let your imagination go wild when it comes to creating new hummus recipes.

SWEET POTATO HUMMUS

SERVES 4

1 small sweet potato

1½ cups drained and rinsed canned chickpeas

2 to 3 tablespoons fresh orange juice

2 tablespoons apple cider vinegar

2 tablespoons tahini

2 tablespoons walnut oil or virgin coconut oil, melted

2 teaspoons grade B maple syrup

⅛ teaspoon garlic powder

Sea salt and freshly ground black pepper

Smoky paprika or cinnamon, for garnish (optional)

1 Preheat the oven to 400°F. Poke a few holes in the potato using a fork. Bake the sweet potato until tender, 30 to 40 minutes. Allow to cool a bit, then remove the skin and place the flesh in a blender.

2 Add the remaining ingredients to the blender and blend until smooth. Spread on a serving platter and serve slightly warmed with paprika sprinkled over the top, if desired.

NUTRITION FACTS
(per serving-104g)

Calories: 231; Fat: 10g; Carbs: 30g; Protein: 7g; Fiber: 7g

Vitamin C: 30%; Iron: 13%; Calcium: 6%; Vitamin A: 194%

CLASSIC HUMMUS DIP

— SERVES 6 —

1 Place the beans in a high-speed blender or food processor. Add the lemon juice, tahini, oil, salt, garlic powder, pepper, lemon zest, and cayenne. Start the blender on low and continue blending until smooth and creamy. If you need to loosen the blend a bit, add the warm water. Taste and add salt and spices to taste, if desired.

2 Pour into a serving dish and smooth with the back of a spoon. Garnish with the olive oil, pepper, cayenne, and parsley. Serve warm, freshly made, or chilled.

1½ cups drained and rinsed canned chickpeas

1½ cups drained and rinsed canned cannellini beans

6 tablespoons fresh lemon juice

2 tablespoons unsalted tahini

2 tablespoons extra-virgin olive oil

1½ teaspoons sea salt, plus more as needed

½ teaspoon garlic powder, plus more as needed

¼ teaspoon freshly ground black pepper, plus more as needed

⅛ teaspoon freshly grated lemon zest

Few pinches of cayenne, plus more as needed

1 to 2 tablespoons warm water (optional)

GARNISH

1 teaspoon extra-virgin olive oil

Freshly ground black pepper

Cayenne or paprika

Chopped fresh flat-leaf parsley

NUTRITION FACTS
(per serving–117g)

Calories: 187; Fat: 9g; Carbs: 21g; Protein: 9g; Fiber: 5g

Vitamin C: 12%; Iron: 12%; Calcium: 7%; Vitamin A: 0%

SUNNY GUACAMOLE

This is how I make guacamole, bright and zesty with a generous amount of lemon juice. Though traditionally guacamole is made with lime juice, I love the brightness of lemon. Garlic, pepper, and salt are must-have spices. And cilantro is needed for that authentic guacamole flavor. If you like your guac on the spicy side, add some jalapeño with the seeds removed. But if you are really brave and crave extra-spicy guac, you can leave the jalapeño seeds in!

SERVES 6

Combine all the ingredients in a medium bowl and mash with a fork until creamy but still chunky, adding more or less lemon juice to taste. Serve freshly made, or cover and refrigerate for up to a few hours before serving.

Variation: For a sweeter version, substitute 1 small orange for one of the lemons.

2 avocados, pitted, peeled, and diced

Juice of 1 to 2 lemons

1 small jalapeño, seeded, if desired, and diced (optional)

½ cup diced red onion

¼ cup finely chopped fresh cilantro

¼ teaspoon sea salt

⅛ teaspoon garlic powder, or 1 clove garlic, finely chopped

⅛ teaspoon freshly ground black pepper

NUTRITION FACTS (per serving–93g) Calories: 138; Fat: 13g; Carbs: 2g; Protein: 2g; Fiber: 5g   Vitamin C: 25%; Iron: 2%; Calcium: 1%; Vitamin A: 3%

8 thickly cut slices French bread

1 tablespoon extra-virgin olive oil, plus more for serving

PEACH CITRUS MINT

¾ cup diced peaches

¾ cup diced navel orange

1 tablespoon chopped fresh mint

Pinch of freshly grated lime zest

1 tablespoon fresh lime juice

1 teaspoon extra-virgin olive oil

Chili salt

SPICY RED PEPPER TOMATO

Handful of chopped fresh basil

1 medium tomato, diced

1 roasted red pepper, thinly sliced

2 cloves garlic, thinly sliced

2 tablespoons fresh lemon juice

2 teaspoons extra-virgin olive oil

1 teaspoon spicy harissa

Sea salt and freshly ground black pepper

CLASSIC TOMATO

1 medium tomato, diced

¼ cup chopped fresh basil

2 tablespoons diced onion

2 tablespoons fresh lemon juice

1 clove garlic, minced

2 teaspoons extra-virgin olive oil

Sea salt and freshly ground black pepper

AVO-MANGO SUNSHINE

1 cup cubed mango

¼ cup cubed avocado

Pinch of freshly grated orange zest

2 tablespoons fresh orange juice

2 tablespoons chopped fresh basil

Pinch of cayenne

Sea salt and freshly ground black pepper

BRUSCHETTA RECIPES

Bruschetta is a fun and easy appetizer to make for a party or for yourself. All you need for a beautiful, delicious bruschetta party platter are some toasted baguette slices and a fresh and lively bruschetta topping. Try classic tomato, summery citrus-peach, or exotic avocado and mango.

───── SERVES 8 ─────

1 Preheat the oven to 400°F.

2 Place the bread slices on a baking sheet and brush the cut surfaces with the oil. Toast the bread in the oven for 5 minutes. Transfer the toast to a serving platter for topping.

3 **For the Toppings:** In a small bowl, toss the topping ingredients. Top each toasted slice of bread with one heaping spoonful of the bruschetta topping. Serve right away. Drizzle extra olive oil over the top to serve.

NUTRITION FACTS (per serving–52g), peach citrus mint:	Calories: 72; Fat: 3g; Carbs: 11g; Protein: 2g; Fiber: 1g	Vitamin C: 23%; Iron: 2%; Calcium: 2%; Vitamin A: 3%
NUTRITION FACTS (per serving–53g), spicy red pepper tomato:	Calories: 69; Fat: 3g; Carbs: 9g; Protein: 2g; Fiber: 1g	Vitamin C: 34%; Iron: 1%; Calcium: 4%; Vitamin A: 9%
NUTRITION FACTS (per serving–53g), classic tomato:	Calories: 114; Fat: 3g; Carbs: 19g; Protein: 4g; Fiber: 1g	Vitamin C: 7%; Iron: 8%; Calcium: 2%; Vitamin A: 3%
NUTRITION FACTS (per serving–48g), avo-mango sunshine:	Calories: 78; Fat: 3g; Carbs: 12g; Protein: 2g; Fiber: 1g	Vitamin C: 16%; Iron: 3%; Calcium: 1%; Vitamin A: 3%

BAKED CASHEW CHEESE

Cashew cheese is a gourmet-looking appetizer that is really quite simple to make once you get the hang of the recipe. The ingredients are simple, but it is the technique and time that takes some patience. Soft cashews are key to successful cashew cheese, so be sure to start the recipe at least a day in advance to give the cashews time to soak. The longer you bake your cheese, the drier the texture will become. You can serve cashew cheese cold or warm, straight from the oven.

SERVES 6

1. At least a day ahead of time, place the cashews in a bowl with enough salted water to cover and soak overnight or for at least 8 hours.

2. Drain the cashews and rinse them well under warm to hot water.

3. In a blender, combine the cashews, lemon juice, nutritional yeast, salt, ¼ cup water, and any spices or seasonings you desire. Blend until as smooth as possible. A high-speed blender really helps here. Over the sink, pour the blended mixture into a cheesecloth or mesh straining bag (nylon or hemp canvas both work). Squeeze out as much of the excess liquid as you can. (You can use this liquid as leftover nut milk! If you'd like to save the liquid, squeeze the mixture over a bowl.)

4. If you'd like a more "cheeselike" cheese, you can hang the bag from a spoon over a bowl for a few hours to strain out more liquid. You can also improve the texture of the cashew cheese by wrapping it in a few bundles of cheesecloth or a clean dish towel and placing the cheese bundle in the fridge for a few hours or overnight. This will also naturally dry out the cheese a bit. You can skip these steps if you are in a hurry, but they are advised for best results.

2 cups raw cashews

¼ cup fresh lemon juice

1 to 2 tablespoons nutritional yeast (optional)

1 teaspoon pink salt

Optional add-ins, such as various spices and seasonings; dry or fresh herbs like lemon-pepper; chipotles; fresh flat-leaf parsley; chopped veggies like kale or red bell pepper; minced or powdered garlic; chopped chives; and freshly ground black pepper

recipe continues

HOW-TO: SOAKING NUTS

- **Uses for soaked nuts:** Nut milks, nut-based desserts, nut-based sauces and dips like cashew cheese

- **How to soak raw nuts:** Place the nuts in a large bowl and add enough water to cover by a few inches. Add a few pinches of salt as well. Set aside to soak on the countertop or in the fridge for at least 6 hours. For faster soaking, use very hot water as your soaking water. Overnight is the standard soaking time, but some recipes may only need a few hours to soften the nuts sufficiently. If you will not be using the soaked nuts right away, store them in the fridge until needed and use within a day or two. Before using the soaked nuts in recipes, be sure to rinse them well with water.

- **Types of nuts:** Standard nuts used for soaking include cashews, almonds, and walnuts. But you can really soak any raw nuts to achieve a somewhat softer texture and sometimes make them easier to digest. You may also want to experiment with soaking seeds, both for blending purposes and digestive purposes.

- **Digestion:** Soaking nuts may improve digestibility and nutrient absorption.

- **How long:** In general, harder nuts take a longer time to soften when soaked. This "hardness" can vary by variety of nut and sometimes even by brand.

continued

5 Preheat the oven to 200°F.

6 Transfer the cashew mixture to an oven-safe serving dish. Top with a pinch of salt and pepper and any dried spices or herbs you desire. Bake the mixture until the surface has darkened and is almost crusty in appearance and texture, about 1 hour. The inside will be firmed up, yet still soft. You can modify the baking time to change the texture of the cheese. Bake longer than an hour for a drier cheese. If you are in a hurry, you can bake the cashew cheese at a higher temperature for as little as 20 minutes to speed up the drying process. The top crust will dry nicely, but the interior will remain quite moist, like a thick dip. Also, the results will vary based on the baking dish size and depth. Cheese that has been spread more thinly will dry out more quickly. Store the cashew cheese in its baking dish in the fridge for up to 2 to 3 days. You can serve it chilled, or reheat in a 350°F oven for 5 to 15 minutes to serve warm. The longer this dish is stored, the drier the cheese texture will become.

NUTRITION FACTS
(per serving–60g)

Calories: 230; Fat: 17g; Carbs: 12g; Protein: 7g; Fiber: 2g

Vitamin C: 8%; Iron: 13%; Calcium: 3%; Vitamin A: 0%

ROMAINE SPEARS
WITH HUMMUS AND DATES

These crunchy spears of romaine topped with hummus and sweet dates are light and lovely. Pile them on a party platter and watch them disappear in a flash. Not just party fare, you can easily gobble up a platter filled with these beauties for snacking. Much better than crunching on breadsticks!

SERVES 6

Spread 1 teaspoon of the hummus on each romaine leaf. Top the hummus with a date half and sprinkle with the paprika and a spritz of lemon juice. Arrange in a fan on a plate to serve.

6 teaspoons Classic Hummus Dip (page 197) or any other hummus

6 romaine leaves

3 Medjool dates, pitted and halved

¼ teaspoon Spanish paprika

Juice of ½ lemon

NUTRITION FACTS
(per serving–20g)

Calories: 37; Fat: 1g; Carbs: 11g; Protein: 1g; Fiber: 1g

Vitamin C: 2%; Iron: 1%; Calcium: 1%; Vitamin A: 1%

EASY BUTTERNUT SQUASH SAGE DIP

This was one of my very first "hit" recipes on my blog. I was so excited that my readers loved this recipe just as much as I did. It is so easy to make and super delicious with savory and sweet flavors in one golden bliss dip. Butternut squash puree combines with garlic, citrus zest, and fresh sage. If you want the flavor and texture a bit more nutty and hearty, blend in a cup of canned white beans. Serve with toasted baguette slices or veggie sticks.

SERVES 4

---

1 Preheat the oven to 350°F.

2 Spoon the butternut squash puree into a medium bowl. Add the hummus, maple syrup, nondairy liquid, orange zest, salt, cinnamon, pepper, and cayenne (if using). Stir well until the dip is smooth and well blended. Fold the chopped sage leaves into the dip. If using the beans, transfer the mixture to a blender, add the beans, and blend until smooth.

3 Transfer the dip to an oven-safe dish and bake for 10 to 15 minutes. For faster prep, you could also microwave the dip for 30 to 60 seconds. Garnish with the whole sage leaf and some orange zest.

1½ cups canned butternut squash puree

4 heaping tablespoons Classic Hummus Dip (page 197)

¼ cup grade B maple syrup

3 tablespoons liquid, such as plain nondairy milk or coconut milk

½ teaspoon freshly grated orange zest, plus more for garnish

½ teaspoon sea salt

⅛ teaspoon ground cinnamon

⅛ teaspoon freshly ground black pepper

Pinch of cayenne (optional)

3 fresh sage leaves, finely chopped, plus 1 whole leaf for garnish

¾ cup drained and rinsed canned white beans or chickpeas (optional)

NUTRITION FACTS (per serving–77g) Calories: 74; Fat: 2g; Carbs: 15g; Protein: 2g; Fiber: 2g Vitamin C: 17%; Iron: 3%; Calcium: 4%; Vitamin A: 75%

PINK BEET WALNUT DIP

Pretty (and delicious) in pink! This bright pink dip is a fun appetizer to serve at a big party or even a party of one. Lightly sweet from the beets, the nutty walnut flavor shines through in each creamy bite.

SERVES 6

1 cup walnuts

¾ cup drained and rinsed canned white beans

½ cup peeled chopped or shredded raw beets

2 tablespoons grade B maple syrup

1 tablespoon apple cider vinegar or fresh lemon or orange juice

Sea salt and freshly ground black pepper

Pinch of cayenne

Few splashes of water, nondairy milk, or fresh lemon or orange juice (optional)

Combine all the ingredients in a high-speed blender or food processor and blend until smooth. If needed, add a few splashes of liquid to loosen the blend. Transfer to a bowl, cover, and refrigerate for at least 1 hour before serving.

NUTRITION FACTS (per serving–67g)	Calories: 189; Fat: 13g; Carbs: 14g; Protein: 6g; Fiber: 3g	Vitamin C: 2%; Iron: 88%; Calcium: 3%; Vitamin A: 0%

GREEN DREAM DIP

Dreamy, healthy, and delicious, this avocado-and-white-bean-infused dip is my favorite recipe for vegging out after a long day or even for snacking when you cannot pry yourself away from your desk. Serve with veggie sticks, rice crackers, or your favorite toasted bread. Best served the same day it's made, to keep the avocado flavor fresh and buttery.

SERVES 6

---

1. In a blender or food processor, combine all the ingredients and blend until smooth. Serve at room temperature, freshly blended.

2 cups fresh baby spinach

1 cup drained and rinsed canned cannellini beans

1 avocado, pitted and peeled

¼ cup fresh lemon juice

1 to 2 tablespoons Candied Walnuts (page 156; optional)

1 teaspoon red pepper flakes

Pinch of sea salt and freshly ground black pepper

NUTRITION FACTS
(per serving–98g)

Calories: 114; Fat: 7g; Carbs: 10g; Protein: 5g; Fiber: 5g

Vitamin C: 18%; Iron: 10%; Calcium: 5%; Vitamin A: 22%

PARTY JALAPEÑO POPPERS

These gently fried little green gems will have your party guests popping with excitement. Crisp and cheesy, you will be thrilled with this vegan version of jalapeño poppers.

SERVES 5

¼ cup vegan cream cheese

¼ cup vegan cheddar cheese shreds

2 tablespoons whole wheat flour

1 tablespoon nutritional yeast

1 teaspoon garlic powder

Few pinches of sea salt and freshly ground black pepper

⅓ cup panko bread crumbs

¼ cup plain soy milk

5 large jalapeños, halved lengthwise and seeded

1 cup safflower oil, plus more as needed

1 Set up a the breading station: In a small bowl, fold the vegan cream cheese with the cheese shreds. In another small bowl, combine the flour, nutritional yeast, garlic powder, and salt and pepper and toss until well combined. Place the panko in a third bowl and the soy milk in a fourth.

3 Stuff each jalapeño with the cheese mixture, then dunk them in the soy milk, roll in the flour mixture, dunk back in the milk, roll in the panko, and set aside. Press the panko crumbs into the wet cheese layer. Continue until all the jalapeño halves are stuffed and breaded.

4 Heat the oil in a saucepan over medium-high heat. Test if the oil is hot enough by dropping one panko crumb into the oil. If it sizzles, the oil is hot enough. Add a few poppers at a time and lightly fry until golden brown, 2 to 3 minutes. If needed, add more oil to the pan between batches, making sure it heats up before adding more poppers.

5 Transfer the poppers to a paper towels to drain and cool for a few minutes before serving. Serve warm.

NUTRITION FACTS (per serving–52g)

Calories: 95; Fat: 5g; Carbs: 11g; Protein: 3g; Fiber: 2g

Vitamin C: 4%; Iron: 8%; Calcium: 4%; Vitamin A: 7%

GOLDEN CASHEW CAKES

These easy appetizer or savory side cakes simmer with enticing aromas: creamy cashews, sizzling onions, warm turmeric, and exotic coconut oil. Cheesy nutritional yeast and garlic accent these tender, toasty cakes. I have used both cashews and walnuts for this recipe and love both versions.

MAKES 5 LARGE OR 10 SMALL CAKES; SERVES 5

1 Place the beans in a large bowl and mash well with a fork.

2 In a blender or food processor, process the cashews and Brazil nuts until they are crumbly and powdery. Add them to the bowl with the beans and fold them in. Fold in the nutritional yeast and turmeric.

3 In a skillet, heat 1 teaspoon of the coconut oil over medium heat. Add the onion and garlic and cook, stirring, until the edges turn brown, 2 to 3 minutes. Pour the onions and some of the pan oil into the bowl with the bean mixture. Fold well. Add the salt and pepper. Fold well until a thick mixture forms.

4 In a skillet, heat 1 tablespoon of the coconut oil over medium-high heat. Form the bean mixture into palm-size patties—work carefully because they will be very delicate and moist. Place the patties in the pan and cook for under a minute on each side. Flip several times to ensure that the nuts in the patties do not burn. When the edges and sides are browned and crisp, transfer to a plate to cool. Repeat until all the bean mixture has been used, refreshing the oil in the pan as necessary. Serve toasty warm, straight from the skillet.

1½ cups drained and rinsed canned white beans

⅓ cup raw cashews

¼ cup Brazil nuts or more cashews

2 tablespoons nutritional yeast

1 teaspoon ground turmeric

2 to 3 tablespoons virgin coconut oil

¼ cup chopped white onion

2 cloves garlic, chopped

Pinch of sea salt and freshly ground black pepper

NUTRITION FACTS (per serving–111g)
Calories: 237; Fat: 12g; Carbs: 25g; Protein: 11g; Fiber: 6g
Vitamin C: 2%; Iron: 7%; Calcium: 23%; Vitamin A: 0%

LENTIL WALNUT CAKES

These skillet-warm cakes with cheesy lentils, walnuts, and citrus-accented flavor have a toasty crisp surface and are moist and tender on the inside. Slice into one with your fork and watch the soft steam escape as you bite into savory bliss. Lentils and walnuts are true superfoods, so embrace this delicious recipe. Serve as an appetizer or entrée.

SERVES 5

1½ cups drained and rinsed canned lentils

1 cup walnuts, ground into crumbly powder

½ cup diced white onion (optional)

⅓ cup nutritional yeast

½ teaspoon sea salt

¼ teaspoon freshly ground black pepper

⅛ teaspoon garlic powder

2 to 4 teaspoons virgin coconut oil

1 teaspoon freshly grated orange zest

Orange slices, for garnish

1. Put the lentils in a large bowl. Using a large fork, mash the lentils until they form a wet, silky, thick paste. Add the ground walnuts, onion (if using), nutritional yeast, salt, pepper, and garlic powder. Fold until the mixture thickens considerably.

2. In a skillet, heat 2 teaspoons of the coconut oil over medium-high heat.

3. Form the lentil mixture into cakes, about 3 inches wide and ¼ to ½ inch thick. Place the cakes in the hot pan and cook for 1 to 2 minutes on each side. Sprinkle ½ teaspoon of the orange zest over the cakes just before flipping. Since the ingredients in the cakes are already cooked, you mostly just want to crisp the outsides and warm the cakes through.

4. Remove the cakes from the skillet and let cool slightly (to help the cakes bind a bit) before serving. Serve warm, with the remaining ½ teaspoon orange zest sprinkled over the top. Garnish with orange slices.

Note: Yes, you could bake these cakes on a greased baking sheet at 350°F until toasty golden on the outsides, about 20 minutes.

NUTRITION FACTS
(per serving–104g)

Calories: 281; Fat: 18g; Carbs: 19g; Protein: 14g; Fiber: 9g

Vitamin C: 3%; Iron: 21%; Calcium: 4%; Vitamin A: 0%

MINI NACHO PIZZAS

These easy snack pizzas are nacho inspired. Melty vegan cheese tops
creamy refried beans, with classic nacho toppings.

SERVES 4

---

1 Preheat the broiler.

2 Slice and toast the English muffins. Set them on a baking
sheet. Spread a heaping spoonful of refried beans on
each half and top with the vegan cheese and other veggie
toppings.

3 Broil the English muffins for a minute until the cheese
bubbles. Serve warm, with the cilantro on top and hot
sauce and lime slices on the side.

2 English muffins

⅓ cup vegan refried beans

¼ cup vegan cheese shreds

4 jalapeños, sliced

1 tomato, diced

1 tablespoon sliced pitted black
olives

4 teaspoons chopped fresh cilantro

Hot sauce

Lime slices

NUTRITION FACTS
(per serving–88g)

Calories: 114; Fat: 3g;
Carbs: 19g; Protein: 4g;
Fiber: 3g

Vitamin C: 9%; Iron:
10%; Calcium: 7%;
Vitamin A: 3%

AVO-DILLA

This creative snack was a recipe I created by accident. I had some extra lavash wraps in my fridge that needed to be used up, so I filled them with avocado (because avocado makes everything better!), folded them up, and sautéed the avocado wraps in a skillet with some coconut oil and agave syrup. I seasoned them with some simple spices and sliced to serve. The layers turned out so bubbly, sweet, and spiced and the avocado was warmed and buttery. This snack experiment was a hit! Try it for yourself.

SERVES 2

½ avocado, diced or gently mashed

1 whole wheat lavash wrap

1 teaspoon virgin coconut oil

2 teaspoons agave or grade B maple syrup

⅛ teaspoon sea salt

⅛ teaspoon freshly ground black pepper

Pinch of cayenne or paprika

1. Add the avocado to the lavash wrap, then using a fork, gently mash or spread it onto the lavash so it sticks. Next, fold half of the lavash wrap over the other half as if you were folding a quesadilla. Alternative method: For a more tightly wrapped Avo-Dilla, fold the lavash as you would fold a burrito, with all sides sealed, then using a spatula, press it into a flattened shape as it cooks in the pan.

2. Heat the coconut oil in a skillet over high heat. Add the lavash wrap; open one folded edge and drizzle syrup inside of the wrap, about a half teaspoon. Fold the wrap to close, flat, long and thin. Be careful since the pan will be hot; use tongs or a spatula.

3. Drizzle the remaining amount of syrup over the outside of the wrap and sprinkle the salt, pepper, and cayenne. Cook, stirring occasionally, until the edges begin to blacken and the syrup becomes very sticky, 1 to 3 minutes on each side should do it.

4. Slice into quarters and serve warm.

NUTRITION FACTS (per serving–53g) Calories: 127; Fat: 8g; Carbs: 10g; Protein: 2g; Fiber: 3g Vitamin C: 5%; Iron: 3%; Calcium: 1%; Vitamin A: 1%

CINNA-CHILI COCONUT OIL POPCORN

This is my favorite popcorn recipe. The corn kernels are popped in virgin coconut oil, which has an amazingly intoxicating aroma when combined with the nutty corn. Then I toss the freshly popped corn with an array of spices like cinnamon, cayenne, and even a splash of maple syrup to mingle with the spices, creating a savory-sweet bowl. Your next movie night needs this popcorn!

SERVES 6

1. In an extra-large soup pot, heat the coconut oil over medium-high heat. Drop in 2 to 3 corn kernels and cover the pot with a lid. Wait until you hear the first kernel pop, then add the rest of the popping corn. Quickly cover with a lid.

2. Shake the pot on the burner for the next minute as the kernels pop, keeping the kernels moving so they don't burn. Once popping starts, keep shaking the popcorn in the pan with the lid still on, to prevent burning.

3. After most of the corn has popped, 3 to 4 minutes, turn off the heat and transfer the popcorn to a large bowl. Toss with the spices, salt, and maple syrup to taste and serve warm.

3 tablespoons virgin coconut oil

½ cup popping corn

2 teaspoons cayenne

½ teaspoon ground cinnamon

¼ teaspoon sea salt

⅛ teaspoon paprika or cayenne

1 to 2 teaspoons grade B maple syrup

NUTRITION FACTS (per serving–30g) Calories: 145; Fat: 8g; Carbs: 16g; Protein: 3g; Fiber: 3g Vitamin C: 0%; Iron: 3%; Calcium: 0%; Vitamin A: 0%

ROASTED RED PEPPER–CREAM SPIRAL WRAPS

I lovingly call these "bull's-eye" spirals because the red-and-white spiral reminds me of a dartboard. Creamy vegan cheese perfectly accompanies tender roasted red peppers in this simple and craveable appetizer or snack roll.

SERVES 2

1 large whole wheat lavash wrap or large flour tortilla

½ teaspoon extra-virgin olive oil

Sea salt and freshly ground black pepper

¼ cup Veggie-Cashew Cream Cheese (recipe follows) or store-bought vegan cream cheese

1 large roasted red pepper, thinly sliced

1 Heat a skillet over medium heat and warm the lavash wrap for 1 to 2 minutes, or warm the wrap in the microwave for 30 seconds.

2 Brush the wrap with the oil and sprinkle with salt and black pepper. Spread the cashew cream cheese on the inside of the wrap. Add the roasted pepper, arranging it evenly across the inside of the wrap.

3 Tightly wrap the lavash just as you would when rolling up sushi or cinnamon buns. Then slice the wrap crosswise into 1-inch-thick pieces, creating large round spirals. Use toothpicks to tightly secure the wraps, if desired. Serve right away or chill until ready to serve. These can be made up to a day ahead of time and stored, covered, in the refrigerator.

NUTRITION FACTS
(per serving–94g)

Calories: 156; Fat: 10g; Carbs: 14g; Protein: 4g; Fiber: 2g

Vitamin C: 137%; Iron: 9%; Calcium: 1%; Vitamin A: 27%

VEGGIE-CASHEW CREAM CHEESE

Store any leftover cheese, covered, in the fridge for 2 to 3 days. You can serve the leftovers on sandwiches, as a veggie or cracker dip, or make more wraps the next day. This cream cheese is also delicious on freshly toasted bagels!

MAKES I CUP, ENOUGH FOR 3 TO 4 WRAPS

---

1 | Combine the soaked cashews, lemon juice, soy milk, and salt and pepper in a blender or food processor and blend until smooth. Fold in the chopped carrots and the parsley.

1 cup raw cashews, soaked overnight

2 tablespoons fresh lemon juice

2 tablespoons plain soy milk

Pinch of sea salt and freshly ground black pepper

1 carrot, finely chopped

¼ cup finely chopped fresh flat-leaf parsley

NUTRITION FACTS
(per serving–77g)

Calories: 214; Fat: 16g; Carbs: 14g; Protein: 6g; Fiber: 2g

Vitamin C: 11%; Iron: 14%; Calcium: 2%; Vitamin A: 5%

GUACAMOLE AND CORN CAKE LETTUCE CUPS

Crispy fresh lettuce wraps take the place of tortillas in this light and lovely appetizer featuring two favorite recipes, guacamole and spoonable sweet corn cakes. The combination of avocado and sweet corn is irresistible!

SERVES 4

---

1 | Place side-by-side scoops of the guacamole and corn cake inside each lettuce leaf. Drizzle a tablespoon of the Salsa Verde or ½ teaspoon of the hot sauce over the top each lettuce cup to serve.

4 scoops Sunny Guacamole (page 199)

4 scoops corn cake (from Feisty Corn Cake Bean Balls on Tomato Moons, page 148)

4 large iceberg or romaine lettuce leaves, washed and dried

2 teaspoons hot sauce

NUTRITION FACTS   see individual recipes

EASY CHEEZY BAKED KALE CHIPS

Kale chips! Every kitchen needs a kale chip baking session. Or two. Or three. These chips go fast, so you will definitely be making them again and again. For guilt-free snacking, kale chips are a favorite in my house. I also add kale chips as garnishes to salad, soups, and over avocado toast—so good! Try them with my cheezy topping, too (variation follows).

SERVES 2

1 large bunch kale

1 teaspoon oil, such as extra-virgin olive, virgin coconut, or safflower oil

⅓ to ½ cup nutritional yeast

3 pinches of Spanish paprika

Sea salt and freshly ground black pepper

1. Preheat the oven to 250°F. Line two baking sheets with parchment paper.

2. Strip the kale leaves from the thick stems. Discard the stems. Rinse the kale leaves in cold water and pat dry. Wet kale will make soggy kale chips, so make sure to dry them well. Toss the dry kale leaves with the oil, nutritional yeast to taste, paprika, and salt and pepper.

3. Arrange the kale in a very thin layer on the lined baking sheets. Overlapping the kale will lead to soggy or unevenly crisped chips, so give the kale plenty of room to breathe.

4. Bake the kale until it is crispy but still slight tender, about 30 minutes. Overcooked kale chips can tasty ashy, so learn to find that sweet spot of crispy yet tender kale. Baking times will vary greatly based on how thick the kale leaves are, so keep a watchful eye on them, checking the oven every 10 minutes or so.

5. Let the baked kale chips cool before piling them into a bowl. This helps keep their crisp texture. Serve warm and crispy or store the leftovers in a sealed container at room temperature or in the fridge. Kale chips are best eaten within a day of making them.

NUTRITION FACTS
(per serving–157g)

Calories: 167; Fat: 5g; Carbs: 21g; Protein: 14g; Fiber: 7g

Vitamin C: 268%; Iron: 26%; Calcium: 19%; Vitamin A: 412%

ENTRÉES

And now, for the main event dishes! I love these family-approved meals inspired by classic entrées like lasagna, pasta, potpie, tacos, and more. I usually pair these dishes with a light soup or side salad. And when you are feeding a crowd, a beautiful vegan entrée makes a delicious centerpiece dish.

CREAMY CASHEW POTPIE

This is my all-time favorite potpie recipe because it is so incredibly rich and creamy yet contains no dairy. The secret? Cashew cream sauce. My creamy nut-based sauce is folded with classic potpie veggies like carrots and peas, baked with a crispy biscuit crust. Comfort food bliss.

SERVES 8

CASHEW BASE

1¾ cups raw cashews, soaked overnight

1 cup vegetable broth

2 tablespoons white miso paste

1 tablespoon apple cider vinegar or fresh lemon juice

½ teaspoon garlic powder

¼ teaspoon sea salt

Few pinches of freshly ground black pepper

VEGGIE FILLING

1¼ cups peeled and diced white potato

1 teaspoon extra-virgin olive oil

1 cup diced carrots

½ cup drained and rinsed canned chickpeas

½ cup diced shiitake mushrooms

⅓ cup chopped sweet onion

1 cup frozen peas, thawed

1. Preheat the oven to 350°F.

2. **For the Cashew Base:** Drain and rinse the cashews. Place them in a food processor or blender and add the veggie broth, miso, vinegar, garlic powder, salt, and pepper. Blend, increasing the speed from low to high, until smooth and creamy; this may take a few minutes depending on how soft the cashews are. Add salt and pepper to taste. Set aside.

3. **For the Veggie Filling:** Place the potatoes in a deep skillet or soup pot and add water to cover by a few inches. Bring to a boil and cover. Reduce the heat to medium and cook the potatoes are until tender but not mushy, 10 to 12 minutes. Drain and set the potatoes aside.

4. In a large, deep skillet, heat the oil over medium heat. Add the carrots, chickpeas, mushrooms, and onions and cook, stirring, until the edges of the onions begin to brown and soften, 2 to 3 minutes. Add the peas and cooked potatoes and cook, stirring, until the peas are warm, 2 to 3 minutes.

5. Pour the blended cashew base over the veggies in the skillet and toss until the veggies are well coated. Raise the heat to high and cook, stirring, for 1 to 2 minutes more so that the flavor of the nutty sauce develops a bit. Pour the heated veggie filling into a potpie serving/baking dish.

6. **For the Biscuit Crust:** In a bowl, quickly mix together the flour, baking powder, and salt. Using your hands, mash

in the coconut oil. Add the water 1 tablespoon at a time, mixing well after each addition. Keep adding water until the dough is kneadable yet still very moist. Knead the dough a bit and then turn it out on a floured surface. (This is a very quick dough, so a lumpy texture is just fine.) Roll out the dough, then place it over the filling, pressing the edges against the edges of the casserole dish to seal. Alternatively, you can just place clumps of the dough over the filling for a more rustic look. Slice a few vents through the top of the dough to allow steam to escape. Brush the top of the dough with the lemon juice, if desired.

7 Bake the potpie, uncovered, until the crust is browned and fluffy and the filling is thickened yet still nice and creamy, 35 to 40 minutes. If you are worried about overbrowning the top crust, you can cover it with foil for the first 30 minutes of baking. Let cool for at least 20 minutes before serving. The potpie is best served warm.

Note: You can use a wide array of casserole dishes—around 5 quarts is best. I like a deep-rimmed dish to retain a lot of moisture and heat in the filling.

BISCUIT CRUST

1½ cups all-purpose flour

1 teaspoon baking powder

½ teaspoon sea salt

⅓ cup virgin coconut oil

6 to 10 tablespoons warm water

2 teaspoons fresh lemon juice or vegan buttery spread, melted (optional)

NUTRITION FACTS
(per serving–171g) Calories: 198; Fat: 21g; Carbs: 43g; Protein: 11g; Fiber: 6g   Vitamin C: 13%; Iron: 20%; Calcium: 5%; Vitamin A: 48%

LASAGNA VERDE

This was a recipe I made in my first few months of blogging. I changed up the traditional red sauce ingredients in lasagna and used an all green sauce, a vegan pesto. I added some creamy cashew ricotta cheese and savory slices of tofu. A touch of jalapeño adds a hint of spiciness. This verde lasagna is a family-style entrée worth gathering at the table for!

SERVES 12

1 Preheat the oven to 350°F. Grease a lasagna baking dish with the oil.

2 Bring a large pot of salted water to a boil. As soon as the water comes to a boil, drop in 4 of the lasagna noodles and cook until tender, 10 to 12 minutes. Remove the cooked noodles and line them up to cover the bottom of the prepared baking dish. Repeat until all the noodles are cooked, transferring the cooked noodles to a side plate once you have covered the bottom of the baking dish. (If you are able to cook more than 4 noodles at a time without having them stick together, you can do that too.) Reserve ½ cup of the pasta cooking water.

3 **For the Spicy Jalapeño Pesto:** In a high-speed blender, combine all the pesto ingredients with ⅓ cup of the pasta cooking water and blend, increasing the speed from low to high, until smooth. The pesto should be thick, yet easy to pour and drizzle, a tad thicker than the consistency of tomato sauce for pizza. Add more of the pasta cooking water, a spoonful at a time, if desired to thin out the texture of the pesto a bit. Pour the pesto into a bowl and set aside.

4 **For the Tofu:** In a sauté pan, heat the oil over medium-high heat. Add the tofu slices and season with salt, pepper, and nutritional yeast (if using). Cook, stirring occasionally, until the tofu edges brown, 3 to 4 minutes. Set aside.

recipe continues

1 tablespoon extra-virgin olive oil

12 to 14 lasagna noodles

SPICY JALAPEÑO PESTO

2 cups fresh basil leaves

2 cups fresh spinach

½ cup fresh lemon juice

½ cup walnuts

¼ cup raw pumpkin seeds

¼ cup extra-virgin olive oil

1 jalapeño, seeded

1 to 3 cloves garlic

TOFU

½ teaspoon extra-virgin olive oil

14 ounces firm or silken tofu, thinly sliced

Few pinches of sea salt and freshly ground black pepper

1 tablespoon nutritional yeast (optional)

ingredients continue

continued

2½ cups Vegan Cashew Ricotta (see page 223)

½ to 1 cup vegan mozzarella cheese shreds

½ cup chopped fresh basil, for garnish

Tip: For a silkier-textured lasagna, blend these mixtures with enough water so that they are at a pourable consistency. For a nuttier, thicker-textured lasagna, use minimal water and spread the ricotta and sauce when
applying to lasagna layers.

5 Add the tofu over the bottom layer of noodles in the baking dish. Top with a generous layer of the cashew ricotta, followed by a layer of pesto, a sprinkle of vegan cheese, and a layer of noodles. Add the remaining cashew ricotta and pesto and any remaining tofu. Top with another layer of noodles. You can layer the lasagna however you'd like, really, just be sure to finish off with a top generous layer of pesto sauce and a sprinkle of vegan cheese.

6 Cover tightly with foil and bake for about 40 minutes. The top of the lasagna will be rippled and drier in texture, and the layers will be moist and tender. The edges should be lightly browned but not overcooked or crispy. Remove the foil, turn the oven to broil, and broil for 1 to 2 minutes. Let cool for at least 20 to 30 minutes in the baking dish before slicing and serving. This cooling time before serving is important. Do not serve too hot or the layers will fall apart too easily. Top with the fresh basil to serve. Serve warm.

Note: The amount of water you add will create either a loose, pourable pesto sauce or a thick, spreadable sauce. Both options are delicious—it all depends on your tastes. Season the sauce to taste based on the water content.

Tip: If you think you may have undercooked the noodles a bit, add a few splashes of vegetable broth to the dish before cooking.

NUTRITION FACTS (per serving–147g) Calories: 388; Fat: 20g; Carbs: 41g; Protein: 15g; Fiber: 2g Vitamin C: 14%; Iron: 13%; Calcium: 9%; Vitamin A: 14%

VEGAN CASHEW RICOTTA

1 Drain the soaked cashews and rinse under warm water. Place the cashews in a food processor or high-speed blender.

2 Add ½ cup of the water and the lemon juice and process on high until smooth, which may take a few minutes depending on the strength of your food processor. The water will create a standard creamy texture, but using nondairy milk as the liquid will create an extra-creamy texture. When blending, if the ricotta is looking too dry, add more nondairy milk or water as needed. You want the end result to be a bit thicker than hummus. Fold in salt and pepper to taste.

Note: Just like with the pesto, the amount of water will create a different texture or cashew cream, pourable versus spreadable.

1½ cups raw cashews, soaked overnight

½ to 1½ cups water or plain nondairy milk (see Note)

2 tablespoons fresh lemon juice

Sea salt and freshly ground black pepper

FAVORITE VEGAN MAC AND CHEESE
WITH VARIATIONS

Mac and cheese seems to be the ultimate dinnertime comfort food. And this version is completely dreamy, dairy-free, and infused with good stuff like nutritional yeast, white beans, healthy turmeric, and baked sweet potato. If you cannot find sweet potato, butternut squash is a good substitute. To liven things up, I love my mac and cheese with some perky green peas or broccoli florets folded in.

SERVES 4

8 ounces elbow macaroni

Pinch of sea salt

CHEESE SAUCE

1 medium sweet potato

1 to 4 tablespoons plain nondairy milk

1 (15-ounce) can cannellini beans, drained and rinsed

½ cup nutritional yeast

¼ to ⅓ cup vegan buttery spread

1½ tablespoons Dijon mustard

¾ teaspoon sea salt

¼ to 1 teaspoon ground turmeric (I like a lot, but start off slow and add more if you like it too)

¼ teaspoon garlic powder

¼ teaspoon freshly ground black pepper

1 Bring 4 cups of water to a boil in a large pot. Add the elbow macaroni and salt. Return to a boil, then reduce the heat to medium-high and boil until the pasta is tender, 8 to 10 minutes. Drain the pasta, reserving at least ½ cup of the pasta cooking water.

2 **For the Cheese Sauce:** Preheat the oven to 400°F. Poke a few holes in the potato using a fork. Bake the sweet potato until tender, 45 to 60 minutes. When cool enough to handle, remove the skin and mash the flesh in a bowl. Measure out about 1½ cups of the mashed potato—a little more is fine if needed to avoid wasting excess potato.

3 In a blender, combine the mashed sweet potato, 1 tablespoon of the nondairy milk, ¼ cup of the reserved pasta cooking water, and the remaining cheese sauce ingredients. Blend until smooth. Add more or less pasta water and nondairy milk based on how thick you want the sauce. Thicker sauce coats the pasta more heavily for a richer dish.

4 If desired, pour the blended cheese sauce into a small saucepan and bring to a boil, then reduce the heat to low and simmer for 5 minutes. (Otherwise, proceed to step 5.)

5 Fold the cheese sauce into the cooked pasta and serve warm. Add any variation ingredients, if desired. If needed, place the pasta, covered, in a warm oven until ready to serve.

VARIATIONS

Cheese and Peas: Fold 1 cup cooked peas into the mac and cheese pasta.

Spicy Fiesta: Add 1 teaspoon chipotle powder or ½ cup spicy salsa to the sauce and add sautéed vegan spicy sausage over the top to serve.

Super Creamy: Add ¼ cup soaked cashews.

NUTRITION FACTS
(per serving–253g)

Calories: 490; Fat: 13g; Carbs: 74g; Protein: 22g; Fiber: 9g

Vitamin C: 25%; Iron: 38%; Calcium: 11%; Vitamin A: 299%

15-MINUTE MARINARA SAUCE WITH VEGAN PARMESAN

This is my go-to marinara sauce to use for everything from vegan lasagna recipes to easy pasta night and even in meatless meatball sub sandwiches! Making your own pasta sauce is easier than you may think, and the results are simply extraordinary. Simmer some from-scratch marinara sauce and feel like a superstar at first taste. To turn this into a pizza sauce, I simply add a few spoonfuls of tomato paste to thicken it a bit and an accent of something sweet like agave syrup. Don't miss the fun sauce variation ideas that accompany this basic recipe.

SERVES 6

EASY VEGAN PARMESAN

½ cup raw nuts (any variety, but walnuts are my favorite)

½ cup nutritional yeast

15-MINUTE MARINARA SAUCE

3 to 4 tablespoons extra-virgin olive oil

1 white onion, chopped

5 to 6 cloves garlic

1 (28-ounce) can crushed San Marzano tomatoes

½ teaspoon sea salt

2 teaspoons dried Italian seasoning

⅛ teaspoon cayenne or red pepper flakes

2 to 4 tablespoons nutritional yeast, plus more for garnish (optional)

Cooked pasta of your choice, for serving

1 **For the Easy Vegan Parmesan:** In a blender or food processor, process the nuts with the nutritional yeast until fine and powdery. No salt is needed since the nutritional yeast is so cheesy and savory.

2 **For the 15-Minute Marinara Sauce:** In a large saucepan, heat 2 tablespoons of the oil over high heat. Add the onion and cook, stirring, until the edges of the onion are brown, 3 to 4 minutes.

3 Add the garlic and cook, stirring, for a minute. Add the tomatoes, salt, remaining oil, Italian seasoning and cayenne. Stir, cover, and reduce the heat to maintain a simmer. Simmer for 15 minutes.

4 Carefully transfer half of the sauce to a food processor or blender. Blend until mostly smooth. Transfer the blended sauce back to the pot and stir to combine with the chunky sauce. Simmer until ready to use.

5 To get a "baked pasta" dish, toss the cooked pasta with the sauce and nutritional yeast (if using), and place in the oven until ready to serve, or simply toss or pour the sauce over the cooked pasta. To serve, sprinkle the vegan Parmesan over plated pasta.

recipe continues

EASY VEGAN PARMESAN

For super-easy vegan Parmesan in a flash, use this recipe!

- **How to make:** In a blender or food processor, combine ½ cup raw walnuts and ½ cup nutritional yeast. Process until powdery.

- **How to use:** Use in place of dairy Parmesan in recipes like lasagna, pizza, salads, and more.

- **Storage:** Store any leftovers in an airtight container in the fridge and use in a few days for optimal flavor.

- **Spice it up:** You can even spice up your sprinkle by adding red pepper flakes, spices, and more.

HAVE A SPAGHETTI AND MEATLESS BALLS NIGHT!

Add Italian Meatless Meatballs (page 150) to serve, on top of the pasta.

continued

SAUCE VARIATIONS

Fresh Basil: Toward the end of the simmering process, add a handful of fresh basil leaves.

Mushroom: While stirring, cook 1½ cups of your favorite mushrooms along with the onion. Add an additional drizzle of olive oil. Season the mushrooms and onions with a hint of freshly ground black pepper.

Garden Veggie: Add ½ cup diced carrot, ½ cup diced bell pepper, and an extra drizzle of olive oil along with the onion.

Caper Olive: Add 2 teaspoons kalamata olives and 1 teaspoon capers while the sauce is simmering.

White Bean: Add 1 cup drained and rinsed canned white beans along with the onions.

NUTRITION FACTS (per serving–169g) Calories: 118; Fat: 8g; Carbs: 11g; Protein: 5g; Fiber: 4g Vitamin C: 35%; Iron: 20%; Calcium: 1%; Vitamin A: 22%

MINI CHICK'N OR VEGGIE POTPIE
(FOR ONE!)

This is a mini potpie made just for you! This cute, cozy potpie is filled to the brim with tender veggies, a creamy sauce, and cubes of protein-rich tofu or veggie chick'n, or just all veggies if you'd prefer. This easy recipe is a keeper. Pull it out on a cozy night made just for you. (Or make two and share the love.)

— SERVES 1 —

1. Preheat the oven to 350°F.

2. **For the Filling:** In a small bowl, whisk the cornstarch into the soy milk to form a slurry.

3. In a skillet, melt the vegan buttery spread over medium-high heat. Add the onion and parsley (if using) and cook, stirring, until tender, about 1 minute. Add the peas and carrots and the black-eyed peas and fold them into the buttery onion mixture.

4. Pour the slurry over the veggies, add the nutritional yeast (if using) and spices, and stir slowly until the mixture begins to bubble and thicken, 2 to 3 minutes. When the mixture has thickened, remove from the heat. (Most of the cooking for the filling will be done in the oven.)

5. Either fold the vegan chick'n cubes right into the veggie mixture or quickly cook them in the drizzle of extra-virgin olive oil, stirring occasionally, until the edges brown, 2 to 3 minutes, and then fold into the veggie mixture. Pour the filling into an oven-safe potpie or casserole dish and set aside.

recipe continues

FILLING

2 teaspoons cornstarch or arrowroot powder

¾ cup plain soy or almond milk

1 teaspoon vegan buttery spread

¼ cup diced white onion

Pinch of chopped fresh flat-leaf parsley, chopped (optional)

¾ cup frozen peas and carrots (veggie blend)

⅓ cup frozen black-eyed peas

1 tablespoon nutritional yeast (optional)

½ teaspoon poultry seasoning

Pinch of garlic powder

Pinch of ground turmeric

Pinch of freshly ground black pepper

Pinch of cayenne

¼ cup cubed vegan chick'n (or simply add more veggies or substitute beans or tofu cubes)

Drizzle of extra-virgin olive oil (optional)

ingredients continue

continued

6 **For the Top Crust:** In a small bowl, quickly mix together the flour, vegan buttery spread, and baking powder. Add 2 tablespoons of room temperature water and the lemon juice. Fold the dough until it thickens. Add another 1 to 2 tablespoons of water if needed to further loosen and soften the dough. The dough should be quite moist, yet still kneadable. Dust your work surface and turn out the dough. Gently knead for a few seconds to soften any lumps, then roll or press out the dough into a round to fit your potpie dish.

7 Gently place the top crust over the veggies. Crimp the edges of the crust to the edges of the dish with your fingers to seal and poke vent holes in the top of the crust to allow steam to escape. Brush the top of the crust with lemon juice.

8 Bake until the top crust is lightly browned and fluffed up a bit, and the insides are thickened yet still creamy, 17 to 20 minutes. Let cool on the counter for at least 10 minutes before serving. The potpie is best served warm.

Note: You can substitute coconut or olive oil in place of the vegan buttery spread. Just be sure to add a few pinches of sea salt along with the oil.

TOP CRUST

½ cup whole wheat flour, plus more for dusting

2 teaspoons vegan buttery spread, softened

½ teaspoon baking powder

1 tablespoon plus ½ teaspoon fresh lemon juice or apple cider vinegar, plus more for brushing

NUTRITION FACTS (per serving—538g)

Calories: 563; Fat: 9g; Carbs: 96g; Protein: 26g; Fiber: 13g

Vitamin C: 21%; Iron: 40%; Calcium: 57%; Vitamin A: 214%

LEMON-PEPPER FETTUCCINE ALFREDO

This dreamy white pasta dish will leave you breathless with glee. It is so lovely with the creamy white sauce coating, tender cooked fettuccine, and lemon zest and chopped parsley bits adding a perk of yellow and green color over the top. Everyone says mac and cheese is the ultimate kid pasta. Fettuccine Alfredo, I think, may be the adult version of it!

SERVES 5

1 Bring a large pot of salted water to a boil. Add the pasta and cook until al dente, 8 to 12 minutes. Drain the pasta, reserving at least 1 cup of the pasta cooking water.

2 **For the Alfredo Sauce:** Drain and rinse the cashews and place them in a food processor or blender. Add ½ cup of the pasta cooking water, the nondairy milk (or an additional ½ cup pasta cooking water), nutritional yeast, lemon juice, miso, garlic powder, lemon zest, and pepper and process until silky smooth. Add more or less pasta cooking water to achieve the consistency you'd like for the sauce. Adding less water thickens the sauce. Taste and add salt to taste.

3 Toss the sauce with the warm pasta and serve with basil, pepper, lemon zest, and vegan Parmesan over the top. Add truffle oil for extra richness, if desired.

Variation: While stirring, cook 1 cup shiitake mushrooms in 1 teaspoon olive oil and finish with a few teaspoons of white wine, sea salt, and freshly ground black pepper to taste.

8 ounces fettuccine pasta

ALFREDO SAUCE

1 cup raw cashews, soaked

½ cup plain nondairy milk (optional)

3 tablespoons nutritional yeast

2 to 3 tablespoons fresh lemon juice

2 teaspoons white miso paste, or sea salt as needed

½ teaspoon garlic powder

Pinch of freshly grated lemon zest

⅛ teaspoon freshly ground black pepper

Sea salt

GARNISH

Fresh basil

Freshly ground black pepper

Freshly grated lemon zest

Easy Vegan Parmesan (page 226)

Drizzle of truffle oil (optional)

Ultra-creamy: Substitute plain soy creamer for the nondairy milk for a super-decadent sauce!

NUTRITION FACTS (per serving–154g) Calories: 400; Fat: 16g; Carbs: 50g; Protein: 16g; Fiber: 4g Vitamin C: 12%; Iron: 26%; Calcium: 4%; Vitamin A: 0%

CAJUN DIRTY RICE-STUFFED PEPPERS WITH GUAC TOPS

Bright and shiny roasted bell peppers are filled to the brim with a bold mixture of red beans and rice, spices galore, and creamy guacamole on top.

— SERVES 2 —

FILLING

1 teaspoon extra-virgin olive oil

½ cup celery

¼ cup diced onion

¼ cup finely chopped fresh flat-leaf parsley

1 cup cooked brown rice

1 cup drained and rinsed canned red kidney or black beans

1 tablespoon nutritional yeast

½ teaspoon Cajun spice blend

Sea salt and freshly ground black pepper

2 large, boxy red or green bell peppers

½ avocado

Juice of 1 lime

Pinch of freshly grated lime zest

Pinch of sea salt and freshly ground black pepper

Pinch of garlic powder

2 sprigs of fresh flat-leaf parsley, for garnish

1   Preheat the oven to 350°F.

2   **For the Filling:** In a large skillet, heat the oil over medium-high heat. Add the celery, onion, and parsley. Cook, stirring, for 1 to 2 minutes. Add the rice, beans, nutritional yeast, and Cajun spice. Reduce the heat to medium and cook, stirring, for 2 to 3 minutes more. Add salt and pepper to taste. Remove from the heat.

3   Slice off the top stems of the peppers and remove any seeds. You want a clean, hollow pepper shell. Tightly stuff the peppers with the filling, stuffing them to the brim. Place the peppers standing up inside a casserole dish or on a baking sheet.

4   Bake the peppers until they are tender and slightly wrinkled in appearance, and the filling has firmed up a bit, about 20 minutes.

5   While the peppers are baking, in a bowl, mash up the avocado with the lime juice, lime zest, salt and pepper, and garlic powder.

6   Serve the peppers hot from the oven with a dollop of mashed avocado on top. Garnish with the parsley.

NUTRITION FACTS (per serving-386g) Calories: 393; Fat: 14g; Carbs: 53g; Protein: 14g; Fiber: 16g   Vitamin C: 285%; Iron: 25%; Calcium: 7%; Vitamin A: 91%

MUSHROOM FAJITA TACOS WITH HOMEMADE CORN TORTILLAS

Homemade corn tortillas are easy to make and so much better than store-bought! They are soft and fluffy with rustic corn flavor. You can fill them with just about any of your favorite veggies or plant proteins for a delicious vegan taco meal. I love my tortillas filled with skillet mushrooms, smashed black beans, and guacamole with spicy salsa on the side.

SERVES 8

1 **For the Tortillas (optional):** At least 1 hour before you start your meal, prepare the tortillas. In a bowl, combine the masa harina, lime zest, and salt with ¾ cup water until a thick dough forms; add another ¼ cup water if needed to achieve the desired consistency. Cover the bowl and let the tortilla dough rest for 1 hour before cooking the tortillas.

2 **For the Cashew Cream:** In a blender or food processor, combine the cashew cream ingredients with ¼ cup water and blend until smooth. Pour into a serving bowl, cover, and refrigerate until needed.

3 **For the Black Bean Spread:** Preheat the oven to 200°F. In a blender, combine the black bean spread ingredients except the vegan cheese and blend until creamy. For chunkier texture, use a fork to mash the spread instead. Spoon this mixture into an oven-safe serving bowl. Add vegan cheese on top, if desired. Place the bowl in the oven to warm the beans for serving.

4 **For the Fajita Filling:** In a large sauté pan, heat the oil over high heat. Add the fajita veggies, jalapeño (if using), garlic, salt, and spices and cook, stirring, for 4 to 5 minutes to soften the mushrooms and peppers. Try not to overcook—you want the veggies to still have lots of color and a crispness to them. When the veggies are done, turn off the heat and sprinkle with the cilantro.

recipe continues

TORTILLAS (OPTIONAL)

1 cup masa harina

¼ teaspoon freshly grated lime zest

¼ teaspoon sea salt

OR

8 to 10 small store-bought corn tortillas

CASHEW CREAM

¼ cup raw cashews, soaked

1 teaspoon fresh lemon juice

Pinch of sea salt and freshly ground black pepper

BLACK BEAN SPREAD

1½ cups drained and rinsed canned black beans

1 to 2 tablespoons extra-virgin olive oil

1 tablespoon tahini

1 tablespoon nutritional yeast

Pinch of vegan cheese shreds (optional)

ingredients continue

continued

FAJITA FILLING

2 teaspoons extra-virgin olive oil

2 cups thinly sliced shiitake mushrooms (any mushroom can be substituted)

1 small red onion, thinly sliced

1 green bell pepper, cut into long strips

½ jalapeño, sliced (optional)

1 clove garlic, chopped

Sea salt

1 teaspoon fajita spice blend, or ¼ teaspoon chipotle powder, ½ teaspoon cumin, and ¼ teaspoon freshly ground black pepper

⅓ cup finely chopped fresh cilantro

Extra-virgin olive, sunflower, or safflower oil, for cooking the tortillas

1 cup shredded romaine lettuce

½ cup salsa or diced fresh tomatoes

½ cup Sunny Guacamole (page 199)

Chopped fresh cilantro

Lime slices

Note: The thinner the tortilla, the easier it will be to fold and roll the taco for filling.

5 Roll the chilled tortilla dough into golf-ball-size balls. Flatten each ball into a thin tortilla. You can use a tortilla press if you have one; otherwise, just do your best with your hands or roll out with a rolling pin. In a skillet, heat a tiny drizzle of oil over medium heat. Cook the tortillas, one at a time, until very slightly brown, about 2 minutes on each side. Repeat until all the tortilla dough has been used up, refreshing the oil in the pan as needed. (If using store-bought tortillas, warm them in a skillet for a minute or two on each side.)

6 Serve the fajita dinner buffet-style, with the tortillas, fajita filling, cashew cream, black bean spread, lettuce, tomatoes, and guacamole in individual serving dishes. Garnish with fresh cilantro and a few lime slices. Fill the tortillas and serve.

NUTRITION FACTS (per serving–185g)
Calories: 243; Fat: 11g; Carbs: 31g; Protein: 8g; Fiber: 8g
Vitamin C: 36%; Iron: 16%; Calcium: 5%; Vitamin A: 12%

MAPLE CHILI BEAN-STUFFED SWEET POTATO

Sweet chili beans and tempeh bacon fill golden baked sweet potatoes for instant comfort food mealtime perfection. The oven method for cooking the sweet potatoes is recommended, but you can microwave them if you're short on time.

— **SERVES 4** —

1. Scrub the sweet potatoes. Preheat the oven to 400°F. Poke a few holes in the potatoes using a fork. Bake the sweet potatoes for 35 to 50 minutes. Set aside to cool while you prepare the filling.

2. **For the Chili Beans:** In a sauté pan, heat the oil over high heat. Add the onions and maple syrup and cook, stirring, until the edges of the onions become translucent, 2 to 3 minutes.

3. Add the remaining chili bean ingredients except the tempeh bacon and peanuts to the pan with the onions and reduce the heat to medium-high. Salt to taste if the canned beans were unsalted. Cook, stirring, until the liquid has been absorbed a bit, 3 to 4 minutes. When the bean mixture is warmed through and saucy, fold in the tempeh bacon and peanuts. Remove from the heat.

4. Slice a slit down the center of each sweet potato. Fill with the warm chili bean mixture. Top with the coleslaw, if desired.

4 medium sweet potatoes

CHILI BEANS

1 teaspoon extra-virgin olive oil

⅓ cup chopped white onion

½ teaspoon grade B maple syrup

1½ cups drained and rinsed canned kidney beans

2 medium tomatoes, diced

2 cloves garlic, chopped

2 tablespoons grade B maple syrup

2 tablespoons apple cider vinegar

1 teaspoon chili powder

½ teaspoon freshly ground black pepper

Sea salt

6 slices or ½ cup Smoky Tempeh Bacon (page 62), finely diced

¼ cup chopped peanuts

2 cups Summer Slaw (page 141; optional)

NUTRITION FACTS (per serving-317g), not including coleslaw: Calories: 370; Fat: 7g; Carbs: 70g; Protein: 12g; Fiber: 13g Vitamin C: 61%; Iron: 25%; Calcium: 6%; Vitamin A: 18%

HOW-TO: ROASTING VEGGIES

Roasting veggies is one of the easiest and most delicious cooking methods around. Have veggies? Roast them! Here is how.

- **Prep:** Wash, scrub, peel, dice—whatever is needed. Leave smaller veggies or long, skinny ones whole, if you'd like, or cut them into cubes.

- **Oven:** Preheat the oven to a high temperature; 400°F is standard, but I like 415°F or higher for veggies that need extra heat due to their hard texture, like carrots, beets, and potatoes.

- **Season:** Toss the veggies in oil before roasting. You can also add vinegar, fresh lemon juice, maple syrup, or other liquid accents.

- **When to spice:** Most of the time, I spice the veggies halfway through and salt at the end. I do not like my spices to burn, so I add them when the veggies are just about finished, but the spices still get enough time in the oven to infuse some flavor into the vegetables. Spicing can be done at the beginning with the oil, but just be sure to watch closely so that you do not overcook any delicate spices. I like to salt and taste at the end of my roasting session just as I pull the veggies out of the oven, still very hot. Coarse pink salt is my choice for roasted veggies.

- **Quick broil:** To add blackened edges to roasted veggies in just a minute, place the veggie tray or dish on the top rack of the oven and broil for a minute or less. That intense heat should add some blackened texture.

ROASTED VEGGIE OLIVE OIL FARRO

Farro salads are light yet satisfying. I love mine tossed with an array of roasted veggies and nuts like toasted almonds. Farro salads are delicious served warmed or chilled from the fridge as a make-ahead dish.

SERVES 6

1. **For the Mixed Roasted Veggies:** Preheat the oven to 400°F. Lightly grease a baking sheet with olive oil.

2. Place the veggies in a large bowl and toss with the oil and lemon juice. Spread in an even layer on the prepared baking sheet. Roast for 10 minutes, then add the nutritional yeast (if using), Italian seasoning, and a few pinches of salt and pepper. Toss in the pan and continue roasting for 10 to 15 minutes more, until the veggies are tender. Let cool for at least 10 minutes before tossing with the grains.

3. While the veggies are roasting, bring the veggie broth to a boil in a saucepan. Add the farro, cover, and reduce the heat to medium. Simmer the farro until tender and all the liquid has been absorbed, 30 to 40 minutes. Fluff the farro.

4. In a large bowl, combine the cooked farro and roasted veggies. Add the parsley, almonds, olives, basil, lemon juice, and lemon zest. Drizzle in additional olive oil, if desired, for added richness. Fold until well combined. Serve warm or refrigerate to serve chilled.

Note: You can substitute any veggies you'd like!

MIXED ROASTED VEGGIES

1 zucchini, diced

1 small red onion, chopped

1 cup chopped shiitake or portobello mushrooms

1 cup broccoli florets

2 to 4 teaspoons extra-virgin olive oil, plus more for greasing the pan

1 tablespoon fresh lemon juice

3 tablespoons nutritional yeast (optional)

1 teaspoon unsalted dried Italian seasoning

Sea salt and freshly ground black pepper

2¾ cups vegetable broth

1 cup farro

½ cup finely chopped fresh flat-leaf parsley

⅓ cup slivered or chopped almonds, toasted, if desired

¼ cup chopped pitted kalamata olives

¼ cup chopped fresh basil

2 teaspoons fresh lemon juice or vinegar

Pinch of freshly grated lemon zest

Extra-virgin olive oil (optional)

NUTRITION FACTS (per serving–276g) Calories: 276; Fat: 9g; Carbs: 38g; Protein: 13g; Fiber: 9g Vitamin C: 51%; Iron: 21%; Calcium: 7%; Vitamin A: 14%

SAGE-ALMOND BUTTERNUT SQUASH RISOTTO

Butternut squash risotto is one of my favorite entrée dishes. I liven things up a bit by adding a touch of apple and sage. This creamy comfort food is a fancy dish that is soothing to prepare. Watching the arborio rice soak up the liquid and become magically creamy and rich is a very meditative process.

SERVES 4

BUTTERNUT SQUASH MIX

2 cups diced butternut squash

½ cup chopped sweet onion

½ cup diced green apple (optional)

1 clove garlic, chopped

1 tablespoon chopped fresh sage leaves

1 tablespoon extra-virgin olive oil

Sea salt and freshly ground black pepper

RISOTTO

1 cup arborio rice

3 to 4 cups vegetable broth

½ cup plain nondairy milk or light coconut milk

Sea salt

⅓ cup sliced almonds

Fresh sage leaves, for garnish

Nondairy milk, warmed (optional)

1 **For the Butternut Squash Mix:** Preheat the onion to 400°F.

2 In a baking dish, toss the squash with the onion, apple (if using), garlic, sage, and oil. Bake until the squash is tender, about 20 minutes (time will vary based on how large the squash cubes are). Sprinkle with a bit of salt and pepper to taste.

3 **For the Risotto:** While the squash is baking, in a deep sauté pan or medium soup pot, combine the rice and 1 cup of the broth. Bring to a boil over medium-high heat. Begin to stir the rice with a large spoon or spatula and keep stirring casually until the liquid has been absorbed, 5 to 8 minutes. Add the remaining broth in small splashes as you keep stirring, waiting until each addition has been absorbed before adding the next, until the rice is tender and all the liquid has been absorbed. Add the nondairy milk and fold it into the risotto until absorbed. Taste and add salt if needed. If you like the rice texture a bit softer, keep simmering for 4 to 6 minutes more, while adding a few more splashes of broth. The rice should be velvety, tender, cooked through, and plumped, with an almost fluffy texture. If the squash is still cooking when the risotto is done, cover the pan, remove from the heat, and set aside until you plate the dish.

recipe continues

continued

4 When both the risotto and butternut squash are cooked, fold them together directly in the serving dish or do a quick stovetop warming for each individual serving dish. I prefer this method for best flavor: For each serving, place 1 cup of the cooked risotto in a clean or lightly oiled sauté pan over medium heat. Fold in a few teaspoons of the almonds and a scoop of the squash mixture. Allow the rice to warm a bit as the flavors from the squash mingle into the risotto rice. After about a minute of allowing the flavors to combine and warm together, transfer the risotto to a serving dish. This way the toppings are folded into the risotto and warmed together. Garnish with sage and add a splash of warmed nondairy milk, if desired.

VARIATIONS

Fancy Version: Add ½ cup white wine to the risotto as you are cooking it. This should not affect the total cooking liquid. As always with risotto, keep adding broth or liquid until the desired texture is reached.

Roasted Corn Variation: Instead of butternut squash, roast fresh corn kernels (from about 2 small ears of corn) with a touch of fresh thyme and vegan buttery spread.

Truffled Rosemary-Mushroom Risotto: In place of butternut squash, roast 2 cups chopped mushrooms (any variety), roast with a splash of balsamic vinegar, truffle oil, fresh rosemary sprigs, extra chopped garlic, and plenty of black pepper, too.

NUTRITION FACTS (per serving–389g) Calories: 342; Fat: 9g; Carbs: 56g; Protein: 11g; Fiber: 5g Vitamin C: 30%; Iron: 12%; Calcium: 11%; Vitamin A: 151%

CHEESELESS QUESADILLAS

Who says you need cheese to make an amazing quesadilla? Not with these luscious, crispy-edged triangles in play! These toasty warm triangles are filled with spiced veggies, avocado, and creamy hummus or black beans. This is a fast and easy dish that your whole family will love.

--- SERVES 2 ---

1 In a large bowl, combine the onion, tomato, avocado, and spices. Add the lime juice and toss well.

2 In a large skillet, heat the oil over high heat. Place the tortillas in the pan, one at a time, to warm them and toast the edges a bit, about 1 minute. Remove the warmed tortillas from the pan and slather the hummus over the inside. Add a generous amount of the avocado-veggie mixture. Close the tortilla and carefully return to the hot pan. Cook for 1 to 2 minutes on each side. Flip carefully and scoot the veggies back inside the tortilla if any fall out.

3 Slice into triangles and serve warm with the fresh lime wedges, hot sauce (if using), and additional avocado mix on the side.

Tip: Adding a generous amount of the hummus helps the veggies stick to the tortilla.

1 small sweet onion, diced

1 tomato, diced

1 avocado, pitted, peeled, and cubed or sliced

¼ teaspoon sea salt

¼ teaspoon freshly ground black pepper

⅛ teaspoon Spanish paprika

Juice of 1 lime

½ to 1 teaspoon oil (try safflower, coconut, or extra-virgin olive oil)

1 extra-large whole wheat flour tortilla or wrap, or 2 small corn tortillas

⅓ cup Classic Hummus Dip (page 197) or vegan refried black beans, warmed

1 lime, cut into wedges

Hot sauce or salsa, for serving (optional)

NUTRITION FACTS (per serving–215g)
Calories: 321; Fat: 19g; Carbs: 26g; Protein: 8g; Fiber: 9g
Vitamin C: 26%; Iron: 11%; Calcium: 3%; Vitamin A: 8%

EASY HASSELBACK BBQ TOFU WITH HOMEMADE BBQ SAUCE

This is a fun dish to set on a dinner table. So easy, too! I take the idea of hasselback potatoes, those super thinly sliced and roasted whole potatoes that create a fanned potato look, and apply that to tofu, using a thick coating of barbecue sauce to flavor. You can use store-bought vegan barbecue sauce or make your own. My homemade barbecue sauce can be used for a wide variety of dishes, not just this one! I love barbecue sauce on pizza, sandwiches, tempeh, beans, vegan chick'n, and more.

SERVES 5

VEGAN BARBECUE SAUCE

¼ cup apple cider vinegar

3 tablespoons blackstrap molasses

3 tablespoons tomato paste

2½ tablespoons agave syrup

1 tablespoon ketchup

2 teaspoons vegan liquid smoke

2 teaspoons extra-virgin olive oil

2 teaspoons tamari

1 teaspoon fresh lime juice

1 teaspoon spicy mustard

1 teaspoon paprika

½ teaspoon sea salt

½ teaspoon freshly ground black pepper

½ teaspoon ground cumin

½ teaspoon onion powder

¼ teaspoon cayenne

1 tablespoon arrowroot powder or cornstarch

1   Preheat the oven to 400°F.

2   **For the Vegan Barbecue Sauce:** In a small saucepan, combine all the barbecue sauce ingredients except the arrowroot powder. Sift in the arrowroot powder so it doesn't clump. Stir well. Bring to a boil over medium-high heat (watch for splattering!), then reduce the heat to low and simmer until thickened, 10 to 20 minutes.

3   Press the tofu dry using a few paper towels. To mimic the look of a hasselback potato, make slices all the way down the tofu block, cutting about three quarters of the way through the block with each slice (do not cut all the way through). You want the tofu in one piece when serving, with the top fanned in many thin slices. Sprinkle a few pinches of salt and pepper over the tofu.

4 Place the sliced tofu, with the sliced side up, in a small oven-safe dish (I use a 6-inch cast-iron skillet). Pour the barbecue sauce over the top, allowing it to seep into the tofu crevices and coat the top thickly. Bake until the top begins to get thick and sticky, about 20 minutes, then broil for 1 to 2 minutes before pulling from the oven. Serve whole, and slice into individual pieces.

1 (12-ounce) block firm tofu

Few pinches of sea salt and freshly ground black pepper

NUTRITION FACTS
(per serving–173g)

Calories: 161; Fat: 5g; Carbs: 23g; Protein: 7g; Fiber: 2g

Vitamin C: 5%; Iron: 22%; Calcium: 21%; Vitamin A: 8%

LOAF

Extra-virgin olive oil for greasing pan

1 cup walnuts

1½ cups drained and rinsed canned lentils

3 slices whole-grain bread (any variety), toasted and cubed

1¼ cups chopped shiitake mushrooms

1 cup vegetable broth

1 cup diced carrots

¾ cup very thinly sliced celery

½ cup chopped fresh flat-leaf parsley

½ cup diced onion

½ cup homemade oat flour (from rolled oats; see Sidebar, page 38) or cooked brown rice

⅓ cup diced peeled white potato

⅓ cup tomato paste

¼ cup nutritional yeast

1½ tablespoons Dijon mustard

1 teaspoon chili powder

½ teaspoon garlic powder

¼ teaspoon sea salt

¼ teaspoon freshly ground black pepper

SASSY RED GLAZE

3 to 4 tablespoons veggie broth

1½ tablespoons tomato paste

1 tablespoon grade B maple syrup

Pinch of sea salt

WALNUT LENTIL MUSHROOM RETRO LOAF

This retro loaf is fluffy, moist and rich with colorful pops of color from diced carrot, peas, and celery. It has a vegtastic "meaty" flavor from the shiitake mushrooms, lentils and walnuts. A sweet sassy red tomato glaze on top makes this oh-so-retro. Serve a slice alongside some mashed potatoes for a cozy 1950s meatloaf style dinner, without the meat!

SERVES 8

---

1. **For the Loaf:** Preheat the oven to 415°F. Lightly grease a loaf pan with oil.

2. Place the walnuts in a food processor and process into flour. Do not overprocess into nut butter. Transfer to a large bowl and add the lentils. Mash the walnuts and lentils together with a fork.

3. Fold in all the remaining ingredients until a thick, wet mixture forms. Pour the mixture into the prepared loaf pan.

4. **For the Sassy Red Glaze:** In a bowl, stir together the glaze ingredients, adding enough broth to bring it to a pourable state. Pour the glaze evenly over the loaf.

5. Bake the loaf for 20 minutes, then reduce the heat to 400°F and bake for 40 minutes more. When the loaf is done, the top will be dark red in color and crinkly with browned edges. The loaf will be cooked through, but still need some time to firm up before slicing. For easiest slicing, let cool in the pan for at least 30 minutes before serving. Otherwise, you can scoop the warm, just-cooked loaf to serve.

NUTRITION FACTS
(per serving–201g)

Calories: 371; Fat: 10g;
Carbs: 61g; Protein:
15g; Fiber: 6g

Vitamin C: 45%; Iron:
22%; Calcium: 24%;
Vitamin A: 11%

SPICY PEANUT SOBA NOODLES WITH VEGGIES

This peanutty noodle dish is delicious, craveable, and healthy. Think of it as comfort food pasta for peanut lovers! Soba noodles are rich in the good-for-you grain buckwheat and the creamy flavorful peanut sauce is the perfect complement. This sauce is delicious both thick and creamy and thin and light, it just depends on what you crave. You can also modify the sweetness and spiciness to suite your taste buds. Add some carrots or choose your own veggie accents to fold into this versatile recipe!

SERVES 4

1. Bring a large pot of salted water to a boil. Add the noodles and cook until tender, about 5 minutes. Drain and rinse the noodles under cold water. For chilled noodles, transfer the noodles to a bowl and refrigerate until ready to use. Otherwise, cover the noodles to keep warm.

2. **For the Sweet and Spicy Peanut Sauce:** In a food processor or blender, combine the peanut sauce ingredients, adding the nondairy milk last a spoonful at a time until you reach a thickness you like, and process until smooth. If the noodles are cold and dry, a wetter sauce may be best, but if the noodles were just cooked and are still steamy and slightly wet, a thinner sauce may be better. If desired, add more or less peanut butter to adjust the consistency.

3. For warm noodles and sauce, pour the sauce in a small saucepan and simmer for 2 to 3 minutes just to warm. Otherwise, pour the sauce directly over the chilled noodles and place back in the fridge until ready to serve.

4. To serve, toss the dressed noodles with the carrots and hemp seeds (if using) over the top. Sprinkle with the cilantro and peanuts to serve.

3 cups soba noodles

SWEET AND SPICY PEANUT SAUCE

3 to 4 tablespoons creamy peanut butter, softened

2 tablespoons grade B maple syrup

2 tablespoons seasoned rice vinegar

1 tablespoon tamari

1 tablespoon chopped fresh cilantro

1 clove garlic

1 teaspoon sesame oil

½ teaspoon grated peeled fresh ginger

Few pinches of cayenne

¼ to ½ cup plain nondairy milk or water (see Note)

1 cup thinly sliced carrots

2 teaspoons hemp or sesame seeds (optional)

¼ cup finely chopped fresh cilantro

1 teaspoon crushed peanuts

Note: Add more or less nondairy milk depending on how thick you like your sauce.

NUTRITION FACTS
(per serving–180 g) Calories: 250; Fat: 8g; Carbs: 38g; Protein: 11g; Fiber: 2g   Vitamin C: 5%; Iron: 15%; Calcium: 1%; Vitamin A: 5%

20-MINUTE PESTO PASTA

This is a fast and delicious fresh pesto meal to whip up on a busy weeknight. For an instant complete meal, serve this pasta with an easy veggie or salad side. This pesto sauce is rich and nutty with a salty accent from the white miso. You can use any raw nuts you'd like, but I prefer walnuts and either pumpkin seeds or pistachios. Healthy tip: For an extra green boost, add a handful of spinach to your blended pesto or fold it into your warm pasta to wilt it. I also like sun-dried tomatoes, cooked chickpeas, or kalamata olives as optional additions.

SERVES 4

8 ounces whole wheat, kamut, or spelt pasta (or another variety)

PESTO SAUCE

Leaves from 1 large bunch fresh basil (3 to 4 cups loosely packed leaves)

Juice of 2 large lemons

¼ cup walnuts

¼ cup raw pumpkin seeds or pistachio nuts

¼ cup nutritional yeast

1½ tablespoons white miso paste

1 to 3 tablespoons extra-virgin olive oil

1 tablespoon agave syrup

2 cloves garlic

1 teaspoon red pepper flakes (optional)

Sea salt and freshly ground black pepper

Fresh basil leaves

Lemon slices

Easy Vegan Parmesan (page 226; optional)

1. Bring a large pot of salted water to a boil. Add the pasta and cook until al dente, following the directions on the package. Drain the pasta and reserve about ½ cup of the pasta cooking water. Set both aside.

2. **For the Pesto Sauce:** In a high-speed blender or food processor, combine the basil, lemon juice, walnuts, pumpkin seeds, nutritional yeast, miso, oil, agave, garlic, red pepper flakes (if using), and salt and black pepper. Add ¼ cup of the reserved pasta cooking water and start blending on low. Add more pasta water as needed to thin the pesto. Blend until nice and smooth.

3. Toss the warm pasta with the fresh pesto sauce. The pesto will warm slightly from the hot pasta. Serve right away for best "fresh pesto pasta" flavor and green color, or warm in the oven until ready to serve. If making ahead of time, note that the pesto will begin to fade in color a bit as it oxidizes. Garnish with basil and lemon slices. Vegan Parmesan is a nice touch, too, if desired.

NUTRITION FACTS (per serving–126g) Calories: 408; Fat: 14g; Carbs: 56g; Protein: 16g; Fiber: 9g   Vitamin C: 17%; Iron: 30%; Calcium: 4%; Vitamin A: 2%

VEGAN "00" PIZZA DOUGH AND PIZZA VARIATIONS

This is an authentic light, crisp, and chewy pizza crust made from "00" or ultrafine flour. You can top this yummy dough with a wide variety of favorite pizza toppings. Vegan pizza night is here.

MAKES 1 MEDIUM OR 2 SMALL PIZZAS; SERVES 4

1. Combine the warm water, yeast, and sugar in a large bowl. Stir until the yeast has dissolved. Add 1 cup of the flour and the salt and stir until sticky. Add the remaining 1⅓ cups flour a scoop at a time, kneading all the way through for a few minutes right in the large bowl until a soft, pillowy ball of dough forms. Yes, your hands will get nice and doughy.

2. Spray a clean bowl with coconut oil spray and flour it so the dough won't stick to the bowl. Transfer the dough to the flour bowl, cover with a clean cloth or a few paper towels, and set aside to rise in a warm spot for a good hour.

3. Preheat the oven to 425°F 10 minutes before you punch down the dough in step 4.

4. Punch down the dough with your fist, add a few pinches of flour, and start kneading the dough. If you are making two mini pizzas, split the dough into two balls.

5. Start rolling, tossing, and stretching the dough to form a pizza shell. Press out the dough on a baking sheet or pizza pan. If using cornmeal, dust the dough with a bit of cornmeal so it lightly coats the bottom of the crust and edges.

recipe continues

1 cup warm water

1 (7-gram) packet active dry yeast

Pinch of vegan sugar

2⅓ cups "00" flour, plus more for dusting

1 teaspoon sea salt

Coconut oil spray

Cornmeal, for dusting (optional)

Extra-virgin olive oil

Red pepper flakes

Vegan Parmesan

continued

Tip: Make sure the oven is nice and HOT! 425°F is a good temp, and if you can go up to 450°F, go for it. Pizza dough loves heat.

Tip: Try 1 teaspoon lemon juice and 1 teaspoon olive oil drizzled over the top of the pizza before baking. I even like to sometimes place a few lemon slices right around the edges of the crust, on top of the sauce before putting on the toppings, and remove them before eating. This leaves behind a wonderful lemon essence baked into the pizza.

6 Top the dough with a drizzle of extra-virgin olive oil, a pinch of red pepper flakes, a pinch of vegan Parmesan. Then add a few generous spoonfuls of sauce, depending on how much and what kind you like. Then place any other toppings over the sauce.

7 Bake until the edges crisp, bubble, and brown and the toppings are cooked, 10 to 15 minutes, depending on size. Slice and serve warm.

PIZZA VARIATIONS

SURFSIDE BBQ CHICK'N PIZZAS

Toppings: chopped vegan chick'n, red onion, green bell pepper, pineapple rings, barbecue sauce (over the top or use in place of marinara), fresh cilantro to serve

BALSAMIC BRUSSELS SPROUT PIZZA

Toppings: Brussels sprouts and cheese with a drizzle of balsamic cream or vinegar

PESTO RICOTTA PIZZA

Toppings: Pesto Sauce (page 250) and Vegan Cashew Ricotta (page 223) plus tomato slices, garlic, and basil

NUTRITION FACTS
(per serving–135g)

Calories: 271; Fat: 1g; Carbs: 56g; Protein: 8g; Fiber: 3g

Vitamin C: 0%; Iron: 20%; Calcium: 1%; Vitamin A: 0%

SOUPS

Cozy soups are one of my favorite go-to vegan meals. I usually pair my giant soup bowl with some sprouted grain toast slathered in vegan mayonnaise. Soups can be creamy and pureed or hearty and veggie-filled with ingredients like noodles and grains to accent them. There is nothing more soothing than simmering a big pot of homemade soup on your stove, just ready to be poured and enjoyed, spoon in hand as steamy goodness wafts in your face.

VEGAN CLAM CHOWDER

This veganized version of clam chowder is rich and creamy, using oyster mushrooms in place of clams and cashew cream in place of dairy. For an extra treat, serve the chowder in bread bowls.

—————————————————— SERVES 4 ——————————————————

1. **For the Creamy Base:** Drain and rinse the cashews. Place the potato in a saucepan with enough water to cover and bring to a boil. Cook until the potato is tender, 10 to 15 minutes. Drain the potato and place in a high-speed blender or food processor.

2. Add the cashews and remaining base ingredients to the blender or food processor and blend until creamy. If you like a thinner soup, add a few more splashes of nondairy milk, vegetable broth, or water. Transfer the soup to a medium saucepan and simmer over very low heat until ready to serve.

3. **For the Mushroom "Clam":** Dice the mushrooms into ¼-inch cubes resembling chopped clams. In a sauté pan, heat the oil over high heat. Add the mushrooms, celery, and onion and cook, stirring, for about 2 minutes. Add the truffle oil (if using) and liquid smoke halfway through the cooking process. Sprinkle in the nori for ocean flavor, if desired. Add a few pinches of salt and pepper. Transfer the mushrooms to the simmering soup base and serve warm in bowls.

Note: Quick soak method: Simmer the cashews over medium heat in salted water for 25 minutes.

CREAMY BASE

1 cup raw cashews, soaked overnight (see Note)

1 medium russet potato

1 cup plain soy creamer

1 cup plain soy milk

⅓ cup white onion

⅓ cup nutritional yeast

1 teaspoon extra-virgin olive oil

½ teaspoon sea salt

¼ teaspoon garlic powder

⅛ teaspoon freshly ground black pepper

Drizzle of truffle oil (optional)

MUSHROOM "CLAM"

4 king oyster mushrooms

2 teaspoons safflower oil

1 cup chopped celery

½ cup chopped white onion

Drizzle of truffle oil (optional)

Few drops of vegan liquid smoke

1 teaspoon crushed nori (optional)

Sea salt and freshly ground black pepper

NUTRITION FACTS
(per serving–369g)

Calories: 448; Fat: 26g; Carbs: 36g; Protein: 16g; Fiber: 10g

Vitamin C: 23%; Iron: 32%; Calcium: 17%; Vitamin A: 5%

PERFECT BAKED SWEET POTATOES

- **More is more:** The longer you bake a sweet potato, the more caramelized and delicious the flesh will become. You want the skin to literally fall off the potato flesh, as sticky-sweet syrup oozes out the ends and through where you pierced the potato with a fork. Keep that potato in the oven until maximum softening has occurred!

- **Poke those holes:** Do not forget to vent that potato! Poke a few holes in the potato to help steam release.

- **Be picky:** Not all potatoes are created equal. Keep a fussy eye out for perfect potatoes. You want potatoes that are firm, heavy, have a hearty skin on them, are free of black or brown spots or "eyes," have firm tips, and basically look like they were pulled out of the ground a few hours ago. Potatoes that have soft spots, weak skins, too many scrapes and dark spots, soft tips, or sprouting eyes should be avoided.

CHIPOTLE SWEET POTATO SOUP
WITH AVOCADO

This quick and easy sweet potato soup, topped with buttery avocados, is a must-try recipe! Sweet potato lovers will adore this creamy, feisty chipotle–sweet potato blend. I even love to add additional spices like ginger, turmeric, paprika, pepper, and cinnamon when I am in a super-spiced mood. I love this soup served extra thick and creamy, but you can easily thin things out simply by adding more liquid and adjusting the seasoning to taste.

SERVES 2

1 Preheat the oven to 400°F. Poke a few holes in the potato using a fork. Bake the sweet potato until tender, sticky, and sweet, about 60 minutes. Remove the skin and place the flesh in a high-speed blender.

2 Add 1 cup water, ¾ cup of the broth, the nondairy milk, maple syrup, chipotle powder, coconut oil (if using), and salt and pepper to taste. Blend until smooth. For thinner soup, add a few more splashes of the broth or any of the liquids.

3 Transfer the soup to a saucepan and simmer over low heat until ready to serve. Serve with the avocado over the top.

Spice It Up! Make things extra spiced by adding a pinch of any of these: cayenne, ground turmeric, grated peeled fresh ginger, paprika, and/or ground cinnamon.

1 large or 2 small sweet potatoes

¾ to 1 cup vegetable broth

1 cup plain nondairy milk

1 teaspoon grade B maple syrup

1 teaspoon chipotle powder

1 teaspoon virgin coconut oil (optional)

Sea salt and freshly ground black pepper

½ avocado, diced and tossed in fresh lime juice, for garnish

NUTRITION FACTS (per serving–457g) Calories: 326; Fat: 12g; Carbs: 45g; Protein: 10g; Fiber: 10g Vitamin C: 74%; Iron: 14%; Calcium: 24%; Vitamin A: 775%

RAINY DAY TOMATO SOUP

This cozy, savory tomato soup will leave you dreaming about rainy days.
Start doing your rain dance now!

SERVES 2

1 (14-ounce) can fire-roasted tomatoes, or 2 cups diced fresh tomatoes

1½ cups vegetable broth

⅓ cup nutritional yeast

2 tablespoons tomato paste

1 clove garlic, minced

½ teaspoon extra-virgin olive oil, plus more as needed

½ teaspoon grade B maple syrup

½ teaspoon sea salt

Pinch of cayenne

Pinch of freshly ground black pepper

1 bay leaf, or 2 to 3 fresh basil leaves

Splash of plain nondairy milk (optional)

Pinch of something green, such as fresh basil, flat-leaf parsley, or kale, for garnish

Soup Tip: Boost this tomato soup by adding in rice and chopped veggies like carrots, kale, and peas.

1. If using fresh tomatoes, preheat the broiler. Place the tomatoes cut-side down in an oven-safe casserole dish. Broil the tomatoes on the top rack until the skins blacken on top, 3 to 5 minutes. (Otherwise, proceed to step 2.)

2. Combine the tomatoes, broth, nutritional yeast, tomato paste, garlic, oil, maple syrup, salt, cayenne, and pepper in a blender and blend, increasing the speed from low to high, until smooth.

3. Transfer the puree to a saucepan, add the bay leaf, and bring to a simmer over medium heat. Simmer for at least 5 minutes, then cover and simmer until ready to serve. If the soup reduces too much and becomes too thick, add a few splashes of nondairy milk. Remove the bay leaf before serving. Serve with a pinch of something green over the top.

NUTRITION FACTS
(per serving–417g) Calories: 185; Fat: 4g; Carbs: 22g; Protein: 15g; Fiber: 8g   Vitamin C: 16%; Iron: 25%; Calcium: 6%; Vitamin A: 8%

EASY SWEET POTATO CHILI

Chocolate-infused sweet potato chili is a comfort food to crave. Wait, chocolate in a savory recipe, with beans and veggies? Oh, yes! This is one secret ingredient to give your vegan chili an extra rich and dreamy flavor. Sweet potatoes accent the spicy bean base quite nicely—plus, they add an extra dose of fiber and vitamins.

SERVES 4

---

1. In a large saucepan, heat the oil over high heat. Add the onion and pepper and cook, stirring, for about 3 minutes.

2. Add the sweet potato, broth, and bay leaf. Cover and bring to a boil. Reduce the heat to medium and simmer until the broth is mostly absorbed and the sweet potatoes are tender, 10 to 12 minutes.

3. Add the lentils, beans, tomato paste, chili powder, and chocolate. Simmer over medium heat until the chili thickens, 12 to 15 minutes. Reduce to very low and simmer until ready to serve. If the chili is quite thick, cover the pan to keep in moisture. If it still seems a bit thin and watery, simmer uncovered to thicken. Taste and add salt and pepper as needed. Remove the bay leaf before serving.

4. Serve warm with one-quarter of the avocado over each bowl, and top with the other garnishes, if desired.

Note: For this recipe I love using vegan chocolate bars that have a high percentage of cacao, 70% and above. But basic semisweet chocolate chips work well, too.

Note: You can toss the avocado in fresh lime juice to prevent browning and add an accent of bright citrus flavor.

1 tablespoon extra-virgin olive oil

1 small onion, diced

1 bell pepper, diced

1 medium sweet potato, peeled and diced

3 cups vegetable broth

1 bay leaf

1 (12-ounce) can lentils, drained and rinsed

1 (12-ounce) can red kidney beans, drained and rinsed

1 (6-ounce) can tomato paste

2 tablespoons chili powder

2 tablespoons chopped vegan dark chocolate chips or bars (see Note)

Sea salt and freshly ground black pepper

1 avocado, pitted, peeled, and thinly sliced or diced (see Note)

OPTIONAL GARNISH

Vegan sour cream or vegan mayonnaise

Sprig of fresh cilantro or flat-leaf parsley

Crushed peanuts

NUTRITION FACTS
(per serving–415g)

Calories: 270; Fat: 7g; Carbs: 41g; Protein: 14g; Fiber: 13g

Vitamin C: 86%; Iron: 29%; Calcium: 6%; Vitamin A: 156%

WELLNESS SOBA NOODLE SOUP

This is my vegan spin on chicken noodle soup. Healthy buckwheat soba noodles swim in steamy broth, studded with thick-cut celery and carrots and optional cubes of vegan chick'n, too. This is my "feel better" soup! Add extra garlic and spices for extra feel-better power.

SERVES 4

1. In a large saucepan, heat the oil over high heat. Add the garlic, bay leaf, celery, carrots, mushrooms, onion, and potato and cook, stirring, until the onions begin to soften, about 3 minutes.

2. Add the broth and water and simmer, covered, for about 5 minutes to allow the potatoes and carrots to become tender.

3. Add the noodles, parsley, cayenne, salt and pepper, and turmeric (if using) to taste. Cover and boil for 4 to 5 minutes. The noodles should be soft by now. Add in the vegan chick'n (if using), and nutritional yeast (if using). For a brothier soup, you can add in another cup or two of broth. Simmer over medium heat for 2 to 3 minutes to warm the added ingredients, then reduce the heat to low and simmer until ready to serve. To reduce the soup for stronger flavors, simmer uncovered for a few minutes. Serve with parsley on top.

1 to 2 tablespoons extra-virgin olive oil

4 to 6 cloves garlic

1 bay leaf

2 cups chopped celery

1¼ cups diced carrots

1 cup thinly sliced shiitake mushrooms

½ cup diced onion

½ cup diced white potato

6 cups vegetable broth

2 cups water (or more broth)

5 ounces or 2 bundles soba noodles

½ cup chopped fresh flat-leaf parsley, plus more for garnish

3 pinches of cayenne

Sea salt and freshly ground black pepper

Ground turmeric (optional)

1 cup chopped vegan chick'n (optional)

Nutritional yeast (optional)

NUTRITION FACTS
(per serving–507g)
Calories: 266; Fat: 10g; Carbs: 35g; Protein: 13g; Fiber: 5g
Vitamin C: 30%; Iron: 16%; Calcium: 8%; Vitamin A: 140%

VEGAN SENATE BEAN SOUP

I first tasted Senate bean soup at a Washington, D.C., Whole Foods store. I fell in love with the smoky flavor that tasted like mashed potatoes and creamy beans all in one spoonful. I later learned that the recipe has a patriotic past and current tradition!

Today, this soup is served daily at the Senate's restaurant, though the recipe dates back to the early twentieth century. One story attributes the recipe to Senator Fred Dubois of Idaho; his version includes mashed potatoes. Another attributes it to Senator Knute Nelson of Minnesota, who, according to the U.S. Senate website, "expressed his fondness for the soup in 1903."

The original recipe calls for ham hock and butter, so I've veganized it with delicious results!

SERVES 3

1 medium white potato

1½ cups drained and rinsed canned navy beans

1½ cups vegetable broth

½ cup chopped fresh flat-leaf parsley

½ cup chopped onion

⅓ cup chopped celery

1 tablespoon garlic powder

1 tablespoon vegan buttery spread

1 large bay leaf

2 teaspoons hot sauce

1 teaspoon vegan liquid smoke

Sea salt and freshly ground black pepper (I like a lot of black pepper in this soup)

⅓ cup plain nondairy milk or soy creamer

Tip: Thin the soup by adding nondairy milk. Thicken the soup by simmering, uncovered, or adding nutritional yeast.

1. Preheat the oven to 400°F. Poke a few holes in the potato using a fork. Bake the potato for 45 minutes, or microwave for 5 to 8 minutes.

2. While the potato is baking, in a large saucepan, combine the beans, broth, parsley, onion, celery, garlic powder, vegan buttery spread, bay leaf, hot sauce, liquid smoke, and salt and pepper to taste. Bring to a boil, then reduce the heat to maintain a simmer and simmer until the potato has finished baking.

3. Roughly slice the baked potato and transfer to a food processor or blender. Remove the bay leaf from the soup. Add 1 to 2 cups of the soup (mostly broth) to the blender as well as the nondairy milk. Blend until smooth. Pour the blended liquid back into the pot with the soup and stir to combine. Simmer the soup, covered, until ready to serve.

NUTRITION FACTS (per serving–319g) Calories: 222; Fat: 4g; Carbs: 36g; Protein: 12g; Fiber: 11g Vitamin C: 32%; Iron: 17%; Calcium: 14%; Vitamin A: 26%

HOW-TO: SOAK AND PREPARE BEANS

In every recipe in this book that calls for canned beans, soaked and cooked dried beans can be substituted if time allows.

- **Why soak?:** Soaking beans is super easy, and the flavor and texture of freshly soaked dried beans is usually much better than canned beans. Soaking and rinsing the beans before cooking also helps to reduce the phytic acid in them. Phytic acid reduces our bodies' ability to absorb the minerals in the beans.

- **Why use canned?:** Canned beans tend to be softer, perfect for recipes in which they will be mashed or pureed. Canned beans are also better if you are in a hurry or for last-minute recipes. But for side dishes or adding beans to soups and stews, give freshly prepared dried beans a try.

- **Freedom to choose:** Both canned and freshly prepared dried beans have an excellent nutritional profile. It really depends on how much time you have and what texture and flavor you desire in your recipe. Freshly prepared dried beans are always my preference when I have time, but for quick meals (and even not-so-quick meals), canned beans work beautifully. So unless you need your beans super soft for mashing, you can usually choose to use either freshly soaked dried beans or canned.

- **How to prepare dried beans:** Rinse the dried beans under warm water. Place the beans in a large bowl and add warm water to cover by at least 2 inches. Discard any beans that look discolored or float to the top of the bowl. Cover the bowl and soak on the counter or in the fridge overnight or for at least 6 hours.

NO-CREAM OF MUSHROOM SOUP

Creamy mushroom soup, without the cream!

———— **SERVES 4** ————

ROASTED MUSHROOMS

8 ounces baby bella mushrooms, quartered

8 ounces portobello mushrooms (2 large), sliced

6 ounces shiitake mushrooms, sliced

2 to 4 cloves garlic, chopped

2 tablespoons extra-virgin olive oil

1 tablespoon apple cider vinegar

2 sprigs fresh rosemary

Few pinches of sea salt and freshly ground black pepper

SOUP BASE

1 medium white cauliflower

3 to 4 cups mushroom or vegetable broth

4 cloves garlic

Sea salt and freshly ground black pepper

2 tablespoons finely chopped fresh flat-leaf parsley

Splash of plain nondairy milk

Freshly ground black pepper

NUTRITION FACTS
(per serving–413g)

Calories: 137; Fat: 8g; Carbs: 16g; Protein: 5g; Fiber: 5g

Vitamin C: 48%; Iron: 7%; Calcium: 3%; Vitamin A: 0%

1 **For the Roasted Mushrooms:** Preheat the oven to 425°F.

2 Rinse and dry the mushrooms, making sure all the woody stems have been removed. In a bowl, toss the mushrooms with the garlic, oil, vinegar, rosemary, and salt and pepper.

3 Lay the mushrooms flat on a baking sheet. Roast the mushrooms until they begin to soften and caramelize around the edges, about 20 minutes. They should be moist, yet fully cooked and flavorful to eat on their own.

4 **For the Soup Base:** While the mushrooms are roasting, bring a pot of water to a boil. Add the cauliflower and cook for 7 to 10 minutes. Drain and set the tender cauliflower aside.

5 In a blender or food processor, or in a saucepan using an immersion blender, combine the cauliflower, about 2 cups of the broth, and the garlic. Blend on low until the cauliflower is smooth. Remove the rosemary sprigs from the baking sheet and reserve. Add ¾ cup of the roasted mushroom mixture to the blender. Blend in a few pinches of the reserved roasted rosemary for added flavor. Continue blending, adding broth until you reach a texture and flavor you like.

6 Transfer the cauliflower mixture to a large saucepan and bring to a simmer. Add salt and pepper to taste and simmer until ready to serve. Garnish with the leftover ¼ cup mushrooms, parsley, and some rosemary from roasting the mushrooms. I like a splash of warm milk and lots of black pepper over the top to serve.

EASY WHITE MISO FRESH PEA SOUP

This is a fresh pea soup that I make every spring when fresh peas are in season. I can make it in just a few minutes, with just a few ingredients, so it is a perfect lunch recipe. The savory white miso and fresh pea flavor combine with buttery avocado for a dreamy bright green soup.

SERVES 2

---

1 Bring 2 cups salted water to a boil. Add the peas to the boiling water and cook for just under 2 minutes.

2 Drain the peas and transfer to a high-speed blender or food processor. Add the avocado and miso.

3 Start blending on low and slowly pour in ½ cup water until a creamy mixture forms. As the peas blend the mixture will thicken nicely. Add pepper to taste. When the mixture is velvety smooth, pour and serve. Enjoy as-is—the temperature will be warm and lovely. A garnish of avocado cubes and fresh mint or lemon juice is nice, if desired.

2 cups shelled fresh English peas

½ avocado

2 teaspoons white miso paste

Freshly ground black pepper

Avocado cubes, for garnish

Fresh mint or lemon juice, for garnish (optional)

NUTRITION FACTS
(per serving–201g)

Calories: 225; Fat: 10g; Carbs: 23g; Protein: 9g; Fiber: 11g

Vitamin C: 105%; Iron: 13%; Calcium: 4%; Vitamin A: 24%

HOME-STYLE SMOKY PEA SOUP

Homemade pea soup is kind of amazing. And just so you know, it actually tastes better the day after you make it, as many soups tend to do. Creamy peas and fresh veggies combine for this smoky pea soup that is incredibly craveable. Serve with a giant slice of crusty bread, slathered in some vegan buttery spread, and enjoy. This hearty soup is rich in protein, fiber, and flavor.

SERVES 4

---

1 cup dried split peas, soaked overnight in salted water

4 cups vegetable broth

1 small onion, diced

1 large carrot, diced or sliced

½ cup diced peeled white potato

¼ cup nutritional yeast

1 tablespoon vegan buttery spread or extra-virgin olive oil

1 tablespoon apple cider vinegar

1 bay leaf

2 teaspoons vegan liquid smoke

1 teaspoon garlic powder

⅛ teaspoon freshly ground black pepper

2 to 3 pinches of cayenne

Sea salt

½ cup Tempeh Bacon Bits (page 62; optional)

Fresh herbs, such as chopped dill, flat-leaf parsley, or cilantro, for garnish (optional)

1 Drain and rinse the peas and place them in a large saucepan.

2 Add the broth, onion, carrot, potato, nutritional yeast, vegan buttery spread, vinegar, bay leaf, liquid smoke, garlic powder, pepper, cayenne, and salt to taste to the pot. Bring to a boil, then reduce the heat to very low, cover, and simmer for at least 1 hour, preferably longer. Check the soup and stir every 20 to 30 minutes. Remove the bay leaf before serving.

3 Serve the soup warm the same day it is made, or allow the soup to sit in the fridge overnight and reheat on the stove. Fold in the tempeh bacon bits and top with fresh herbs just before serving, if desired.

NUTRITION FACTS
(per serving—374g)

Calories: 300; Fat: 5g; Carbs: 43g; Protein: 21g; Fiber: 15g

Vitamin C: 17%; Iron: 65%; Calcium: 5%; Vitamin A: 22%

CREAMY CAULI-POTATO SOUP WITH TURMERIC, GINGER, AND COCONUT MILK

This enchanting soup combines creamy cauliflower, silky coconut milk, spicy ginger, and warming turmeric. The exotic blend is simply lovely! Add some saffron for an even more fragrant blend.

_____ SERVES 4 _____

1 Bring a large pot of salted water to a boil. Add the cauliflower, potato, and garlic and cook until the potatoes and cauliflower are tender, 7 to 10 minutes.

2 Drain the boiled veggies and transfer to a blender or food processor. Add the broth. Blend on low, then increase the speed with caution until the veggies are blended into a smooth puree.

3 Transfer the puree to a medium saucepan. Add the coconut milk, turmeric, ginger, cayenne, saffron (if using), and salt and pepper. Stir so the turmeric and saffron infuse the soup with a golden color. Simmer on low for at least 10 minutes before serving.

2 cups cauliflower florets

1 russet potato, peeled and diced

2 cloves garlic

1½ cups vegetable broth

1 cup full-fat or light coconut milk

1 teaspoon ground turmeric, or to taste

1 teaspoon grated peeled fresh ginger

⅛ teaspoon cayenne

Pinch of saffron (optional)

Sea salt and freshly ground black pepper

NUTRITION FACTS
(per serving–245g)
Calories: 201; Fat: 15g; Carbs: 15g; Protein: 5g; Fiber: 4g
Vitamin C: 56%; Iron: 11%; Calcium: 3%; Vitamin A: 0%

SOUTHERN PEANUT SWEET POTATO STEW

Oh, my, do I love this soup recipe. I first tried "peanut stew" a few years ago and fell in love. I love peanut butter, so to find it in a savory stew was just perfect! I got creative for this recipe and added chopped collard greens, cubed sweet potatoes, sweet onion, and garlic. I really love using white sweet potatoes for this recipe, but golden or garnet yams will work, too.

SERVES 3

½ teaspoon virgin coconut oil

2 cloves garlic, chopped

1 small sweet onion, chopped

2 cups plain soy milk

2 cups vegetable broth

1½ cups white or golden sweet potato

2 to 3 tablespoons peanut butter

1 teaspoon grade B maple syrup

1 to 3 cups water or broth (optional)

2 cups thinly sliced collard greens

¼ cup chopped fresh cilantro

1. In a large saucepan, heat the coconut oil over high heat. Add the garlic and onion and cook, stirring, for 1 minute.

2. Add the soy milk, broth, potatoes, peanut butter, and maple syrup. Bring to a boil, then reduce the heat to low and simmer until the potatoes are tender, 10 to 15 minutes. Thin out the soup by adding water or broth, if desired. Thicken the soup by simmering until ready to serve.

3. Fold in the collard greens and cilantro about 5 minutes before you plan on serving the soup. You want the collards nice and tender, but still perky. Serve warm.

NUTRITION FACTS
(per serving–552g) Calories: 300; Fat: 10g; Carbs: 43g; Protein: 14g; Fiber: 7g   Vitamin C: 55%; Iron: 17%; Calcium: 29%; Vitamin A: 21%

ROASTED VEGGIE GOLDEN RAISIN SOUP

This soup recipe is inspired by a stew I enjoyed when I visited the Golden Door Spa Resort in Escondido, California. The stew had a sweet tomato base, roasted veggies, and some surprising soup ingredients like kalamata olives and golden raisins. I was pleasantly surprised by the flavor and craved that bowl when I returned home. I did my best to re-create that delicious bowl, and this is what I came up with. I really love the unique flavor that the raisins add to the savory tomato broth and plentiful veggies. Feel free to substitute your own blend of roasted veggies in place of the ones I've listed below.

—————— **SERVES 4** ——————

1 **For the Roasted Veggies:** Preheat the oven to 400°F.

2 In a bowl, toss the chopped vegetables with the garlic, lemon juice, oil, rosemary, and salt and pepper. Spread on a rimmed baking sheet and roast until tender, 25 to 30 minutes. Remove from the oven and let rest a few minutes before adding to the soup.

3 **For the Tomato Broth Base:** In a large saucepan, combine the tomato base ingredients and bring to a boil. Reduce the heat to maintain a simmer.

4 Fold in the roasted veggies, kale (if using), and nutritional yeast (if using). Simmer for at least 10 minutes, and remove the bay leaf before serving.

ROASTED VEGGIES

2 portobello mushrooms, chopped

1 small sweet onion, chopped

1 zucchini, chopped

1 red bell pepper, chopped

4 cloves garlic, chopped

2 tablespoons fresh lemon juice

2 tablespoons extra-virgin olive oil

1 large sprig fresh rosemary

Few pinches of sea salt and freshly ground black pepper

TOMATO BROTH BASE

1 can (28-ounce) can crushed fire-roasted tomatoes, or 4 cups diced broiled fresh tomatoes (see step 1, page 258)

6 cups vegetable broth

1 cup chopped celery

10 kalamata olives, halved and pitted

⅓ cup golden raisins

⅓ cup finely chopped fresh flat-leaf parsley

1 bay leaf

¼ teaspoon cayenne, or more to taste

2 cups chopped kale (optional)

2 to 3 tablespoons nutritional yeast (optional)

NUTRITION FACTS
(per serving—516g)

Calories: 193; Fat: 7g; Carbs: 24g; Protein: 7g; Fiber: 5g

Vitamin C: 97%; Iron: 12%; Calcium: 5%; Vitamin A: 44%

ROASTED VEGGIE CREAMY SOUPS

I adore making roasted veggie soups. My favorites are carrots and sweet potatoes. Winter squash, mushrooms, beets, corn and more veggies also work! The process is simple: First, you roast the veggies until soft and tender. Place the roasted veggies in a blender and add as much liquid as needed to achieve your desired creamy soup texture. I use vegetable broth, nut milks, or soy milk depending on how creamy I want my soup. Blend until smooth and season to taste. I love adding loads of spices like turmeric, grated peeled fresh ginger, ground cinnamon, cayenne, paprika, pepper, and more. Garlic, too. Pour the blended soup into a soup pot and simmer on low until fully warmed and ready to serve.

WHITE VELVET ROASTED YAM SOUP

This ultra-creamy soup is flavored with sweet white yam, savory garlic, and rustic white beans. Japanese white sweet potatoes have a dense white flesh that becomes sticky-sweet and caramelized when roasted. This simple soup will leave a big impression. Fill your bowl and sink into white velvet bliss. I like to pair my soup with some whole-grain toast, a drizzle of walnut oil, and a dash of cinnamon and cayenne.

SERVES 4

1 Preheat the oven to 400°F.

2 Cut the sweet potatoes into 1-inch-thick rounds. Place the rounds in an oven-safe casserole dish with the garlic and drizzle with the coconut oil and maple syrup. Roast until tender and easily cut with a fork, 20 to 25 minutes.

3 Transfer the potatoes to a high-speed blender and add the beans, 1½ cups of the nondairy milk, the ginger (if using), cinnamon, salt, and pepper. Blend on low until creamy. Add the remaining nondairy milk to thin the soup, if desired. Taste and add salt and pepper as needed.

4 Pour the soup into a medium saucepan and simmer on low until ready to serve. Top with a few pinches of pepper and cinnamon.

4 cups white sweet potatoes (about 2 medium or 3 small), peeled

4 cloves garlic

2 teaspoons virgin coconut oil

Drizzle of grade B maple syrup

¾ to 1 cup drained and rinsed canned white beans

1½ to 2 cups plain nondairy milk

½ teaspoon ground ginger, or 1 teaspoon grated peeled fresh ginger (optional)

¼ teaspoon ground cinnamon, plus more as needed

¼ teaspoon sea salt, plus more as needed

Pinch of freshly ground black pepper, plus more as needed

NUTRITION FACTS (per serving–192g) Calories: 212; Fat: 4g; Carbs: 42g; Protein: 6g; Fiber: 7g Vitamin C 22%; Iron: 12%; Calcium: 16%; Vitamin A: 6%

SIMPLE CURRIED ROASTED CARROT SOUP

Simple carrot-ginger stew has been a longtime favorite of mine. But for this recipe, I used roasted carrots and added optional canned pumpkin, plus a wide array of warming spices like turmeric, cayenne, ginger, pepper, and optional curry powder. This soup is simple and loaded with vitamin A, which is great for healthy skin!

―――――――――――――――― SERVES 2 ――――――――――――――――

9 medium carrots (about 1 bunch), sliced or chopped

1 tablespoon extra-virgin olive oil or virgin coconut oil

2 teaspoons agave syrup or grade B maple syrup

Sea salt

2 cups vegetable broth

1 to 2 cups plain almond milk

1 cup canned unsweetened pumpkin puree (optional)

1 teaspoon grated peeled fresh ginger

1 teaspoon ground turmeric or sweet curry spice blend

¼ teaspoon cayenne (optional)

¼ teaspoon freshly ground black pepper

VARIATION

You can easily substitute the pumpkin puree with sweet potato or butternut squash, or omit it entirely if you have trouble finding this seasonal ingredient.

1 Preheat the oven to 415°F.

2 In a bowl, toss the carrots with the oil, agave, and salt. Lay flat on a rimmed baking sheet and roast until tender, 25 to 35 minutes. Reserve the "roasting juices" from the carrot pan.

3 Place the roasted carrots in a blender, leaving out a few small carrots for garnish. Add the remaining ingredients to the blender and blend, increasing the speed from low to high, until silky smooth. I personally love my soup very rich and creamy, so I use minimal amounts of liquid. But for a more traditional soup consistency, start with 2 cups broth and 1 cup nondairy milk, and go from there. If you add too much liquid you can always simmer the soup uncovered to thicken. After blending, taste the soup and adjust the spices and salt to taste.

4 Pour the soup in a saucepan and simmer until ready to serve. Garnish with the reserved roasted carrots and a drizzle of the carrot juices from the roasting pan.

NUTRITION FACTS
(per serving–893g)

Calories: 322; Fat: 12g; Carbs: 46g; Protein: 10g; Fiber: 13g

Vitamin C: 36%; Iron: 23%; Calcium: 44%; Vitamin A: 1309%

DESSERTS

Creating healthy, happy, vegan desserts always catches me off guard a bit. I grew up eating desserts that were mostly loaded with refined sugar, white flour, eggs, and butter. But on the flip side, I always loved healthy sweet things like fruits and healthy baked goods from the natural foods store even more than those classic unhealthy desserts. As a vegan adult, I love taking classic dessert recipes and infusing them with plant-based ingredients.

Instead of looking at desserts as "bad" foods, I have reinvented many of them to actually have nutrient-dense properties! They're desserts you feel good about indulging in.

Dessert recipes present an opportunity to take sweet treat foods and infuse them with superfoods, healthy ingredients, and more. Sweet fruits, healthy nuts and seeds, healthy fats, and more can all find their way into vegan dessert recipes, making them something to feel good about. This collection of desserts has something for every mood. In this chapter are a few classic recipes turned vegan, recipes that may be more traditional in scope and be thought of as "treat" foods. There are other desserts included that you truly could eat every day, after every meal, and feel good about them! Actually, some of these desserts could even be eaten for breakfast or as snacks! So embrace the flavors and textures that you love when it comes to dessert, and start feeling good about treating yourself. We all deserve dessert when a craving calls.

CHOCOLATE-COVERED STRAWBERRY LAYER CAKE

This is the cake recipe I make for my husband every year for his birthday. He adores chocolate and strawberries and anything exploding with rich dark chocolate flavor. If you love chocolate-covered strawberries, this cake will impress!

SERVES 12

CAKE

Virgin coconut oil or cooking spray, for the pans

12 ounces silken tofu

3 cups all-purpose white flour

1 cup vegan sugar

½ cup plain nondairy milk

¼ cup vegan chocolate chips

5 tablespoons cocoa powder

2 to 3 tablespoons virgin coconut oil, melted

2 tablespoons vital wheat gluten, homemade oat flour (from rolled oats; see Sidebar, page 38), or ground flaxseeds

1 tablespoon baking powder

2 teaspoons sea salt

2 teaspoons apple cider vinegar

2 teaspoons pure vanilla extract

1. **For the Cake:** Preheat the oven to 375°F. Grease two 8-inch round cake pans with coconut oil.

2. In a large bowl, combine all the cake ingredients and beat until smooth. Pour the batter into the prepared cake pans.

3. Bake the cakes until fluffy and smooth, and the tops are firm to the touch, not moist, 20 to 24 minutes. Let cool in the pans on wire racks.

4. **For the Berry Filling:** In a small bowl, toss the strawberries in the lemon juice. Refrigerate until ready to use.

5. **For the Chocolate-Covered Strawberries:** Line a plate with parchment paper. In a small bowl, combine the chocolate chips and coconut oil and microwave for 20 seconds. Briskly stir until smooth. Dry the berries completely and dip in the melted chocolate. Lay flat on the lined plate. Place the berries in the fridge or freezer to harden. (Not shown. Fresh berries are used in the accompanying recipe photo.)

6. **For the Chocolate Frosting:** Combine all the frosting ingredients except the nondairy milk in a large bowl and beat until smooth. Gradually add the nondairy milk, using more or less as needed to smooth out the frosting. Cover and refrigerate for 15 minutes before applying to the cake; the frosting should be firmed up a bit but still soft enough to spread on the cake.

7 Remove the cooled cakes from the pans. Place one layer one a serving plate or cake stand. Begin spreading the frosting on the cake layer, covering it completely. If the frosting has firmed up too much, let soften at room temperature until spreadable.

8 Drain the chilled strawberries of any excess liquid and pat dry. Top the frosted cake layer with a thin layer of the chilled berries. Set the second cake layer on top and frost the top and sides. Top the cake with the chocolate-dipped strawberries and any excess sliced berries. Garnish with fresh mint. Serve chilled or at room temperature. Store the leftover cake, covered, in the fridge for 3 to 4 days.

BERRY FILLING

1 cup thinly sliced strawberries

1 teaspoon fresh lemon juice

CHOCOLATE-COVERED STRAWBERRIES

¼ cup vegan chocolate chips

2 teaspoons virgin coconut oil

5 to 6 large strawberries

CHOCOLATE FROSTING

3 cups confectioners' sugar

1 cup cocoa powder

½ cup vegan buttery spread, softened

¼ cup virgin coconut oil, softened

1 teaspoon pure vanilla extract

Pinch of sea salt

¼ cup plain nondairy milk, give or take a little

Fresh mint leaves, for garnish

| **NUTRITION FACTS** (per serving–170g) | Calories: 490; Fat: 19g; Carbs: 77g; Protein: 9g; Fiber: 8g | Vitamin C: 15%; Iron: 16%; Calcium: 10%; Vitamin A: 1% |

GINGERBREAD BUNDT CAKE
WITH VANILLA BEAN COCONUT GLAZE

Fluffy and dark caramel in color, this spicy-sweet gingerbread Bundt cake is perfect for a fall or holiday party. The white vanilla bean glaze streaming down the sides is quite beautiful and oh so delicious.

SERVES 8

CAKE

Virgin coconut oil, for the pan

1½ cups whole wheat flour

1 cup all-purpose white flour

1½ tablespoons ground flaxseeds

1 tablespoon baking powder

½ teaspoon ground cinnamon

½ teaspoon sea salt

10 ounces silken tofu, at room temperature

1 cup plain almond milk, at room temperature or warmed

½ cup blackstrap molasses

½ cup grade B maple syrup

½ cup vegan sugar

½ cup virgin coconut oil, softened

½ cup vegan buttery spread, softened

2 tablespoons fresh orange juice

1 teaspoon pure vanilla extract

1 teaspoon grated peeled fresh ginger, or ½ teaspoon ground ginger

½ teaspoon freshly grated orange zest

1. **For the Cake:** Preheat the oven to 400°F. Grease a Bundt cake pan with a generous amount of coconut oil.

2. In a large bowl, combine the flours, flaxseeds, baking powder, cinnamon, and salt.

3. In a blender, combine the tofu, almond milk, molasses, maple syrup, sugar, coconut oil, vegan buttery spread, orange juice, vanilla, ginger, and orange zest. Blend, increasing the speed from low to high, until smooth. Add the tofu mixture to the flour mixture and fold until a silky batter forms. Pour the batter into the prepared Bundt pan.

4. Bake for 15 minutes, then reduce the oven temperature to 350°F and bake for 45 to 50 minutes more. When done, the cake will be lightly browned on edges, and the surface visibly darkened and fluffy to the touch.

5. Let the cake cool for 10 to 15 minutes in the pan, then carefully loosen the edges and invert the cake pan onto a plate. Let cool almost completely. Place the cake in the freezer for 1 to 2 minutes just before glazing to give the surface of the cake an extra chill. This makes it easier for the glaze to cling to the cake.

6 **For the Glaze:** In a small bowl, whip together the glaze ingredients. Pour the glaze over the slightly chilled cake. Serve. Store in the fridge if not consuming immediately.

GLAZE

2 cups sifted confectioners' sugar

3 tablespoons virgin coconut oil, melted

2 tablespoons coconut milk

¼ teaspoon vanilla bean powder, or 1 vanilla bean, split, seeds scraped, pod discarded

NUTRITION FACTS (per serving–140g)	Calories: 444; Fat: 21g; Carbs: 59g; Protein: 5g; Fiber: 2g	Vitamin C: 4%; Iron: 16%; Calcium: 18%; Vitamin A: 1%

GERMAN CHOCOLATE LOAF CAKE

German chocolate cake was always my favorite cake to make as a kid. I made it using a boxed mix and a plastic tub of frosting. Milk, eggs, butter. Well, this veganized version uses healthy coconut oil, all silky and rich, sticky brown rice syrup, chopped nuts, and coconut frosting to top a rich vegan chocolate cake. I used a loaf pan for this cake to keep things super simple. One pan. Easy. You could also make these into cupcakes. Indulge, chocolate lovers!

SERVES 10

CAKE

Virgin coconut oil, for the pan

1½ cups all-purpose white flour

½ cup cacao powder

1½ tablespoons baking powder

1 teaspoon ground flaxseeds or chia seeds

¾ teaspoon sea salt

1 cup drained and rinsed canned white beans, or 1 cup silken tofu

1 cup agave syrup, or 1 cup plus 1 tablespoon vegan sugar

½ cup plain nondairy milk

⅓ cup virgin coconut oil, melted

¼ cup vegan chocolate chips, melted

1 shot prepared espresso

½ teaspoon apple cider vinegar

1 **For the Cake:** Preheat the oven to 400°F. Grease a loaf pan with coconut oil.

2 In a large bowl, combine the flour, cacao powder, baking powder, flaxseeds, and salt.

3 In a blender, combine the beans, agave, nondairy milk, and coconut oil and blend until smooth.

4 Combine the chocolate chips with the hot espresso to melt. Stir briskly. If needed, microwave for 20 to 30 seconds to further melt. Stir the apple cider vinegar into the melted chocolate chip mixture and then put this into the blender with the other liquid ingredients. Blend on low until smooth. Stir the bean mixture into the flour mixture and whip until fluffy. Pour the batter into the prepared pan.

5 Bake the cake for 10 minutes, then reduce the oven temperature to 350°F and bake until the cake cooks through and the edges pull away from the pan, 25 to 35 minutes more. Remove the cake from the oven and let cool in the pan for 5 to 10 minutes. Carefully loosen the edges of the cake with a butter knife and unmold the cake onto a serving plate. Let cool completely before frosting.

6 **For the Frosting:** In a small bowl, whip together the frosting ingredients until fluffy and soft. Place in the freezer for about 5 minutes to firm up a bit.

7 Slice the cake loaf horizontally into two layers. Set one layer aside. Spread frosting on the bottom layer, top with the second layer, and then frost the top layer. Slice and serve. Store the cake in the fridge. The frosting will firm up in the fridge, so allow the leftover cake to warm to room temperature slightly before serving.

FROSTING

1 cup brown rice syrup

¾ cup chopped walnuts or pecans

½ cup virgin coconut oil, softened

½ cup unsweetened shredded coconut

Pinch of sea salt

Pinch of ground cinnamon

NUTRITION FACTS
(per serving–157g)

Calories: 540; Fat: 27g; Carbs: 76g; Protein: 7g; Fiber: 4g

Vitamin C: 0%; Iron: 54%; Calcium: 14%; Vitamin A: 1%

FEEL-GOOD GLUTEN-FREE CARROT CAKE

This carrot cake is bursting with fresh carrot flavor, gluten-free made with oat flour, creamy sweet vegan cream cheese frosting on top. Don't hesitate to enjoy a slice as an afternoon snack, or even a sweet treat for breakfast. Each slice contains fiber, vitamin A, and protein.

**MAKES ONE 13X9-INCH SHEET CAKE OR
ONE 9-INCH ROUND DOUBLE-LAYER CAKE; SERVES 15**

CAKE

Virgin coconut oil, for the pan

4 cups rolled oats

2 tablespoons ground flaxseeds

1 tablespoon baking powder

¾ teaspoon ground cinnamon

8 ounces silken tofu

1½ cups plain nondairy milk

1 cup agave or grade B maple syrup (vegan sugar could also be used)

3 tablespoons fresh orange juice

2 tablespoons vegan buttery spread, melted

1 teaspoon pure vanilla extract

½ teaspoon freshly grated orange zest

2¾ cups shredded carrots

⅓ cup chopped walnuts

⅓ cup raisins

CREAM CHEESE FROSTING

8 ounces vegan cream cheese

3 to 4 ounces vegan buttery spread, melted, or 3 to 4 ounces coconut oil and a pinch of sea salt

1¼ cups pitted Medjool dates

Freshly grated orange zest, for garnish

1 **For the Cake:** Preheat the oven to 350°F. Grease a 13x9-inch cake pan or two 9-inch round cake pans with coconut oil.

2 Grind the oats in a blender, increasing the speed from low to high, until a flour forms. Pour the mixture into a large bowl. Add the flaxseeds, baking powder, and cinnamon.

3 In a bowl, stir the tofu until smooth. Stir in the nondairy milk, agave, orange juice, vegan buttery spread, vanilla, and orange zest. Pour this mixture into the bowl with the dry ingredients and stir. Fold in the carrots, walnuts, and raisins.

4 Pour the batter into the prepared pan(s), smooth the top with a spatula, and bake until the edges brown and start to pull away from the pan, 30 to 40 minutes. Let cool completely in the pan, at least 30 minutes.

5 **For the Cream Cheese Frosting:** While the cake is baking, combine all the frosting ingredients in a food processor and process until smooth. Using a spatula, scoop the frosting into a small bowl, cover, and refrigerate until ready to use.

6 For ease, frost the cake while it is in the pan. Frost the cooled cake and top with orange zest. Serve chilled. Store any leftovers, covered, in the fridge.

NUTRITION FACTS (per serving–143g) — Calories: 322; Fat: 15g; Carbs: 42g; Protein: 6g; Fiber: 5g; Vitamin C: 7%; Iron: 12%; Calcium: 12%; Vitamin A: 70%

PEANUT BUTTER CUP CUPCAKES

Chocolate and peanut butter in a sweet, dreamy cupcake.

───────────── MAKES 12 CUPCAKES ─────────────

1 **For the Chocolate Cupcakes:** Preheat the oven 375°F. Grease a standard 12-cup muffin tin with coconut oil or line with paper liners.

2 In a large bowl, combine the flour, sugar, cocoa powder, baking powder, cinnamon, and salt.

3 In a separate bowl, stir together the applesauce, vegan buttery spread, nondairy milk, flax egg, vanilla, and vinegar. Using a handheld mixer, blend the applesauce mixture into the flour mixture.

4 Fill the cups of the prepared muffin tin with the batter. Bake the cupcakes until the tops become firm and shiny, 16 to 20 minutes. Cool for 2 to 3 minutes in the pan, then loosen the cupcakes and transfer to a plate or wire rack to cool for 30 minutes more before frosting.

5 **For the Peanut Butter Frosting:** In a bowl, combine the frosting ingredients and use a handheld mixer to whip the frosting. Place the frosting in the fridge to firm up a bit, 15 to 25 minutes. Transfer the frosting to a pastry bag fitted with a star tip and pipe the frosting onto the cooled cupcakes, or simply spoon the frosting on top in a casual swirl.

CHOCOLATE CUPCAKES

Virgin coconut oil, for the pan (optional)

1½ cups all-purpose white flour

1 cup vegan sugar

⅓ cup cocoa powder

1 tablespoon baking powder

¼ teaspoon ground cinnamon

½ teaspoon sea salt

½ cup plus 1 tablespoon applesauce

½ cup vegan buttery spread, melted

½ cup plain nondairy milk

1 flax egg (⅓ cup water mixed with 1 teaspoon ground flaxseeds)

1 teaspoon pure vanilla extract

¼ teaspoon apple cider vinegar

PEANUT BUTTER FROSTING

1 cup confectioners' sugar

⅓ cup creamy salted peanut butter

⅓ cup vegan buttery spread, chilled

2 to 3 tablespoons plain nondairy milk

Few drops of pure vanilla extract

NUTRITION FACTS (per serving–99g)

Calories: 327; Fat: 16g; Carbs: 43g; Protein: 4g; Fiber: 2g

Vitamin C: 2%; Iron: 11%; Calcium: 8%; Vitamin A: 1%

VANILLA-CINNAMON FROSTED BANANA CUPCAKES WITH STICKY PEANUT BUTTER CARAMEL SAUCE

Peanut butter caramel sauce is drizzled over fluffy banana cupcakes with cinnamon frosting.

MAKES 12 CUPCAKES

CUPCAKES

Virgin coconut oil, for the pan (optional)

6 ounces silken tofu, at room temperature

2 extra-ripe bananas, mashed

½ cup vegan sugar

2 tablespoons virgin coconut oil, softened

1 teaspoon fresh lemon juice

Pinch of vanilla bean seeds, or ½ teaspoon pure vanilla extract

1 cup all-purpose white flour

2 teaspoons baking powder

½ teaspoon sea salt

½ teaspoon ground cinnamon

STICKY PEANUT BUTTER CARAMEL SAUCE

⅓ cup vegan sugar

2 tablespoons vanilla bean frosting

2 tablespoons creamy peanut butter

1 tablespoon coconut milk (or coconut oil leftover from a chilled can of full-fat coconut milk; see page 304)

1 **For the Cupcakes:** Preheat the oven to 375°F. Grease a standard 12-cup muffin tin with coconut oil or line with paper liners.

2 In a blender, combine the tofu, bananas, sugar, coconut oil, lemon juice, and vanilla seeds and blend until smooth.

3 In a large bowl, combine the flour, baking powder, salt, and cinnamon. Fold in the blended tofu mixture until a silky batter forms.

4 Fill the cups of the prepared muffin tin with batter. Bake until the cupcakes have lightly browned, slightly puffed tops and are firm to the touch, 18 to 20 minutes. Let cool completely before frosting.

5 **For the Sticky Peanut Butter Caramel Sauce:** Combine the caramel sauce ingredients in a small saucepan and heat over medium-high heat, stirring, until the mixture begins to boil and bubble, 1 to 2 minutes. Continue to cook for about a minute more, then remove from the heat. Pour into a small bowl, cover, and refrigerate.

6 **For the Vanilla Bean Frosting:** In a bowl, combine the coconut cream from the chilled can of coconut milk with the remaining frosting ingredients and use a handheld electric mixer to whip until smooth and fluffy. Transfer the

frosting to a pastry bag fitted with a star tip and pipe a swirl of frosting on top of each cooled cupcake. Transfer the cupcakes to a wire rack set over a baking sheet and drizzle the chilled caramel sauce over each cupcake. Serve. These are best eaten the same day they are baked. Store any leftovers in the fridge, covered, for 2 to 3 days.

VANILLA BEAN FROSTING

1 can coconut milk, fully chilled

2 cups confectioners' sugar

2 tablespoons virgin coconut oil, melted

Pinch of sea salt

Tip: If the caramel is too thick to drizzle, allow it to come to room temperature before drizzling.

NUTRITION FACTS (per serving–88g)	Calories: 265; Fat: 15g; Carbs: 30g; Protein: 4g; Fiber: 2g	Vitamin C: 3%; Iron: 7%; Calcium: 7%; Vitamin A: 0%

KATHY'S FAVORITE CHOCOLATE CHIP COOKIES

This is my favorite chocolate chip cookie recipe, which means I make these a lot! If there is one thing I have learned in life, it is that everyone loves chocolate chip cookies. I add coconut oil as my fat because it creates crispy edges and a rich flavor. And I add a hint of peanut butter for a subtle nutty accent.

--- **SERVES 12** ---

Virgin coconut oil, for the pan

½ cup plus 2 tablespoons all-purpose white flour (see Note)

½ cup spelt or homemade oat flour (from rolled oats; see Sidebar, page 38)

1½ tablespoons ground flaxseeds

1½ teaspoons baking powder

½ teaspoon sea salt

Pinch of ground cinnamon

½ cup plus 2 teaspoons virgin coconut oil, softened

½ cup plus 2 tablespoons vegan sugar

2 tablespoons plain almond milk, warmed

2 teaspoons salted creamy peanut butter, softened

½ teaspoon pure vanilla extract

¾ cup vegan semisweet chocolate chips

½ teaspoon apple cider vinegar

1. Preheat the oven to 400°F. Grease two baking sheets with coconut oil.

2. In a large bowl, combine the flours, flaxseeds, baking powder, salt, and cinnamon.

3. In a medium bowl, combine the coconut oil, sugar, almond milk, peanut butter, and vanilla. Fold the coconut oil mixture into the flour mixture. Fold in the chocolate chips and vinegar.

4. Place the dough in the fridge just long enough for it to become sticky and firm, at least 10 minutes (this makes it easier to handle). Roll the dough into balls and place them on the prepared baking sheets.

5. Place the cookies in the oven, then reduce the oven temperature to 375°F right away. Bake until the tops begin to very slightly brown, 10 to 12 minutes. The cookies will be very soft when you take them out of the oven, but as they cool they will become buttery and crisp on the outside. When cool enough to move without breaking, transfer the cookies to a wire rack. These are delicious served warm or cooled but are best served the same day they are baked. Store any leftovers, covered, on the countertop for 1 to 2 days. For longer storage, place the cookies in sealed containers or baggies and store in the freezer. Rewarm frozen cookies in the microwave for 30 seconds, or allow to come to room temperature on a plate on the counter.

NUTRITION FACTS
(per serving–44g)

Calories: 214; Fat: 13g; Carbs: 23g; Protein: 3g; Fiber: 2g

Vitamin C: 0%; Iron: 5%; Calcium: 6%; Vitamin A: 1%

TRAIL TREKKER OAT COCONUT COOKIES

These are my "everything but the kitchen sink" cookies. I adore them because I can see all the nutty, bumpy, healthy things inside them—things like coconut, nuts, chocolate, oats, banana, and spices. These cookies are oil free and very textured, and bake into cluster-looking shapes. They are nutty, sweet, and ready to make you swoon. Grab a few just before you hit the road on an adventure-filled trek!

SERVES 14

1 Preheat the oven to 375°F. Lightly grease two baking sheets with coconut oil or line with parchment paper.

2 In a large bowl, combine the oat flour, oats, baking powder, cinnamon, salt, and cayenne.

3 In a separate bowl, combine the bananas, brown rice syrup, peanut butter, flaxseeds, orange juice, chia seeds, vanilla, and orange zest. Stir the banana mixture into the flour mixture until a thick dough forms. Fold in the chocolate chips, coconut, and walnuts. Place the dough in the fridge or freezer for about 20 minutes or longer to chill and firm up.

4 Spoon the cookie dough onto the prepared baking sheets. Really pile on the dough so that you get large, tall, clumpy mounds of cookie dough. These should be big, hearty, tall, textured cookies. Bake for about 12 minutes, more or less if you modify the cookie size a bit. When the cookies are done, they will have puffed up in size and have golden brown edges where the oats and nuts creep out of the cookies. These cookies are best served the same day they are baked, but leftovers are convenient for grab-and-go enjoyment as well. Store the leftovers, covered, on the countertop for 1 to 2 days. For longer storage, place the

recipe continues

Virgin coconut oil, for the pan (optional)

1½ cups homemade oat flour (from rolled oats; see Sidebar, page 38) or whole wheat white flour

1 cup rolled oats

1 tablespoon baking powder

1 teaspoon ground cinnamon

¾ teaspoon sea salt

Pinch of cayenne or freshly grated nutmeg (optional)

2 medium very ripe bananas, mashed

¾ cup brown rice syrup (another liquid sweetener could be used if needed, but I like the stickiness of brown rice for these)

⅓ cup salted creamy peanut butter, softened

2 tablespoons ground flaxseeds

1 to 2 teaspoons fresh orange juice

ingredients continue

continued

1 teaspoon chia seeds

½ teaspoon pure vanilla extract

Few pinches of freshly grated orange zest

½ cup vegan semisweet chocolate chips

⅓ cup unsweetened shredded coconut

¼ cup chopped walnuts (pecans or peanuts also work nicely)

cookies in sealed containers or baggies and store in the freezer. Rewarm the frozen cookies in the microwave for 30 seconds, or allow to come to room temperature before serving. For treks: Pull a cookie from the freezer in the morning, pack it in your out-the-door bag, and enjoy it at room temperature in a few hours.

NUTRITION FACTS (per serving–75g)	Calories: 214; Fat: 8g; Carbs: 34g; Protein: 6g; Fiber: 4g	Vitamin C: 5%; Iron: 23%; Calcium: 9%; Vitamin A: 0%

SOFT AND CHEWY PEANUT BUTTER COOKIES

Peanut butter cookies are classic and also easily veganized. I use flaxseeds and water as my egg replacer for this easy recipe then let the luscious peanut butter, sweetener, and spices do the rest.

SERVES 18

---

1. Preheat the oven to 350°F. Lightly grease two baking sheets with coconut oil or line with parchment paper.

2. In a small bowl, whisk together the flax egg and set aside to thicken for at least 3 minutes.

3. In a large bowl, beat together the vegan buttery spread, peanut butter, sugars, vanilla, and vinegar. Fold or beat in all the dry ingredients except coarse sugar. Place the dough in the fridge to chill for at least 20 minutes.

4. Using your hands, roll the dough into balls and dip them in the coarse sugar. Place the balls on the prepared baking sheets. Use a fork to imprint a classic peanut butter cookie grid in the dough, flattening the dough balls with the fork twice and rotating the fork 90 degrees on the second press.

5. Bake until the cookies are darkened in color with chewy, light golden edges, about 12 minutes. Cool the cookies on the baking sheet for 1 to 3 minutes before transferring to a wire rack to cool for 5 to 10 minutes more before serving. These are best served warm the same day they are baked. Store the leftovers, covered, on the countertop for 1 to 2 days. For longer storage, place the cookies in sealed containers or baggies and store in the freezer. Rewarm the frozen cookies in the microwave for 30 seconds, or allow to come to room temperature on a plate on the counter.

Virgin coconut oil, for the pan (optional)

1 flax egg (⅓ cup water mixed with 1 teaspoon ground flaxseeds)

½ cup vegan buttery spread, softened

½ cup salted creamy peanut butter, softened

¾ cup coconut sugar or another vegan sugar

¼ cup brown or unrefined sugar

1 teaspoon pure vanilla extract

½ teaspoon apple cider vinegar

1 cup whole wheat white, oat, or spelt flour

1 teaspoon baking powder

1 teaspoon baking soda

½ teaspoon ground cinnamon

¼ teaspoon sea salt

½ cup coarse sugar, such as turbinado (or use more coconut sugar)

NUTRITION FACTS
(per serving-34g)

Calories: 160; Fat: 9g; Carbs: 18g; Protein: 3g; Fiber: 2g

Vitamin C: 0%; Iron: 5%; Calcium: 1%; Vitamin A: 0%

WHITE CHOCOLATE MACADAMIA COOKIES

My favorite cookie before I went vegan was a white chocolate macadamia nut cookie, all soft and chewy, studded with creamy sweet white chocolate. Well, when I discovered that vegan white chocolate chips exist, this is the first recipe I made with them! I found the chips online. You may need to special order them, but if you love this flavor of cookie, you will be wildly impressed with how similar these cookies taste to the original!

SERVES 12

½ banana, mashed

½ cup vegan buttery spread

¼ cup grade B maple syrup

¼ cup vegan sugar

½ teaspoon pure vanilla extract

½ teaspoon apple cider vinegar

¾ cups whole wheat white flour

1 tablespoon vital wheat gluten flour

½ teaspoon baking soda

¼ teaspoon ground cinnamon

½ cup chopped macadamia nuts

¼ cup vegan white chocolate chips

1 Preheat the oven to 350°F. Line two baking sheets with parchment paper.

2 In a large bowl, combine the banana, vegan buttery spread, maple syrup, sugar, vanilla, and vinegar. Blend with a handheld mixer until the butter is creamy. Blend or fold in the flours, baking soda, and cinnamon until a thick dough forms. Fold in the nuts and chocolate chips.

3 Either spoon the sticky dough onto the prepared baking sheets or place the dough in the fridge for at least 30 minutes for easier scooping of dough. Warm dough will spread better, cool dough will stay a bit thicker in shape.

4 Bake until the cookies are slightly puffed up and spread with lightly browned edges, 14 to 16 minutes. Let cool on the baking sheets for 2 to 3 minutes before transferring to a wire rack to cool for 10 minutes more. Serve warm. These cookies are best served the same day they are baked. Store any leftovers, covered, on the countertop for 1 to 2 days. For longer storage, place the cookies in sealed containers or baggies and store in the freezer. Rewarm the frozen cookies in the microwave for 30 seconds, or allow to come to room temperature on a plate on the counter.

NUTRITION FACTS
(per serving–43g)

Calories: 190; Fat: 13g;
Carbs: 18g; Protein: 3g;
Fiber: 2g

Vitamin C: 1%; Iron: 3%;
Calcium: 3%; Vitamin
A: 0%

SOFT GINGER MOLASSES COOKIES

These ginger cookies are soft and tender with a fresh ginger bite. Molasses, nutmeg, ground ginger, and cinnamon bring on that unique ginger cookie flavor.

SERVES 10

1. Preheat the oven to 375°F. Lightly grease a baking sheet with coconut oil.

2. In a large bowl, combine the flour, baking powder, ground ginger, cinnamon, nutmeg, baking soda, and salt.

3. In a separate bowl, combine the maple syrup, vegan buttery spread, molasses, fresh ginger (if using), vanilla, and 1 tablespoon water. Fold the wet ingredients into the dry ingredients. Refrigerate the dough for at least 20 minutes.

4. If you want perfectly shaped ginger cookies, roll out the dough and use a round cookie cutter to cut out cookies. Alternatively, simply roll the dough into moist balls using your hands. Roll or toss each cookie in sugar and place on the prepared baking sheet.

5. Bake until the cookies have puffed up slightly and have crinkled, darkened tops, 8 to 10 minutes. Carefully transfer the cookies to a wire rack to cool. The cookies will firm up as they cool. These are best served slightly warm or room temperature the same day they are baked. Store any leftovers, covered on the countertop for 1 to 2 days. For longer storage, place the cookies in sealed containers or baggies and store in the freezer. Rewarm the frozen cookies in the microwave for 30 seconds, or allow to come to room temperature on a plate on the counter.

Virgin coconut oil, for the pan

1 cup all-purpose white flour

1 teaspoon baking powder

1 teaspoon ground ginger

½ teaspoon ground cinnamon

¼ teaspoon freshly grated nutmeg

¼ teaspoon baking soda

Pinch of sea salt

⅓ cup grade B maple syrup or vegan sugar

¼ cup vegan buttery spread, softened

2 tablespoons molasses

½ teaspoon grated peeled fresh ginger, or an additional ¼ teaspoon ground ginger (optional)

½ teaspoon pure vanilla extract

Vegan sugar, for coating

Note: Do not overbake or you will have gingersnaps instead of chewy cookies.

NUTRITION FACTS (per serving–31g)

Calories: 124; Fat: 5g; Carbs: 20g; Protein: 2g; Fiber: 1g

Vitamin C: 0%; Iron: 0%; Calcium: 3%; Vitamin A: 5%

PEANUT BUTTER BUCKWHEAT BEAUTIES

These tender, moist cookies are made using buckwheat flour and classic peanut butter cookie ingredients. Buckwheat is a healthy vegan flour and works beautifully in this sweet treat.

—— SERVES 16 ——

Virgin coconut oil, for the pan (optional)

¾ cup buckwheat flour

¾ cup creamy peanut butter

¾ cup grade B maple syrup

1 tablespoon virgin coconut oil, softened

1 teaspoon apple cider vinegar

1 teaspoon baking powder

1 teaspoon ground flaxseeds

½ teaspoon pure vanilla extract

¼ teaspoon ground cinnamon

¼ teaspoon sea salt

1½ ounces vegan dark chocolate bar (half of a 3-ounce bar), broken into nickel-size pieces

1. Preheat the oven to 350°F. Lightly grease a baking sheet with coconut oil or line with parchment paper.

2. In a large bowl, combine all the ingredients, except the chocolate, and whip until a smooth, soft dough forms. Refrigerate the dough for at least 20 minutes.

3. Roll the chilled dough into balls and place on the prepared baking sheet. Press down the cookies with a fork.

4. Bake until the cookies are smooth and round and dark golden brown in color, 9 to 12 minutes. A few minutes after pulling the cookies from the oven, push a small piece of chocolate into the top of the cookie, so it sticks out from the cookie. Let cool for 2 to 3 minutes on the baking sheet, then carefully transfer to a wire rack to cool for 5 to 10 minutes more before serving. These are best served warm the same day they are baked. Store any leftovers, covered, on the countertop for 1 to 2 days. For longer storage, place the cookies in sealed containers or baggies and store in the freezer. Rewarm the frozen cookies in the microwave for 30 seconds, or allow to come to room temperature on a plate on the counter.

NUTRITION FACTS
(per serving–36g)

Calories: 146; Fat: 8g; Carbs: 18g; Protein: 4g; Fiber: 2g

Vitamin C: 0%; Iron: 4%; Calcium: 3%; Vitamin A: 0%

GLUTEN-FREE ALMOND BUTTER–JAM THUMBPRINT COOKIES

These jam-filled gems are simple and sweet, gluten-free, and cute on a plate.

SERVES 8

1. Preheat the oven to 400°F. Line a baking sheet with parchment paper.

2. In a bowl, combine all the ingredients, except the jam, until a soft dough forms.

3. Carefully roll the dough into balls and place on the prepared baking sheet. Press a small thumbprint into each cookie. Place the cookies in the freezer for 10 minutes to solidify the shape for baking.

4. Bake the chilled cookies until they are rounded and lightly puffed and darkened on the edges, 8 to 10 minutes.

5. Pull the cookies from oven and dab a small bit of the jam in the center thumbprint of each cookie. Remove the cookies from the pan and transfer to a plate. Place the cookies in the fridge to chill. Serve the cookies once they have cooled and firmed up a bit, otherwise at room temperature they will be slightly soft in texture. These cookies are best served the same day they are baked. Store any leftovers, covered, in the fridge, for 1 to 2 days. For longer storage, place the cookies in sealed containers or baggies and store in the freezer. Rewarm the frozen cookies in the microwave for 30 seconds, or allow to come to room temperature on a plate on the counter.

¾ cup homemade oat flour (from rolled oats; see Sidebar, page 38)

½ cup vegan sugar or coconut sugar

2½ tablespoons almond butter, softened

2 teaspoons virgin coconut oil, softened

¼ teaspoon ground cinnamon

Pinch of sea salt

Pinch of baking soda

2 tablespoons fruity jam, any flavor

Note: If the dough is too soft to work with, place it in the fridge a few minutes to firm up a bit.

COOKIE TIPS

* **Fold-ins:** Use slightly chilled fold-ins like nuts or chocolate chips—this helps firm up the dough a bit faster.

* **Flour:** If desired, replace the wheat flour with oat flour or an all-purpose gluten-free flour blend. The cookie texture will vary a bit.

NUTRITION FACTS
(per serving–32g)

Calories: 135; Fat: 5g; Carbs: 22g; Protein: 3g; Fiber: 2g

Vitamin C: 1%; Iron: 4%; Calcium: 2%; Vitamin A: 0%

PEANUT BUTTER BROWNIES

These ultra-moist brownies are just like the ones I used to love to make with my girlfriends at slumber parties when I was a teenager, drizzled with a heavy hand of peanut butter then baked until gooey-delicious, each nibble falling apart as a warm, delicious chocolate mess in your fingers. But these brownies have beans in them (shhhh!). I know—I used to think it sounded crazy to include beans in a dessert, but they actually fit seamlessly into this veganized dish. You can add pureed beans to cakes, muffins, and more as an egg replacer. They add texture and nutrients, and trust me, you will not even taste them as "beans." So grab some cocoa powder and whip up this chocolate bliss.

—————————— SERVES 12 ——————————

BROWNIES

Virgin coconut oil, for the pan

1½ cups drained and rinsed canned black beans (not low-sodium)

¼ cup vegan semisweet chocolate chips

½ teaspoon virgin coconut oil

1 shot prepared espresso

¾ cup raw cacao powder or cocoa powder

¾ cup vegan sugar

½ cup homemade oat flour (from rolled oats; see Sidebar, page 38)

2 teaspoons ground flaxseeds

½ teaspoon pure vanilla extract

¼ teaspoon sea salt

¼ teaspoon baking powder

ingredients continue

1 **For the Brownies:** Preheat the oven to 400°F. Grease an 8- or 9-inch square or round pan with coconut oil.

2 Place the black beans in a food processor and process until smooth. Transfer to a large bowl.

3 Place the vegan chocolate chips and coconut oil in a small microwave-safe cup and microwave until softened, 30 to 50 seconds. Briskly stir the mixture until silky and melted. Add the melted chocolate and espresso to the bowl with the beans. Whip until well combined.

3 Fold in the remaining ingredients. To get the batter extra creamy, use a handheld mixer to whip until smooth, 1 to 2 minutes.

recipe continues

continued

PEANUT BUTTER TOPPING

⅓ cup creamy peanut butter

2 tablespoons virgin coconut oil

Sprinkle of vegan chocolate chips (optional)

4 Pour the brownie batter into the prepared pan, smoothing the top well.

5 **For the Peanut Butter Topping:** In a small microwave-safe dish, combine the peanut butter and coconut oil and microwave until melted, 30 to 50 seconds. Stir to combine, then pour the mixture over the brownies, swirling it a bit into the batter. Add a few whole chocolate chips to the top, if desired.

6 Bake for about 30 minutes. The brownies are done when the edges firm up and pull away from the sides of the pan. Let cool in the pan for at least 30 minutes before slicing, if you want the brownies to stay in one piece. These are best served warm the same day they are baked. Store any leftovers in their baking pan, covered, for 2 to 3 days. Serve the brownies chilled, or rewarm individual brownies in the microwave for 30 seconds, or allow to come to room temperature on a plate on the counter. You could also rewarm in a 350°F oven for 5 to 8 minutes.

NUTRITION FACTS (per serving-61g) Calories: 237; Fat: 8g; Carbs: 36g; Protein: 9g; Fiber: 6g   Vitamin C: 0%; Iron: 5%; Calcium: 5%; Vitamin A: 0%

COZY PUMPKIN-PECAN CINNAMON ROLLS WITH MAPLE-GINGER CREAM CHEESE GLAZE

I do not make cinnamon rolls all that often, but when I do, I ensure that they are rich and gooey, just like sticky-sweet cinnamon rolls should be. This special treat will make any brunch or breakfast extra special. And yes, these are pretty sweet and rich, so I treat them as a dessert more than a breakfast item. These cinnamon rolls are infused with pumpkin, pecan, maple, and ginger flavor. Start on the dough at least 3 hours before you bake the rolls.

MAKES 8 ROLLS; SERVES 16

1 **For the Pumpkin Cinnamon Dough:** In a large bowl, combine the warm water with the yeast. Stir well to dissolve. Stir in the nondairy milk and shortening. Add 1 cup of the flour, the sugar, pumpkin, and salt. Using a handheld mixer, beat on low until smooth. Fold in the remaining 4 cups flour with a spoon until the dough is easy to handle and less sticky. Roll the dough into a ball and knead gently for a minute. Place the dough in a floured bowl. Cover with a clean towel and place in a warm spot. Let rise for about 2 hours. You can either proceed to make the rolls or place the dough in the fridge overnight to bake the next day.

2 Preheat the oven to 400°F. Grease an 8- to 9-inch cake pan with coconut oil.

3 Punch down the dough. Roll out the dough to about ⅓ inch thick on a clean well-floured surface with a rolling pin.

4 **For the Pecan Cinnamon Sugar Filling:** In a bowl, combine the sugar with the melted vegan buttery spread and vanilla. Fold in the pecans and cinnamon. The mixture should be

recipe continues

PUMPKIN CINNAMON DOUGH

½ cup warm water

1 (7-gram) packet active dry yeast

1 cup plain nondairy milk

½ cup vegan shortening or vegan buttery spread, melted

5 cups whole wheat white flour, plus more for kneading

¾ cup vegan sugar or coconut sugar

¾ cup canned unsweetened pumpkin puree

1 teaspoon sea salt (reduce to ½ teaspoon if using vegan buttery spread)

Virgin coconut oil, for the pan

ingredients continue

continued

PECAN CINNAMON SUGAR FILLING

¾ cup brown sugar or raw turbinado sugar

½ cup vegan buttery spread, melted

½ teaspoon pure vanilla extract

¾ cup roughly chopped pecans

1 tablespoon ground cinnamon

2 tablespoons vegan buttery spread (optional)

GINGER CREAM CHEESE GLAZE

1 cup vegan cream cheese

½ cup grade B maple syrup

½ cup soy creamer

⅓ cup vegan buttery spread, melted

¼ cup confectioners' sugar, sifted

1½ teaspoons ground ginger

thick yet spreadable. Spread the filling over the rolled-out dough.

5 Roll the dough tightly into a log and slice it crosswise into 1½-inch-thick rolls. Place the rolls about ⅛ inch apart in the prepared pan. Add a few dots of vegan buttery spread on top of the rolls, if desired. Bake until the rolls are fluffy and lightly browned on the edges, 25 to 35 minutes.

6 **For the Ginger Cream Cheese Glaze:** Combine all the glaze ingredients in a large bowl and beat with a handheld mixer until smooth.

7 When the rolls are pulled from the oven, pour the glaze over the top. Allow the glaze to soak into the rolls for at least 10 minutes before serving warm. Chill any leftover rolls. To reheat, warm individual rolls for 30 to 60 seconds in the microwave, or warm the entire pan in a 350°F oven for 10 to 15 minutes.

NUTRITION FACTS (per serving–122g) Calories: 428; Fat: 24g; Carbs: 49g; Protein: 7g; Fiber: 6g Vitamin C: 1%; Iron: 9%; Calcium: 5%; Vitamin A: 32%

COUNTRYSIDE DOUBLE BERRY PIE WITH HOMEMADE LATTICE CRUST

This rustic berry pie with a buttery homemade lattice crust reminds me of all things "country": sunshine, wooden picnic tables, tall glasses of lemonade, blue skies, long lazy afternoons, and wildflowers. Fresh or frozen berries will work, although you will get a bolder flavor and better texture from fresh berries. Allow extra time for the berries to soften if you are using frozen berries. Serve up a slice of this homestyle pie when fresh berries are in season and embrace some chill time as you satisfy your sweet tooth.

SERVES 12

1   Make the crust ahead of time. Split the dough into two equal rounds, wrap each in plastic wrap, and store in the freezer until needed the day of baking. Pull the rounds from the freezer a good 25 to 45 minutes before ready to use, depending on how warm your kitchen is, so that they can soften to room temperature. You want the rounds very chilled, but also pliable and soft when ready to roll out.

2   Preheat the oven to 400°F.

3   Roll out one dough round to fit a 9-inch pie dish. Fit the dough into the pie dish. Bake until the crust is slightly puffed up and a darker shade of gold, 5 to 8 minutes. Set aside to cool. Raise the oven temperature to 425°F.

4   In a soup pot, with the stove off, whisk the cornstarch into the fruit juice until it begins to dissolve. Turn the heat to medium and add the remaining ingredients. Stir the filling mixture and bring to a slow boil so the blueberries soften. Reduce the heat to low and simmer for 2 to 3 minutes to allow the filling to reduce a bit.

recipe continues

1 recipe Homemade Pie Crust (page 301)

2 tablespoons cornstarch or arrowroot powder

2 tablespoons fruit juice, water, or nondairy milk

2 cups blueberries

1½ cups blackberries

½ cup vegan sugar, plus more for sprinkling

2 tablespoons vegan buttery spread

½ teaspoon pure vanilla extract

Pinch of sea salt

continued

Note: Start the crust either the night before or at least 2 hours before you cook the pie.

5 Pour the warm filling into the partially baked crust. Roll out the remaining dough round and cut into ¾-inch-wide strips. Arrange the strips over the pie filling in a lattice design. Crimp the edges of the pie and sprinkle some sugar over the top. Cover the pie with foil if you do not like a crispier crust. Remove the foil halfway through baking.

6 Bake the pie for 15 minutes, then reduce the heat to 350°F and bake until the crust browns and bubbles, 25 minutes more. Let cool for at least 1 hour before slicing. Serve warm or completely cooled. Store leftovers in the fridge and rewarm as desired.

NUTRITION FACTS
(per serving–109g)

Calories: 293; Fat: 17g; Carbs: 33g; Protein: 3g; Fiber: 2g

Vitamin C: 7%; Iron: 6%; Calcium: 1%; Vitamin A: 1%

HOMEMADE PIE CRUST

This is my homemade vegan pie crust recipe. I use it for a wide variety of fruit pies, as well as cream pies and more. I also love it for making mini hand pies and for this blueberry pie recipe. Make sure the vegan buttery spread is well chilled before using. I also like to chill the flour in the freezer. Starting with the cold ingredients will help you achieve a buttery, flaky crust.

**MAKES 2 BALLS OF DOUGH,
ENOUGH FOR 1 DOUBLE-CRUST PIE, 12 SERVINGS**

1 Place the vegan buttery spread in the freezer for at least 30 minutes before using.

2 In a blender or food processor, pulse the flour, sugar, and salt. Add the vegan buttery spread and pulse until the mixture resembles coarse crumbs. You want all the butter to combine with the flour and become dry little beads. (If you are using a blender, transfer the mixture to a bowl at this point.)

3 Add the chilled water to the dough a little bit at a time until the dough is kneadable but still fluffy.

4 Dust your work surface with flour and turn out the dough. It's okay if the dough feels a bit sticky at this point. Add more flour if necessary to properly work with the dough. Also, if there are a few clumps of buttery spread left in the dough, that's okay, too.

5 Separate the dough into two rounds. They will be incredibly soft and delicate right now. Satiny and fluffy, more so with lighter grain flours. Wrap the dough balls in plastic wrap and place them in the freezer for at least 1 hour before working with the dough. You can freeze the dough overnight, if needed.

1 cup vegan buttery spread, chopped into small cubes

2¼ cups all-purpose white flour, plus more for rolling

1 tablespoon vegan sugar or coconut sugar

1 teaspoon sea salt

¼ to ½ cup ice water

recipe continues

continued

6 Pull the rounds from the freezer a good 25 to 45 minutes before ready to use, depending on how warm your kitchen is, so that they can soften to room temperature. You want the rounds very chilled, but also pliable and soft when ready to roll out.

7 Roll out one round of dough and fit it into a pie dish. The crust doesn't have to be perfect. You can always mold the dough in the dish with your fingers. Press it out through the sides as you'd like.

8 Bake the crust for 5 to 7 minutes at 400°F before adding filling, if you like, for a crisper cooked pie crust. Otherwise, simply fill the raw crust with filling and proceed from there. Roll out the second round of dough if you'd like your pie to have a top crust and bake as directed in the recipe.

NUTRITION FACTS
(per serving–43g)

Calories: 222; Fat: 15g; Carbs: 19g; Protein: 3g; Fiber: 1g

Vitamin C: 0%; Iron: 6%; Calcium: 0%; Vitamin A: 0%

MAPLE-CASHEW PUMPKIN PIE

My secret for perfect vegan pumpkin pie has always been using soaked cashews to blend with the pumpkin puree. The cashews are incredibly creamy and rich and bake beautifully. This maple-infused vegan pumpkin pie is a perfect way to finish any fall feast.

SERVES 10

1 Preheat the oven to 400°F.

2 In a blender or food processor, combine the pumpkin, maple syrup, coconut oil, pumpkin pie spice, salt, and vanilla. Blend until smooth. Add the cashews ¼ cup at a time to ensure the blender can handle the thickness of the blend. You may need to stop between additions and scrape sides of the blender. Blend until smooth. If you are having a rough time due to the power of your machine, add the nondairy milk to loosen the mixture.

3 Pour the blended pumpkin mixture into the crust. Smooth the top and arrange the reserved ⅓ cup cashews around the edges of the pie. Bake for 15 minutes, then reduce the heat to 350°F and bake for 25 minutes more. When done, the top of the pie will have darkened in color and the edges will be golden brown. The cashews will be lightly browned as well.

4 Cool the pie on the counter, then place in the fridge for at least 3 hours to firm up—overnight is best. Store any pie leftovers, covered, in the fridge for 3 to 4 days. Serve the leftovers chilled from the fridge or warm to room temperature for 5 to 15 minutes on the countertop.

1 (15-ounce) can unsweetened pumpkin puree

½ to ¾ cup grade B maple syrup (use the full ¾ if you like a sweet pie)

1 tablespoon virgin coconut oil, melted

½ teaspoon pumpkin pie spice

½ teaspoon sea salt

¼ teaspoon pure vanilla extract

1½ cups plus 1 tablespoon raw cashews, soaked in salted water for at least 6 hours and drained (reserve ⅓ cup for garnish)

¼ cup plain nondairy milk or water

Homemade Pie Crust (page 301) or store-bought graham cracker crust

Creamy variation: For a creamier pumpkin pie, substitute 8 ounces vegan cream cheese for ½ cup of the cashews.

NUTRITION FACTS
(per serving—98g)
Calories: 276; Fat: 16g; Carbs: 31g; Protein: 4g; Fiber: 4g
Vitamin C: 3%; Iron: 12%; Calcium: 5%; Vitamin A: 132%

HOW-TO: COCONUT WHIP

Fluffy, silky coconut whip is just a recipe away!

To make coconut whip, you will be using the "coconut cream" part of a can of coconut milk. Place the can(s) of coconut milk (full-fat only!) in the fridge until fully chilled. Open the can without shaking it or turning it upside down—you will notice that a thick, opaque white substance has separated from the layer of glossy, clear-ish oily liquid. You want only the thick opaque layer for coconut whip. Tip: You can also buy cans of "coconut cream," which have already separated the coconut cream out for you.

You can now whip this mixture with a hand beater for basic unsweetened whip. But for sweet, extra-fluffy, and whipped cream–like whip, add 2 to 3 tablespoons or more of confectioners' sugar for each can of coconut milk. Whip the mixture until fluffy; it may take a few minutes to fluff air into the mixture. If the coconut milk becomes too warm, place in the fridge for a few minutes to chill so the cream doesn't melt. Here is the process laid out in steps:

- **Go shopping:** Buy a can of full-fat coconut milk.

- **Chill it:** Place it in the fridge overnight. Also place a stainless-steel bowl in the freezer.

- **Open the can:** The next day, remove the can of coconut milk from the freezer, without shaking it or turning it upside down, and open it. Remove the bowl from the freezer as well.

- **Spoon the cream:** Carefully spoon out the layer of opaque white stuff that has gathered at the top of the can into the chilled bowl. You will be left with about ½ cup of a syrupy translucent liquid. Leave this in the can. (I use this leftover liquid in numerous coconut-y recipes. Plus, it makes a great coconut syrup, almost like a hydrated extract of coconut flavor. Or you can toss it.) To prevent waste, seek out cans of just "coconut cream," such as those available at Trader Joe's.

- **Sweeten and flavor it:** Add 2 to 3 tablespoons confectioners' sugar to the coconut cream in the bowl. You can also add ground cinnamon, vanilla bean seeds, or any small amount of flavoring you'd like.

- **Whip it:** Using a whisk or handheld electric mixer, whip the coconut cream until thick. Start on low and move to a higher speed, moving the beater in an up and down motion to infuse the mixture with as much air as possible.

- **Serve:** Spoon on top of ice cream, try it for making cream pies, use it for coffee lattes, mix it with strawberries, or eat it with a spoon. I guarantee you'll be licking those beaters. And the bowl.

NO-BAKE WALNUT PUMPKIN PIE

This no-bake recipe is silky and creamy with pure pumpkin flavor in every bite. Healthy raw walnuts, rich in healthy fats, provide a sturdy accent to the pumpkin puree. If you want a chilled, no-bake pumpkin pie recipe, give this nutty spin a try. Top with soy or coconut whip to serve!

SERVES 10

1. **For the Crust:** In a blender or food processor, combine the oats, walnuts, sugar, flaxseeds, and salt and blend until fine and crumbly.

2. Generously grease a pie dish with the vegan buttery spread. Press the ground oat mixture into the dish. It should firm up quite nicely as you pack and press it into a flat layer on the bottom and up the sides of the dish.

3. **For the Filling:** In a blender or food processor, combine all the filling ingredients except the coconut oil. Blend until very smooth and silky. With the blender on low, slowly pour in the melted coconut oil until the mixture is smooth and silky. Do a quick taste test of the filling. Salt and sweeten to taste or adjust the spices as desired.

4. Pour the filling into the crust and place in the fridge for at least 4 to 5 hours to fully firm up—overnight is best.

5. Slice and serve chilled, topped with soy whip, if desired! Store any pie leftovers, covered, in the fridge for 3 to 4 days. Serve the leftovers chilled from the fridge or warm to room temperature for 5 to 15 minutes on the countertop.

CRUST

½ cup rolled oats

⅓ cup walnuts

2 tablespoons brown sugar or grade B maple syrup (or another hint of sweetener)

2 tablespoons ground flaxseeds or chia seeds

½ teaspoon sea salt

2 tablespoons vegan buttery spread or virgin coconut oil

FILLING

1 (15-ounce) can unsweetened pumpkin puree

½ cup walnuts

⅓ cup agave syrup or grade B maple syrup

¼ cup brown sugar

¼ cup plain nondairy milk

1½ teaspoons pumpkin pie spice

¾ teaspoon sea salt

½ cup virgin coconut oil, melted

Soy or coconut whip (see page 304; optional)

NUTRITION FACTS
(per serving–94g)

Calories: 273; Fat: 21g; Carbs: 20g; Protein: 3g; Fiber: 3g

Vitamin C: 3%; Iron: 40%; Calcium: 4%; Vitamin A: 133%

FREEZER GINGERBREAD MEN AND TRUFFLES

This raw version of gingerbread cookies is a healthy way to indulge in your holiday cookie craving.

— MAKES 2 TO 3 GINGERBREAD MEN OR 12 TRUFFLES —

1 cup raw almonds

¼ cup unrefined cane sugar

1½ tablespoons virgin coconut oil

1 teaspoon blackstrap molasses

¼ teaspoon chia seeds

¼ teaspoon ground cinnamon

⅛ teaspoon vanilla bean powder or extract

Pinch of sea salt

1 In a blender or food processor, process the almonds into a crumbly flour. Do not process too long or the nuts will turn into almond butter. You will need ½ cup almond flour, but make a bit more than that so you can use the nut flour as a nonstick surface to press out the dough.

2 In a small bowl, combine all the ingredients, folding them together until a wet, thick dough forms. Place in the fridge for about 5 minutes to firm up a bit.

3 If making truffles, roll the dough into balls and place them in the freezer to chill until ready to serve. If making gingerbread men, spread 1 to 2 tablespoons of the ground almonds on your work surface and carefully press out the dough to at least ¼ inch thick. Cut out the gingerbread cookies. Carefully transfer the cookies to parchment paper and place in the freezer to chill for at least 10 minutes before serving. Store in the freezer.

NUTRITION FACTS
(per serving–57g)

Calories: 275; Fat: 19g; Carbs: 24g; Protein: 6g; Fiber: 4g

Vitamin C: 8%; Iron: 52%; Calcium: 9%; Vitamin A: 0%

CARAMEL APPLE PIE

Confession: I used to hate apple pie. Or so I thought. How silly, yes? But then I realized that I simply hated certain types of apple pie. Once I made my own from scratch and I was able to make a flaky vegan crust, a sweet-tart apple-cinnamon filling, and then top everything off with caramel sauce, my mind was forever changed about apple pie. This is now one of my favorite pies! Mission accomplished.

--- SERVES 8 TO 10 ---

APPLE CIDER CARAMEL SAUCE

2 teaspoons cornstarch or arrowroot powder

½ cup apple cider

1 cup vegan sugar

½ cup vegan shortening or vegan buttery spread

2 tablespoons grade B maple syrup

2 tablespoons fresh lemon juice

½ teaspoon ground ginger

¼ teaspoon ground cinnamon

Pinch of sea salt

FILLING

4 large tart apples, peeled, cored, and sliced

2 tablespoons cornstarch or arrowroot powder

2 tablespoons grade B maple syrup

2 tablespoons fresh lemon juice

1 teaspoon ground cinnamon

1 teaspoon ground ginger

½ teaspoon pure vanilla extract

Pinch of sea salt

1 Preheat the oven to 425°F.

2 **For the Apple Cider Caramel Sauce:** In a medium saucepan, dissolve the cornstarch into the cider. Add the remaining caramel ingredients. Bring the mixture to a boil, stirring continuously. After about 2 minutes of bubbling, reduce the heat to medium and continue to cook, stirring, until the mixture thickens even more, 2 to 3 minutes more. Note that it will be watery when hot and fully thicken as it cools in the fridge. Remove from the heat. Set aside 2 tablespoons of the warm caramel sauce for the apple filling. Pour the remaining sauce into a bowl and refrigerate.

3 **For the Filling:** Place the apples and remaining filling ingredients in a large bowl, pour over the 2 tablespoons caramel sauce, and fold well to coat the apples.

4 Roll out one round of the pie dough and fit it into a pie dish greased with ½ teaspoon of the vegan butter. Pour the filling over the top and dot with 1 to 2 tablespoons vegan buttery spread. Roll out the remaining dough and layer over the filling, or cut strips and arrange them in a lattice design over the filling. Poke venting holes if doing a flat crust. Brush the top crust with melted vegan buttery spread and sprinkle with sugar, if desired.

5 Bake for 15 minutes, then reduce the oven temperature to 350°F and bake for 25 to 35 minutes more. The crust will be golden brown and the pie filling will be firmed up when done.

6 Let cool for at least 1 hour before slicing and serving. Pour the caramel over each slice, or over the entire pie before slicing. You may need to let the caramel warm up a bit to pour it. Store any leftovers, covered, in the fridge and consume within 3 to 4 days. Serve leftovers chilled or reheat the pie slices in the microwave for 30 to 60 seconds or in a 350°F oven for 10 minutes.

1 recipe Homemade Pie Crust (page 301)

1 to 2 tablespoons plus ½ teaspoon vegan buttery spread

1 tablespoon vegan buttery spread, melted, or fresh lemon juice (optional)

1 tablespoon vegan sugar (optional)

NUTRITION FACTS
(per serving–205g)

Calories: 465; Fat: 22g; Carbs: 65g; Protein: 2g; Fiber: 3g

Vitamin C: 13%; Iron: 2%; Calcium: 2%; Vitamin A: 1%

COCONUT OIL FOR NO-BAKE DESSERTS

What did I do before coconut oil? Coconut oil is what dreamy, raw, no-bake desserts are made of. This magical oil can help you make firmed-up, oven-free pies, cheesecakes, treats, bars, truffles, and more.

- **Temperature-sensitive oil:** The trick to coconut oil is that at room temperature it is soft and velvety. When warmed over 70°F, it becomes liquid. And when chilled, it becomes rock-hard. The magic is easy.

- **Basic use:** Add coconut oil to raw dessert recipes in a liquid state, making sure all the ingredients are at room temperature so the oil doesn't bead up, then chill the dessert and watch it magically firm up to be a sliceable treat. No heat required!

- **How much oil?:** One standard cheesecake or pie usually contains around ½ cup melted coconut oil. But if you are using other high-fat, firmable ingredients like processed nuts and seeds, you can easily reduce that amount for nutritional purposes.

- **Chocolate lovers:** Coconut oil is also wonderful for making homemade chocolate desserts in a flash! Make homemade peanut or almond butter cups in just a few minutes—try the recipe on page 321. Use your creativity and fall in love with this healthy oil.

- **What kind of coconut oil?:** I use extra-virgin coconut oil, unrefined and organic preferred. Read labels carefully—not all coconut oil is created equal. I also look for coconut oil labeled "raw" so I know it has been processed without intense heat.

RAW ALMOND BUTTER CHEESECAKE

This no-bake cheesecake includes almond butter flavor in every creamy, silky bite. Cashews and coconut oil create vegan cheesecake magic. No oven required for nutty cheesecake bliss. You may substitute peanut butter for the almond butter, if desired.

SERVES 12

1. **For the Crust:** Grease a pie dish with coconut oil. In a blender or food processor, process the crust ingredients and press them into the prepared dish until a loose crust forms.

2. **For the Cheesecake:** Drain the soaked cashews and rinse with warm water. Place the cashews, salt, and cinnamon in a blender or food processor. Start blending on low and pour in the agave, coconut oil, and almond butter. Keep blending until the mixture is silky smooth. You may need to stop and scrape down the sides of the blender if a few cashews get stuck. Add a splash of water if the mixture is too thick to blend (this can happen if the cashews have not been soaked long enough).

3. Pour filling into the pie dish and smooth the top. Chill in the fridge until firm enough to slice, at least 2 hours—overnight is best. Place in the freezer for 1 hour just after pouring filling, then back in the fridge, to speed up chilling time. Serve chilled. Store any leftovers, covered, in the fridge and consume within 2 to 3 days.

CRUST

Virgin coconut oil, for the pan

¾ cup almonds

½ cup pitted Medjool dates

1 teaspoon flaxseeds

1 teaspoon virgin coconut oil

CHEESECAKE

3 cups raw cashews, soaked

1 teaspoon sea salt

¼ teaspoon ground cinnamon

¾ cup agave syrup or grade B maple syrup

½ cup virgin coconut oil, melted

⅓ cup raw unsalted almond butter

NUTRITION FACTS (per serving–69g)
Calories: 385; Fat: 29g; Carbs: 24g; Protein: 8g; Fiber: 2g
Vitamin C: 0%; Iron: 13%; Calcium: 6%; Vitamin A: 0%

PEANUT BUTTER CHOCOLATE SILK PIE WITH PEANUT COOKIE CRUST

This silky tofu-based pie has rich chocolate flavor swirled with dreamy peanut butter, all on top of a dreamy peanut butter cookie crust. This is a decadent dessert for any peanut butter–chocolate lover to try.

──────── **SERVES 12** ────────

COOKIE CRUST

Virgin coconut oil, for the pan

1 cup almonds

½ cup creamy peanut butter, softened

½ cup coconut sugar

2 teaspoons virgin coconut oil, softened

Pinch of sea salt

FILLING

24 ounces silken tofu, at room temperature

½ cup agave syrup

4½ tablespoons cocoa powder

¼ cup virgin coconut oil, melted

½ teaspoon pure vanilla extract

¼ teaspoon sea salt

¼ teaspoon ground cinnamon

PEANUT BUTTER SWIRL

2 tablespoons creamy peanut butter, melted

1 tablespoon agave syrup

1 teaspoon virgin coconut oil, melted

1 **For the Cookie Crust:** Preheat the oven to 400°F. Grease a pie dish with coconut oil.

2 In a high-speed blender or food processor, process the almonds into flour. Do not overprocess or they will turn into nut butter. Place the almond flour in a large bowl, add the remaining crust ingredients, and fold together until thickened.

3 Press the cookie crust mixture into the prepared pie dish in an even layer. Bake the crust until golden brown and crispy, about 10 minutes. Let cool a bit while you make the filling.

4 **For the Filling:** In a blender or food processor, combine all the filling ingredients and blend until silky smooth. Pour the filling over the warm cookie crust.

5 **For the Peanut Butter Swirl:** In a bowl, whip together the peanut butter swirl ingredients and pour over the filling. Swirl the peanut butter into the chocolate with a butter knife.

6 Cover the pie with plastic wrap and place in the fridge. Chill for at least 8 hours—overnight is best. Slice and serve chilled. Store any leftovers, covered, in the fridge and consume within 3 to 4 days.

NUTRITION FACTS (per serving–109g) — Calories: 291; Fat: 18g; Carbs: 27g; Protein: 10g; Fiber: 3g — Vitamin C: 0%; Iron: 9%; Calcium: 5%; Vitamin A: 0%

EASY BAKED BROADWAY CHEESECAKE
WITH BLUEBERRY TOPPING

When I used to live in New York City, I noticed that one thing on most tourist to-do lists was to grab a slice of classic New York cheesecake. Well, now I can have my vegan cheesecake and eat it, too. I gladly gave a classic blueberry-topped cheesecake a vegan spin by using vegan cream cheese, coconut oil, and sassy lemon juice and a fresh blueberry sauce on top. You could also substitute cherries or cherry sauce.

———— SERVES 12 ————

CRUST

1 cup walnuts

1 tablespoon virgin coconut oil, softened

OR

1 vegan graham cracker pie crust

CHEESECAKE FILLING

16 ounces vegan cream cheese, at room temperature

1 cup agave syrup, or 1 cup plus 1 tablespoon vegan sugar

3 tablespoons virgin coconut oil, softened

2 tablespoons fresh lemon juice

1 teaspoon sea salt

1 teaspoon pure vanilla extract

⅛ teaspoon baking soda

1 **For the Crust:** Preheat the oven to 400°F.

2 In a food processor, process the walnuts until fine and crumbly and toss with the coconut oil. Press into the bottom of pie dish. Bake for 7 to 10 minutes.

3 **For the Cheesecake Filling:** Combine all the cheesecake ingredients in a large bowl. Beat with a handheld mixer until smooth.

4 Pour the cheesecake filling into the baked crust. Bake the cheesecake for 15 minutes, then reduce the oven temperature to 350°F and bake for 30 minutes more. The edges will be lightly browned and the top firmed and velvety when done. Let cool for 15 minutes, then place in the fridge to cool completely, at least a few hours, before slicing and serving.

5 **For the Blueberry Topping:** In a small saucepan, dissolve the arrowroot in the agave. Add the blueberries and salt. Heat the mixture over medium-high heat, stirring continuously, for a few minutes, until the blueberries soften and begin to bubble. Reduce the heat to low. Transfer

half of the mixture to a blender and blend until smooth. Return the blended blueberry mixture to the pan and stir to combine. Remove from the heat and let cool before serving over the cheesecake. Store any leftovers, covered, in the fridge and consume within 3 to 4 days.

BLUEBERRY TOPPING

1 teaspoon arrowroot powder or cornstarch

¼ cup agave syrup

1½ cups fresh blueberries (or try sliced pitted cherries!)

Pinch of sea salt

NUTRITION FACTS
(per serving–101g), with a graham cracker pie crust

Calories: 264; Fat: 12g; Carbs: 37g; Protein: 2g; Fiber: 1g

Vitamin C: 7%; Iron: 5%; Calcium: 5%; Vitamin A: 0%

PEANUT BUTTER CARAMEL APPLES

Vegan caramel apples are made even tastier by using peanut butter–infused caramel! Crushed peanuts finish things off.

SERVES 2 TO 3

PEANUT BUTTER CARAMEL

3 tablespoons vegan sugar

2 tablespoons salted creamy peanut butter

2 tablespoons coconut cream (scooped from a chilled can of full-fat coconut milk)

3 small or 2 medium apples, chilled

½ cup chopped salted peanuts

1 **For the Peanut Butter Caramel:** Combine the sugar, peanut butter, and coconut cream in a sauté pan. Cook over high heat, stirring, until melted together, 1 to 2 minutes. Continue stirring as the mixture begins to bubble, 45 seconds to 1 minute more. Reduce the heat to low and stir for a minute more. Remove from the heat and pour the mixture into a small dish. Continue stirring the caramel for about a minute so it doesn't separate. Once the caramel has cooled a bit, place the bowl in the fridge to chill until sticky (10 to 20 minutes should do it).

2 Skewer the apples with wooden lollipop sticks or wooden chopsticks. Roll the chilled apples in the caramel until well coated. Let the caramel warm just a bit if it is too sticky. Place the peanuts in a shallow dish and roll the caramel-coated apples in the crushed peanuts.

3 Place the apples on a parchment paper–lined plate and refrigerate for 5 minutes before serving.

NUTRITION FACTS
(per serving–227g)

Calories: 294; Fat: 14g; Carbs: 41g; Protein: 6g; Fiber: 6g

Vitamin C: 14%; Iron: 11%; Calcium: 2%; Vitamin A: 2%

EASY HOMEMADE APPLESAUCE

This spiced, sweet applesauce is delicious as an ultra-healthy dessert and perfect for using in a variety of baked good recipes. When a recipe calls for applesauce, use this recipe if you can!

SERVES 3

1 In a blender, combine the apples, lemon juice, maple syrup, cinnamon, and 2 tablespoons water. Blend, increasing the speed from low to high, until pureed, 30 to 60 seconds. For fastest blending, use a high-speed blender. In a less powerful blender you may need to add additional water.

2 Serve immediately for a raw sauce, or pour into a dish, cover, and refrigerate to serve chilled. For simmered sauce, transfer the applesauce mixture into a small saucepan and simmer on medium-high heat, stirring constantly, for 1 to 2 minutes. Add additional cinnamon, ginger, cayenne, and nutmeg or a few drops of vanilla extract, if you'd like.

3 Pour the applesauce into a serving dish and serve immediately, or cover and chill in the fridge until ready to serve. Raw applesauce should be eaten the same day it is prepared. Simmered applesauce can be stored, covered, in the fridge for 1 to 3 days.

Note: For smoother applesauce you can peel the apples before blending. However, I usually keep the skins on because I find that my high-speed blender pulverizes them enough, and that way I don't lose any of the nutrition and fiber in the peel.

2 large apples, cored and roughly chopped

1 to 2 teaspoons fresh lemon juice

½ teaspoon grade B maple syrup

Few pinches of ground cinnamon, plus more as needed

Ground ginger (optional)

Cayenne (optional)

Freshly grated nutmeg (optional)

Few drops of pure vanilla extract (optional)

NUTRITION FACTS
(per serving–151g)

Calories: 81; Fat: 0g; Carbs: 21g; Protein: 0g; Fiber: 4g

Vitamin C: 13%; Iron: 1%; Calcium: 1%; Vitamin A: 2%

CHOCOLATE SILK AND BANILLA SWIRL

White banana-vanilla pudding swirls with rich chocolate pudding for a soothing dessert treat.

SERVES 3

BANILLA PUDDING

6 ounces silken tofu, at room temperature

1 large extra-ripe banana

2 tablespoons virgin coconut oil, melted

1 tablespoon agave syrup or grade B maple syrup

½ teaspoon pure vanilla extract, or 1 vanilla bean pod, split, seeds scraped, pod discarded

¼ teaspoon ground cinnamon

CHOCOLATE SILK

¼ cup vegan dark chocolate chips

2 teaspoons virgin coconut oil, melted

6 ounces silken tofu, at room temperature

2 tablespoons agave syrup or grade B maple syrup

¼ teaspoon sea salt

1. **For the Banilla Pudding:** In a blender, combine all the banilla pudding ingredients and blend until silky smooth. Pour the banilla pudding into three serving glasses, retaining a few teaspoons to add later. No need to wash the blender.

2. **For the Chocolate Silk:** Place the chocolate chips and coconut oil in a small bowl and microwave for 10 seconds. Stir briskly, then microwave for another few seconds. Repeat until the chips are melted. Do not overheat or the chocolate will burn—30 seconds max should do it.

3. Transfer the melted chocolate mixture to the blender and add the remaining chocolate silk ingredients. Blend until smooth.

4. Pour the chocolate silk over the banilla pudding in the serving cups. Top with the reserved banilla pudding and swirl the colors gently with a toothpick. Refrigerate for at least 2 hours before serving.

NUTRITION FACTS
(per serving–192g)

Calories: 276; Fat: 15g; Carbs: 32g; Protein: 7g; Fiber: 2g

Vitamin C: 6%; Iron: 8%; Calcium: 5%; Vitamin A: 1%

CHOCO-PEANUT-BANANA SNOWSTORM

This is my go-to recipe when I crave something frosty, sweet, and creamy for dessert or an indulgent snack. This frosty shake includes frozen bananas, soothing cinnamon, and creamy peanut butter. Use as little liquid as possible to ensure a thick and creamy blend.

SERVES 2

In a blender, combine all the ingredients and blend, increasing the speed from low to high, until frosty and creamy. Serve in tall frosted glasses.

2½ bananas, frozen

1 cup plain nondairy milk

2 tablespoons creamy peanut butter

2 tablespoons raw cacao nibs (optional)

1 tablespoon cacao powder

¼ teaspoon ground cinnamon

NUTRITION FACTS (per serving–286g) Calories: 262; Fat: 10g; Carbs: 42g; Protein: 7g; Fiber: 6g   Vitamin C: 21%; Iron: 13%; Calcium: 24%; Vitamin A: 7%

EASY ALMOND BUTTER CUPS

These fast and easy almond butter cups taste just like the real thing. Maybe even better. You can use any nut or seed butter you'd like, including peanut or sunflower. I love almond butter best. For those pretty crimped edges, you can buy specialty candy molds online or in gourmet cooking stores, or simply use paper or foil muffin liners that have crimped edges built in.

SERVES 12 TO 15

1 Place the chocolate chips and coconut oil in a small bowl and microwave for 20 seconds. Stir briskly. If not fully melted after 1 minute of stirring, microwave for 10 to 15 seconds more. Stir again until melted and well combined.

2 Place the almond butter, agave, and vanilla, if desired, in a separate bowl and microwave for 20 seconds. Stir until thin and smooth.

3 Grease candy molds or muffin cup liners with coconut oil spray. Place a tiny amount, 1 to 2 teaspoons, of the melted chocolate in the bottom of the molds, then place the molds in the freezer until firm, 5 minutes. Remove from the freezer and add the nut filling, about 1 teaspoon for each cup. Smooth the filling as much as possible to a flat glob. Add a few more spoonfuls of chocolate over the top until it reaches the top of the candy mold and covers the filling. If using a muffin liner, you can make the filling as thick as you'd like, but about ½ inch is a good size for a homemade cup.

4 Place the filled cups in freezer for 15 to 20 minutes. Enjoy straight from the freezer or allow to warm up for about a minute for softer cups. Store these delicate cups in the freezer.

1 cup vegan chocolate chips

2 tablespoons virgin coconut oil, melted

¼ cup almond butter or peanut butter

1 tablespoon agave syrup or grade B maple syrup

Drop of pure vanilla extract (optional)

Coconut oil spray

NUTRITION FACTS (per serving–12g)

Calories: 71; Fat: 6g; Carbs: 4g; Protein: 1g; Fiber: 0g

Vitamin C: 0%; Iron: 3%; Calcium: 3%; Vitamin A: 0%

CANDIED CINNAMON BRANDY ORANGE PEELS

This is such a fun recipe because I love making a fancy treat out of an ingredient that usually gets tossed aside: orange peels! These sweet, cinnamon-spiced candied orange peels can be prepared with just a few simple ingredients, and they really add a gourmet tone as a garnish for desserts or salads. Or simply eat them as a sweet treat. My recipe is infused with cinnamon-sugar and brandy.

SERVES 10

1 orange, scrubbed
¾ cup vegan sugar
1 teaspoon brandy or cognac
2 pinches of ground cinnamon

SUGAR TOSS
¼ cup vegan sugar
¼ teaspoon ground cinnamon
Pinch of sea salt

1 Peel the rind from the orange, taking as little of the white pith as possible, and slice the rind into thin strips. Set aside.

2 In a small saucepan, combine the sugar and ½ cup water and bring to a boil. Add the brandy and cinnamon.

3 Add the orange peel to the sugar mixture and reduce the heat to maintain a simmer. Simmer for 15 minutes. No need to stir the peels.

4 Remove the pot from the heat and drain the syrupy liquid (reserve as a simple syrup for citrus-sweetened beverages, if you'd like).

5 **For the Sugar Toss:** In a small bowl, combine the sugar, cinnamon, and salt. Toss the warm, wet orange peels in the cinnamon-sugar mixture and lay flat on a sheet of parchment paper. Allow to dry and cool for at least 1 hour before using. Store the leftovers in the fridge or freezer for up to 2 months.

NUTRITION FACTS
(per serving–37g)
Calories: 65; Fat: 0g; Carbs: 17g; Protein: 0g; Fiber: 1g
Vitamin C: 22%; Iron: 0%; Calcium: 2%; Vitamin A: 1%

DRINKS, SIPS, AND SMOOTHIES

This is just a taste of a few of my favorite sips. I love a homemade latte, all steamy and warm. But my favorite lattes do not include espresso, but rather wellness ingredients like turmeric and matcha green tea! Okay, and the occasional pumpkin spice espresso latte or mocha, too. I also adore my smoothie-a-day habit. I have included a few of my favorite smoothies. And aside from recipe sips, remember that the most important sip of all is pure, refreshing water. Stay hydrated and your body will thank you. I also adore coconut water and kombucha as healthy sips.

BASIC VANILLA ALMOND OR CASHEW MILK

Homemade nut milks taste so much better than store-bought versions. The fresh, creamy, nutty, sweet flavor is something you have to taste to fall in love with. All you need to get started are a few basic tools and plenty of soaked raw nuts. See my how-to on page 326. Here are a few recipes to get you started.

SERVES 4

I See full instructions on page 326.

VARIATIONS

Chocolate: Add 2 tablespoons of cacao powder.

Strawberry: Add ½ cup fresh strawberries.

Coconut: Substitute coconut water for the purified water.

1 cup raw almonds or cashews

4 cups purified water

2 tablespoons grade B maple syrup or agave syrup

½ teaspoon ground cinnamon

Seeds from ½ vanilla bean, or ½ teaspoon pure vanilla extract

¼ teaspoon sea salt

NUTRITION FACTS
(per serving–277g),
without variations*

Calories: 196; Fat: 15g; Carbs: 13g; Protein: 6g; Fiber: 4g

Vitamin C: 0%; Iron: 7%; Calcium: 9%; Vitamin A: 0%

*does not account for the pulp that is strained out

HOW-TO: MAKING NUT MILKS

Nut milk is easy to make once you have the required tools:

Raw nuts, soaked overnight
Nut milk straining cloth (hemp canvas or nylon mesh)
High-speed blender
Glass containers for storing the milk
Large bowl
Flavorings: pink salt, vanilla bean seeds, ground cinnamon, sweeteners, cocoa, and more
Funnel (optional)

- **Soak:** Soak the nuts overnight. Drain and rinse.

- **Blend:** In a high-speed blender, combine the nuts and water, and process until it is as smooth as you can get it. The standard nut to water ratio is 1 cup soaked nuts to 3 cups water, but you can stray a bit depending on how thick and creamy or watery you like your nut milk.

- **Strain and Squeeze:** Strain the blended liquid through your nut milk bag into a bowl. Squeeze, squeeze, squeeze. The silky white liquid will fill the bowl, while leaving nut pulp in the bag. Pour the pulp back in the blender and add a bit more water to try and blend out some more milk. Strain again. Continue blending and straining until as little nut pulp is left as possible.

- **Reblend:** Rinse the blender. Pour the strained, silky nut milk back into the blender and blend on low with the desired flavorings. Salt, sweeten, and flavor to taste. I like a pinch of ground cinnamon, vanilla bean seeds, salt, maple syrup, and sometimes cacao for chocolate nut milk!

- **Flavor:** Pour the flavored milk into glass containers (a funnel is helpful here) and store in the fridge. Use within a few days.

PUMPKIN SPICE LATTE

Pumpkin-infused lattes and warm mugs are so cozy during the fall and winter months. This first recipe is a vegan version of a classic pumpkin spice latte, and the second recipe, my hot pumpkin mug, is a caffeine-free sip that makes pumpkin the star of the show! My hot pumpkin mug does for pumpkin what hot cocoa does for chocolate.

SERVES 2

1 In a small saucepan, combine the nondairy milk, maple syrup, pumpkin puree, pumpkin pie spice, and vanilla. Whisking briskly, bring the mixture to a boil over medium-high heat, 3 to 4 minutes. Reduce the heat to low and simmer for 2 to 3 minutes more.

2 Transfer the pumpkin mixture to a blender and blend for 30 seconds on low. This whips some frothy air into the liquid for a lighter beverage. Taste and sweeten to taste. Pour from the blender into two serving mugs.

3 Pour a shot of espresso into each mug. Serve hot, with a dollop of whip on top, if desired.

Hot Pumpkin Mug Variation: Exclude the espresso shots and add an additional 1 to 2 tablespoons pumpkin puree. This creates a pure pumpkin flavor that is caffeine-free and perfect for serving to kids or drinking around bedtime. Sweeten to taste and add a pinch of sea salt, if desired.

2 cups nondairy milk, unsweetened (if using sweetened or vanilla, reduce maple syrup to 1 tablespoon or add to taste)

2 tablespoons grade B maple syrup

2 tablespoons canned unsweetened pumpkin puree

½ teaspoon pumpkin pie spice

Few drops of pure vanilla extract

2 shots prepared espresso

Soy or coconut whip (page 304; optional)

NUTRITION FACTS (per serving-349g) Calories: 141; Fat: 2g; Carbs: 23g; Protein: 8g; Fiber: 2g   Vitamin C: 1%; Iron: 10%; Calcium: 55%; Vitamin A: 59%

WELLNESS LATTES

These espresso-free lattes are two of my favorite wellness blends. The rich green and golden colors remind me of all the healthy properties of these sips. Matcha green tea swirls with creamy nondairy milk and sweetener for a simple matcha tea blend. Mint optional. And my turmeric latte is bright golden in color, with accents of cinnamon and cayenne, and maple syrup to sweeten the deal. Both turmeric and matcha could be considered acquired tastes, but once you fall in love with these flavors, I promise you will be craving them for their delicious appeal, and for the way they make you feel!

Basic Latte Directions:

1 Place the nondairy milk in a serving mug and microwave until steamy hot, 1 to 3 minutes. You could also warm it on the stovetop over medium-high heat until the liquid comes to a slow boil.

2 Pour the hot nondairy milk into a blender and turn the blender on low. With the blender running, add the sweetener, powder, and spices. Allow to blend until the powder is fully dissolved and the milk becomes frothy. I blend from low to high to ensure that plenty of air is whipped into the milk, making it frothy, foamy, and light when served. You will know the blending worked because the amount you pour back into the mug will be more than what you started with! The foam and air-infused liquid takes up more room in the mug. If you do not want too much foam, simply blend on low speed only. You could also briskly stir the beverage in the mug with a spoon, and skip the blending step.

3 Pour back into the warm serving mug and serve warm. Sweeten to taste, if desired.

MATCHA

NUTRITION FACTS
(per serving–248g)

Calories: 144; Fat: 3g; Carbs: 25g;
Protein: 8g; Fiber: 1g

Vitamin C: 1%; Iron: 6%; Calcium:
29%; Vitamin A: 10%

Follow the directions on page 328 to prepare the latte.

1 cup plain nondairy milk

1 tablespoon agave syrup or grade B maple syrup

¾ to 1 teaspoon matcha green tea powder

1 to 2 drops peppermint extract (optional)

SERVES 1

TURMERIC

NUTRITION FACTS
(per serving–248g)

Calories: 144; Fat: 3g; Carbs: 25g;
Protein: 8g; Fiber: 1g

Vitamin C: 1%; Iron: 6%; Calcium:
29%; Vitamin A: 10%

Follow the directions on page 328 to prepare the latte.

1 cup plain nondairy milk

1 tablespoon agave syrup or grade B maple syrup

½ to 1 teaspoon ground turmeric

Few pinches of ground cinnamon

Pinch of cayenne

SERVES 1

FAVORITE SMOOTHIES

You guys may know this already, but I am a smoothie kind of girl. My first book, *365 Vegan Smoothies*, shared a full year's worth of smoothie recipes! But I do admit to having my handful of favorite smoothie recipes that I make again and again. These are my favorites. The Watermelon Frosty is sweet and frosty. My Matcha Shake is my go-to lunch smoothie recipe. I always add a scoop of vanilla protein powder, too. My Golden Wellness Shake is a glow of deliciousness and wellness featuring the anti-inflammatory super spice turmeric. And the Green Glow Smoothie is a favorite leafy green blend, sweet in flavor and packed with healthy nutrients.

WATERMELON FROSTY

In a high-speed blender, combine all of the ingredients and blend from low to high until smooth.

1 banana

2 cups frozen watermelon cubes

½ cup coconut water or plain nondairy milk

2 tablespoons fresh lime juice (omit if using nondairy milk)

1 to 2 tablespoons grade B maple syrup

NUTRITION FACTS
(per serving–584g)

Calories: 275; Fat: 1g; Carbs: 70g; Protein: 3g; Fiber: 4g

Vitamin C: 173%; Iron: 17%; Calcium: 5%; Vitamin A: 35%

SERVES 1

GREEN GLOW SMOOTHIE

In a high-speed blender, combine all of the ingredients and blend from low to high until smooth.

1 orange, peeled

1 banana

2 cups leafy greens (try kale or fresh spinach)

1 cup plain nondairy milk or coconut water

½ cup green grapes

½ cup ice

NUTRITION FACTS
(per serving–916g)

Calories: 348; Fat: 2g; Carbs: 85g; Protein: 8g; Fiber: 11g

Vitamin C: 693%; Iron: 25%; Calcium: 31%; Vitamin A: 421%

SERVES 1

GOLDEN WELLNESS SHAKE

SERVES 1

1 cup vanilla almond milk

1 teaspoon ground turmeric

1 teaspoon grade B maple syrup

¼ teaspoon ground cinnamon

Pinch of cayenne (optional)

1 large banana, frozen

1 cup frozen orange segments

1. Place the almond milk in a blender and blend on the lowest speed. With the blender on, add the turmeric, maple syrup, cinnamon, and cayenne (if using). Blend until the turmeric has dissolved into the liquid, creating a smooth golden color, 1 to 2 minutes.

2. Turn off the blender and add the frozen fruit. Blend again from low to high speed until smooth. Be sure to blend at a high speed for at least 30 seconds or more so that the orange fully smoothes out. Pour and serve.

NUTRITION FACTS
(per serving—565g)

Calories: 292; Fat: 3g; Carbs: 66g; Protein: 4g; Fiber: 10g

Vitamin C: 193%; Iron: 22%; Calcium: 54%; Vitamin A: 18%

PERFECT SMOOTHIES AND SHAKES

Here are a few tips for better smoothies. Also check out my book *365 Vegan Smoothies*.

- **Blend at high speed:** When blending green smoothies with plenty of whole food ingredients like kale or apples or spinach, be sure to turn the blender to max/high for a few seconds. This will ensure that all those little bits of fiber from the foods get blended smoothly and that all the leafy green bits blend smoothly.

- **Creative cubes:** Try flavored ice cubes when using ice so that you do not water down the flavor of the smoothie. Try coconut water, juice, nondairy milk, or even coffee ice cubes. I also like to use frozen watermelon in place of ice.

- **Less is more:** For the thickest, creamiest smoothies and shakes, use as little liquid as possible to blend. Frozen bananas are wonderful for adding "ice cream–like" texture to your smoothies.

- **Frozen melon:** I am obsessed with adding frozen watermelon cubes to my smoothies. I just adore the texture they create. Give them a try! Frozen cantaloupe and honeydew also work and provide varying colors and flavors.

- **Superfood add-ins:** Experiment with a variety of wellness add-ins for your smoothies. Try ingredients like matcha green tea, turmeric powder, aloe vera juice, cayenne, vegan yogurt, a handful of nuts or seeds, vegan protein powder, açaí and pomegranate, spirulina, maca powder, and more.

FAVORITE MATCHA SHAKE

1 In a high-speed blender, combine the almond milk, protein powder, and matcha. If using, add the spirulina, maca, and chia seeds. Blend on low. Turn off the blender, break the banana into quarters if you have frozen it whole, and add it to the blender along with half of the watermelon cubes. Blend from low to high until smooth, adding a few more splashes of liquid as needed to blend. When the shake is nearly perfectly smooth, add the remaining watermelon cubes. This will thicken everything up and you will be left with a thick and frosty shake. Add 1 to 2 more cubes of watermelon at this point if you want the texture a bit thicker.

2 Pour the shake into your serving glass and top with the pumpkin seeds, if desired. Serve with a spoon!

Tip: You can substitute coconut water for half of the nondairy milk to lighten things up a bit and add healthy electrolytes.

¾ cup vanilla almond or soy milk

1 scoop vegan vanilla protein powder

1 teaspoon matcha green tea powder

½ teaspoon spirulina (optional)

1 teaspoon maca powder (optional)

1 teaspoon chia seeds (optional)

1 banana, frozen

1 to 1½ cups frozen watermelon cubes

1 teaspoon raw pumpkin seeds (I like sprouted and salted seeds), for garnish (optional)

NUTRITION FACTS (per serving–561g) Calories: 368; Fat: 7g; Carbs: 64g; Protein: 23g; Fiber: 13g   Vitamin C: 110%; Iron: 87%; Calcium: 56%; Vitamin A: 101%

EVERY MORNING LEMON TEA

This is the lemon water tea I drink almost every morning right after I wake up. Some people like to do a basic combo of warm water with lemon juice, but I make my tea a bit fancier by adding cayenne, green tea, maple syrup, and sometimes a spoonful of goji berries and a few pinches of turmeric, too. This wellness tea will help cleanse your digestive system for a new day of healthy eating and digesting. It also may help keep your body in a healthy alkaline state.

SERVES 1

8 ounces purified water

1 green tea bag or herbal tea bag of your choice (detox teas are great, too!)

1 tablespoon grade B maple syrup, plus more as needed

1 to 2 pinches of cayenne

Pinch of ground turmeric (optional)

Juice of 1 large or 2 small lemons

1 tablespoon goji berries (optional)

1 Heat the water in a mug for 2 minutes in the microwave, or boil the water on the stovetop.

2 Add the tea bag, sweetener, and spice(s). Add the lemon juice. Add the goji berries (if using). If adding the goji berries, allow the tea to sit for at least 2 minutes so that the berries soften and plump. You can squeeze the berries into the tea a bit and eat them after you drink the tea. Sweeten to taste, depending on how much lemon was used.

Tip: I also like to eat 2 to 3 Brazil nuts in the morning right after this tea. Brazil nuts are rich in selenium.

NUTRITION FACTS
(per serving–277g)

Calories: 64; Fat: 0g; Carbs: 15g; Protein: 0g; Fiber: 0g

Vitamin C: 35%; Iron: 2%; Calcium: 2%; Vitamin A: 2%

TRIO OF HOLIDAY SIPS

When cool temperatures roll in and the holiday lights start twinkling, these are my three favorite festive sips to warm me up. Mulled Wine is spiced and soothing. My Hot Toddy is bright with sweet citrus and spice flavor. And of course, a classic hot cocoa is everyone's favorite. I spice mine with cinnamon, cayenne, and a hint of mesquite!

KATHY'S SPICY LEMON MULLED HOT TODDY

SERVES 2

1. Combine all the ingredients in a medium saucepan with 2 cups water and bring to a low boil over medium-high heat. Reduce the heat to low and simmer for 5 to 15 minutes. Pour through a mesh strainer into glasses to serve. Garnish with either a cinnamon stick or a fresh slice of lemon, if desired.

Note: For a sweeter citrus sip, substitute fresh orange juice or apple cider for half the water (you may want to decrease the amount of maple syrup if you do this, depending on how sweet you'd like it).

Juice of 2 small or 1 large lemon

1 tea bag (I like black tea when I do not mind the caffeine, or ginger or chamomile tea for an evening sip)

2 shots brandy or cognac

2 tablespoons grated peeled fresh ginger

3 to 4 whole cloves

1 star anise

1 cinnamon stick, plus 2 cinnamon sticks, for garnish

Pinch of freshly grated lemon zest

Pinch of cayenne

Lemon slices, for garnish

NUTRITION FACTS (per serving–330g)
Calories: 121; Fat: 0g; Carbs: 18g; Protein: 1g; Fiber: 1g
Vitamin C: 51%; Iron: 3%; Calcium: 4%; Vitamin A: 0%

KATHY'S MULLED WINE

SERVES 2

16 ounces leftover red wine (you do not need anything too fancy, a $10 to $15 bottle is perfect)

Juice of 1 orange

1 orange, sliced

½ apple, cored and diced

3 to 4 whole cloves

1 star anise

1 cinnamon stick

1 to 2 tablespoons grade B maple syrup

1 shot brandy or cognac

½ teaspoon freshly grated orange zest

Combine all the ingredients in a medium saucepan and bring to a boil. Reduce the heat to low and simmer for 5 to 15 minutes. The longer you simmer, the more intense the flavor will become and the stronger the intensity of the alcohol, since the liquid will reduce as it simmers. Pour the liquid through a mesh strainer into glasses to serve. Garnish each glass with a few pieces of the apple or a simmered orange slice, if desired. Serve warm.

Note: For a lighter/sweeter sip, add ½ cup apple cider or pomegranate juice.

NUTRITION FACTS (per serving–343g)

Calories: 289; Fat: 0g; Carbs: 23g; Protein: 1g; Fiber: 1g

Vitamin C: 82%; Iron: 6%; Calcium: 6%; Vitamin A: 4%

KATHY'S AZTEC HOT COCOA

SERVES 1

1. Fill a microwave-safe mug with the nondairy milk and microwave until hot, 2 to 3 minutes. You could also heat in a small saucepan over medium-high heat until the liquid starts to boil, 2 to 3 minutes.

2. Pour the hot milk into a blender and turn the blender on low. Add the sweetener, cacao, cinnamon, cayenne, salt, and mesquite powder (if using). Blending until frothy and light.

3. Pour the liquid back into the mug. Add soy whip or vegan marshmallows on top, if desired, and serve.

VARIATIONS

Add a sprig of fresh mint or peppermint extract for minty cocoa.

Add vanilla bean seeds or pure vanilla extract for vanilla-infused cocoa.

Add a teaspoon of peanut butter for peanut butter cup cocoa.

---

1 cup plain nondairy milk (preferably soy)

1 heaping tablespoon grade B maple syrup, agave syrup, coconut sugar, or vegan sugar, plus more as needed

1 tablespoon cacao powder

Few pinches of ground cinnamon

Pinch of cayenne

Pinch of sea salt

Pinch of mesquite powder (optional)

1 to 2 tablespoons soy or coconut whip (page 304), or 1 tablespoon vegan marshmallows (optional)

Tip: For extra-frothy cocoa, after pouring the cocoa back into the mug, microwave the cocoa for 10 seconds. This will fluff the foam up even more.

NUTRITION FACTS
(per serving–244g) Calories: 180; Fat: 5g; Carbs: 29g; Protein: 8g; Fiber: 2g   Vitamin C: 0%; Iron: 11%; Calcium: 6%; Vitamin A: 0%

FOR THE KIDS

Here are a few fun and healthy kid-approved vegan recipes to try! Get your child started off on the right fork! Er, foot. Kids love colors, so embrace fresh fruits and veggies in your kid-friendly meals. You can also give kids small pieces of info about the foods they are eating, and they might proudly remember them the next time they eat those foods! Anecdotes like, "Oranges are rich in vitamin C. Vitamin C helps you stay healthy and well!" Or, "Broccoli is rich in calcium. Calcium helps you stay strong!" Or even, "Bananas are rich in fiber. Fiber keeps your tummy happy!"

FRUITY RAINBOW WRAPS

These fun rainbow wraps are like a creative art project for kids, but this is edible art they can eat instead of hanging on the fridge door! You can make these rainbow wraps using all fruit, all veggies, or a mixture of both.

───────── SERVES 2 ─────────

1 Spread the vegan cream cheese on the tortillas. Allow your kids to arrange the fruit over the cream cheese in a rainbow design.

2 Roll up the wraps tightly in a spiral. Slice crosswise into 1-inch-thick circles, and serve!

NUTRITION FACTS (per serving–166g)

Calories: 223; Fat: 10g; Carbs: 33g; Protein: 3g; Fiber: 5g

Vitamin C: 17%; Iron: 6%; Calcium: 6%; Vitamin A: 1%

¼ cup vegan cream cheese

2 medium flour tortillas or 1 lavash wrap

2 cups fruit in rainbow colors—try:

Red: cherries, strawberries, apples, raspberries

Orange: oranges, apricots, peaches

Yellow: banana, mango

Green: kiwi, green grapes

Blue: blueberries

Purple: purple grapes, blackberries

MAGIC CHIA SEED PUDDING

Chia seed pudding is pretty magical for adults, so just imagine how much kids will love watching those tiny purple seeds turn into plump little beads, making a sweet and silky pudding.

───────── SERVES 2 TO 3 KIDS ─────────

1 Have the kids combine the nondairy milk, chia seeds, agave, and "magic dust" cinnamon in a tall glass, then let them briskly stir the chia seed milk for 1 to 3 minutes. This is when the "magic" starts to happen! Place the chia pudding in the fridge overnight and in the morning, the pudding will be magically thickened and the magic chia seeds plumped up! Stir briskly before serving.

1¼ cups plain nondairy milk

3 to 4 tablespoons chia seeds

1 tablespoon agave syrup or grade B maple syrup

Pinch of ground cinnamon (a.k.a. magic dust!)

NUTRITION FACTS (per serving–230g)

Calories: 213; Fat: 11g; Carbs: 20g; Protein: 10g; Fiber: 11g

Vitamin C: 0%; Iron: 28%; Calcium: 46%; Vitamin A: 5%

"I KNOW MY ALPHABET" TOMATO SOUP WITH CHEDDAR APPLE LOGS

This cozy day soup and side is a favorite kid-friendly recipe. Instead of serving tomato soup from a can, you can easily whip up this yummy red bowl. Paired with some crunchy sweet apple grilled cheese "log" sandwiches, any rainy day is made better!

SERVES 2

SOUP

2 ounces alphabet pasta

1 (14-ounce) can crushed tomatoes

1 cup vegetable broth

¾ cup plain soy or almond milk

¼ cup chopped onion

2 tablespoons nutritional yeast

2 tablespoons agave syrup

1 to 2 tablespoons tomato paste

Sea salt and freshly ground black pepper

APPLE CHEDDAR LOG SANDWICHES

½ teaspoon vegan buttery spread

2 slices bread

½ apple, sliced

4 thin slices vegan cheddar cheese

1 **For the Soup:** Bring a small pot of salted water to a boil. Add the alphabet pasta and cook until tender, 8 to 10 minutes. Drain and set the pasta aside.

2 In a blender, combine the tomatoes, broth, nondairy milk, onion, nutritional yeast, agave, and 1 tablespoon of the tomato paste and blend until silky smooth. Add the remaining 1 tablespoon tomato paste if a thicker texture is desired.

3 Pour the tomato mixture in a small saucepan and add the pasta. Bring the mixture to a boil and then reduce the heat to low and simmer until ready to serve. Season with salt and pepper to taste.

4 **For the Apple Cheddar Log Sandwiches:** In a sauté pan, melt the vegan buttery spread over high heat. Add a slice of the bread and top with the sliced apple and vegan cheddar. Place the remaining slice of bread on top and warm until the edges of the toast become golden, 2 to 4 minutes. Flip once. Cook until the cheese has melted as much as desired. Slice the sandwich into thin strips, like logs, and serve alongside the warm tomato soup.

NUTRITION FACTS (per serving–479g)

Calories: 263; Fat: 3g; Carbs: 47g; Protein: 13g; Fiber: 4g

Vitamin C: 24%; Iron: 16%; Calcium: 16%; Vitamin A: 26%

BEST DAY GRILLED CHEESE

Grilled cheese is a classic kid-friendly food. Here is my easy vegan version!

1 Slather ½ teaspoon of the vegan buttery spread over one side of each slice of bread.

2 In a sauté pan, heat the oil over medium-high heat. Add one slice of the bread, vegan buttery spread side up, and top with the vegan cheese and tomato slices. Top with the other slice of bread, vegan buttery spread side down. To help melt the cheese, splash a few drops of cold water on the pan and cover the pan. Reduce the heat to low so you do not burn the bread. Flip after a few minutes and cook until the cheese has melted, 3 to 4 minutes. You could also use a panini press for faster cooking.

3 Slice the sandwich into quarters and serve alongside the carrot sticks and apple slices.

1 teaspoon vegan buttery spread

2 slices sprouted grain bread

½ teaspoon extra-virgin olive oil (or vegan buttery spread)

½ cup vegan cheese shreds

2 tomato slices

Carrot sticks, for serving

Cinnamon-sprinkled apple slices, for serving

NUTRITION FACTS
(per serving–131g)

Calories: 275; Fat: 10g; Carbs: 37g; Protein: 8g; Fiber: 7g

Vitamin C: 9%; Iron: 11%; Calcium: 2%; Vitamin A: 8%

BEAN NICE CHEEZY BURRITO

This simple cheesy bean burrito is a great entrée for kids who love fiesta flavors. The added nutritional yeast not only adds yummy cheesy flavor, but plenty of additional nutrients. Tip: If your kids do not like whole beans, you can either mash the beans before adding to the tortilla or use vegan refried beans.

SERVES 1

¾ cup drained and rinsed canned pinto beans or refried beans

1 to 2 tablespoons vegan cheddar cheese shreds

1 medium whole wheat tortilla

1 tablespoon mashed avocado

1 tablespoon diced tomatoes

1 teaspoon nutritional yeast

1 teaspoon finely chopped fresh cilantro

1 Place the beans and cheese on the tortilla and warm in the microwave until the cheese has melted, 30 seconds to 1 minute.

2 Add the avocado, tomatoes, nutritional yeast, and cilantro to the tortilla. Roll up the burrito, slice in half, and serve warm.

NUTRITION FACTS (per serving–214g) Calories: 304; Fat: 6g; Carbs: 50g; Protein: 14g; Fiber: 12g   Vitamin C: 5%; Iron: 21%; Calcium: 5%; Vitamin A: 2%

STRAWBERRY ALMOND BUTTER SANDWICH SUSHI

This fun little recipe is a creative, cute way to serve a PB&J sandwich. Use soft bread for easy rolling. Thick, grainier breads may not mold into rolls very well.

SERVES 1

---

1 Slather the almond butter and jam on the bread, leaving a 1-inch dry space on one side.

2 Roll up the bread in a tight spiral toward the dry side, as the bread rolls, the jam and almond butter will squish to coat the dry space.

3 Slice the roll crosswise into 1-inch-thick pieces and serve as sandwich sushi. These pieces hold together well when squeezed inside a small container.

1 tablespoon almond butter, softened

2 teaspoons strawberry jam

1 slice soft wheat bread, crusts removed

NUTRITION FACTS
(per serving–46g)
Calories: 153; Fat: 7g; Carbs: 20g; Protein: 4g; Fiber: 2g
Vitamin C: 0%; Iron: 6%; Calcium: 5%; Vitamin A: 0%

PINK LADYBUGS ON A LOG

Switch out those raisin ants for some cute little pink goji ladybugs! Goji berries make the perfect little ladybugs for your favorite nut or seed butter–filled celery log. Tip: If the goji berries are too firm or chewy, simply soak them in water or fruit juice for a few minutes (or longer) and they will soften up quite nicely. For quickie softening, use hot water or juice.

SERVES 1

2 teaspoons peanut, sunflower, or almond butter

1 to 2 stalks celery, rinsed and dried

1 tablespoon goji berries

Spread the nut butter in the channel of the celery stalk(s). Add the goji berries on top of the nut butter in a long line. Serve or chill until ready to serve.

NUTRITION FACTS
(per serving–50g)

Calories: 90; Fat: 6g;
Carbs: 8g; Protein: 3g;
Fiber: 2g

Vitamin C: 6%; Iron: 8%;
Calcium: 3%; Vitamin
A: 37%

12 HAPPY LIFE MENUS

1 RAINY DAY COMFORT LUNCH

Entrées: Rainy Day Tomato Soup (page 258), Avocado Toast (page 96)

Dessert: Trail Trekker Oat Coconut Cookie (page 285)

2 VEGAN PIZZA NIGHT

Entrée: Vegan Pizza (page 251)

Salad: Avocado Dreamboat Salad with Hummus Crostini (page 164)

Dessert: Chocolate Silk and Banilla Swirl Pudding (page 318)

3 COMFORT FOOD MAC 'N' CHEEZ DINNER

Entrée: Favorite Vegan Mac and Cheese (page 224)

Veggies: Easy Cheezy Roasted Broccoli (page 134)

Dessert: Soft and Chewy Peanut Butter Cookies (page 287)

4 PRE- AND POST-WORKOUT FUEL

Pre-Workout: No-Bake Chewy Energy Bars or Balls (page 70)

Post-Workout: Favorite Matcha Shake (page 333)

5 VEGGIE BURGER NIGHT

Entrée: Sweet Potato Veggie Burger with Avocado (page 120)

Side: Summer Slaw (page 141) or Oven-Roasted Crispy Taters (page 138)

Salad: Mango Avocado Arugula Salad (page 168)

Dessert: Kathy's Favorite Chocolate Chip Cookies (page 284)

6 CALIFORNIA GIRL (OR BOY!) LUNCH

Entrée: The Californian: Sprout Avocado Sandwich (page 90)

To Share: Sunny Guacamole with carrot sticks and romaine spears (page 199)

Dessert: Favorite Matcha Shake to share (page 333) or Raw Almond Butter Cheesecake (page 311)

7 "KID" LUNCH – ALL AGES

Entrée: Fruity Rainbow Wraps (page 339)

Side: Pink Ladybugs on a Log (page 344)

To sip: Watermelon Frosty (page 330)

Dessert: Gluten-Free Almond Butter–Jam Thumbprint Cookies (page 293)

8 BREAKFAST IN BED

Entrée: Chocolate-Covered Strawberry Oatmeal (page 55) with vegan buttered toast

Side: Maple-Lime Papaya (page 48)

To sip: Espresso, Tea, or Matcha Latte (page 329)

9 FEEL BETTER MEAL

Entrée: Wellness Soba Noodle Soup (page 261)

Side: Avocado Toast with citrus (page 96)

To Sip: Turmeric Latte (page 329)

10 FAMILY-STYLE BRUNCH FEAST

Mom's Apple Pancakes (page 41)

Easy Tofu Scramble (page 34) or Garden Veggie Frittata (page 36)

Cinnamon Maple Citrus Sweet Potato Home Fries (page 64)

Smoky Tempeh Bacon (page 62)

Chop 'n' Toss Rainbow Fruit Salad (page 47)

Easy Hummus Spiral Wraps (page 104)

Pumpkin Spice Lattes (page 327)

11 HEALTHY WINTER MORNING BLISS

Entrée: Cranberry-Nut Farro Porridge (page 56)

Side: Fresh seasonal fruit or freshly squeezed winter citrus juice

To sip: Hot Pumpkin Mug (page 327) or Pumpkin Spice Latte (page 327)

12 KATHY'S FAVE TO-GO MEAL

Starter: Chipotle Sweet Potato Soup with Avocado (page 257)

Entrée: 5-Step Raw Kale Salad (page 153)

Side: Smoky Tempeh Bacon (page 62)

Dessert: Trail Trekker Oat Coconut Cookies (page 285)

INDEX

Note: Page references in *italics* indicate photographs.